Study Guide

Volume 1: To 1815

A HISTORY OF WESTERN SOCIETY

Study Guide

Volume 1: To 1815

A HISTORY OF WESTERN SOCIETY

Third Edition

James A. Schmiechen
Central Michigan University, Mt. Pleasant

John P. McKay
University of Illinois at Urbana-Champaign

HOUGHTON MIFFLIN COMPANY • BOSTON

Dallas   Geneva, Illinois   Lawrenceville, New Jersey   Palo Alto

Copyright © 1987 by Houghton Mifflin Company.

All Rights Reserved. No part of this work may be reproduced or transmitted in any form or by any means, electronic or mechanical, including photocopying and recording, or by any information storage or retrieval system, except as may be expressly permitted by the 1976 Copyright Act or in writing by the Publisher. Requests for permission should be addressed in writing to Permissions, Houghton Mifflin Company, One Beacon Street, Boston, Massachusetts 02108.

Printed in the U.S.A.

Library of Congress Catalog Card Number: 86-81468

ISBN: 0-395-42409-7

ABCDEFGHIJ–FFG–89876

CONTENTS

TO THE STUDENT

HOW TO STUDY HISTORY AND PREPARE FOR EXAMS

The study of history can be rewarding but also perplexing. Most history courses require you to read and understand large bodies of detailed information. The history student is expected to perform many tasks—memorize information, study the reasons for change, analyze the accomplishments and failures of various societies, understand new ideas, identify historical periods, pick out broad themes and generalizations in history, and so forth. These jobs often present difficulties. This guide will make your study easier and increase your efficiency. It has been developed to help you read, study, and review *A History of Western Society*, and regular and systematic use of it will improve your grade in this course. You may use the guide in a variety of ways, but for best results you might choose the following approach:

1. *Preview the entire chapter* by reading the chapter objectives and synopsis; then quickly read through the study outline, noting the reading with understanding exercises. All of this will take only a few minutes but is an important first step in reading. It is called *previewing*. By pointing out what the chapter is about and what to look for, previewing will make your reading easier and improve your reading comprehension.

2. *Now read your assignment in the textbook*. Pay attention to features that reveal the scope and major emphasis of a chapter or section, such as the chapter title, chapter and section introductions, questions, headings, conclusions, and illustrative material (e.g., maps and photographs). Note study hint 3 on page ix about underlining.

3. After reading, *review what you have read* and check your comprehension by going over the chapter outline once again—but this time make sure that you understand

all the points and subpoints. If you do not fully understand a particular point or sub-point, then you need to return to the text and reread. It is not at all uncommon to need to read the text at least twice.

4. Continue your review. *Answer the review questions* that follow the study outline. It is best to write out or outline your answer on a sheet of paper or a note card. Be sure to include the supporting facts. Reread your answers periodically. This process will help you build a storehouse of information and understanding to use at the time of the exam.

5. Now work on the definitions, identifications, and explanations in the study-review exercises provided in each chapter of the *Study Guide*. This will help you to under-stand and recall both concepts and specific facts. Know not just who or what, but also why the term is significant. Does it illustrate or represent some fundamental change or process? Note that if a particular term appears in the text *and* in your lec-ture notes, it is of special importance. Do the geography exercises found in all appro-priate chapters. This is important because they will enable you to visualize the sub-ject matter and thus remember it better. It will take a few minutes, but the payoff is considerable.

6. Last, *complete the multiple-choice and fill-in exercises* for each *Study Guide* chapter. Some of these questions look for basic facts, while others test your under-standing and ability to synthesize material. *The answers are at the end of the Guide.* If you miss more than two or three, you need to restudy the text or spend more time working on the *Guide*.

ADDITIONAL STUDY HINTS*

1. *Organize your study time effectively*. Many students fail to do well in courses be-cause they do not organize their time effectively. In college, students are expected to read the material before class, review, and do the homework on their own. Many history teachers give only two or three tests during the semester; therefore, assuming personal responsibility for learning the material is vital. Mark up a semester calendar to show scheduled test dates, when term projects are due, and blocks of time to be set aside for exam study and paper writing. Then, at the beginning of each week, check the calendar and your course outlines and notes to see what specific preparation is

*For a complete text and workbook written to meet the needs of students who want to do their best in college, see James F. Shepherd, *RSVP, The Houghton Mifflin Reading, Study, and Vocabu-lary Program*, Second Edition (1984).

necessary for the coming week, and plan your time accordingly. Look at all the reading with understanding exercises in this *Study Guide* and try to estimate how much time you will need to master study skills. Set aside a block of time each day or once every several days for reading your text or studying your lecture notes and working in the *Study Guide*. Despite what one observes on college campuses, studying is not done most effectively late at night or with background music. Find a quiet place to study alone, one where you can tune out the world and tune into the past.

2. *Take good lecture notes.* Good notes are readable, clear, and above all reviewable. Write down as much of the lecture as you can without letting your pen get too far behind the lecturer. Use abbreviations and jot down key words. Leave spaces where appropriate and then go back and add to your notes as soon after the lecture as possible. You may find it helpful to leave a wide margin on the left side for writing in subject headings, important points, and questions, as well as for adding information and cross-references to the text and other readings. One way to use your notes effectively is by *reciting*. Reciting is the act of asking a question and then repeating the answer silently or aloud until you can recall it easily. Above all, do not wait until the night before an exam to use lecture notes you have not looked at for weeks or months. Review your lecture notes often and see how they complement and help you interpret your reading.

3. *Underline.* Too often students mark almost everything they read and end up with little else than an entire book highlighted in yellow. Underlining can be extremely helpful or simply a waste of time in preparing for exams; the key is to be selective in what you underline. Here are some suggestions:

a. Underline major concepts, ideas, and conclusions. You will be expected to interpret and analyze the material you have read. In many cases the textbook authors themselves have done this, so you need to pinpoint their comments as you read. Is the author making a point of interpretation or coming to a conclusion? If so, underline the key part. Remember, learning to generalize is very important, for it is the process of making history make sense. The author does it and you must learn to identify his or her interpretation as well as conflicting interpretations; then to make your own. Here is where your study of history can pay big rewards. The historian, like a good detective, not only gathers facts but also analyzes, synthesizes, and generalizes from that basic information. This is the process of *historical interpretation*, which you must seek to master.

b. Underline basic facts. You will be expected to know basic facts (names, events, dates, places) so that you can reconstruct the larger picture and back up your analysis and interpretations. Each chapter of this guide includes several lists of important items. Look over these lists before you begin to read, and then underline these words as you read.

c. Look at the review questions in the *Study Guide*—they will point to the major themes and questions to be answered. Then, as you read, underline the material that answers these questions. Making marginal notations can often complement your underlining.

4. *Work on your vocabulary*. The course lectures and each chapter in the text will probably include words that you do not know. Some of these will be historical terms or special concepts, such as *polis, feudalism,* or *bourgeoisie*—words that are not often used in ordinary American speech. Others are simply new to you but important for understanding readings and discussion. If you cannot determine the meaning of the word from the context in which it appears or from its word structure, then you will need to use a dictionary. *Keep a list of words* in your lecture notebook or use the pages in the back of this guide. Improving your historical and general vocabulary is an important part of reading history as well as furthering your college career. Most graduate-school entrance exams and many job applications, for instance, have sections to test vocabulary and reading comprehension.

5. *Benefit from taking essay exams*. Here is your chance to practice your skills in historical interpretation and synthesis. Essay exams demand that you express yourself through ideas, concepts, and generalizations as well as by reciting the bare facts. The key to taking an essay exam is preparation. Follow these suggestions:

a. *Try to anticipate the questions on the exam*. As you read the text, your notes, and this guide, jot down what seem to be logical essay questions. This will become easier as the course continues, partly because you will be familiar with the type of question your instructor asks. Some questions are fairly broad, such as the chapter-objective questions at the beginning of each chapter in this guide; others have a more specific focus, such as the review questions. Take a good look at your lecture notes. Most professors organize their daily lectures around a particular theme or stage in history. You should be able to invent a question or two from each lecture. Then answer the question. Do the same with the textbook, using the *Study Guide* for direction. Remember, professors are often impressed when students include in their essay textbook material not covered in class.

b. *Aim for good content and organization*. Be prepared to answer questions that require historical interpretation and analysis of a particular event, series of events, movement, process, person's life, and so forth. You must also be prepared to provide specific information to back up and support your analysis. In some cases you will be expected to give either a chronological narrative of events or a topical narrative (for example, explaining a historical movement in terms of its social, political, and economic features). Historians often approach problems in terms of cause and effect, so spend some time thinking about events in these terms. Remember, not all causes are of equal importance, so you must be ready to make distinctions—and to back up these distinctions with evidence. This is all part of showing your skill at historical interpretation.

When organizing your essay, you will usually want to sketch out your general thesis (argument) or point of interpretation first, in an introductory sentence or two. Next move to the substance. Here you will illustrate and develop your argument by weighing the evidence and marshaling reasons and factual data. After you have completed this stage (writing the body of your essay), go on to your conclusion, which most likely will be a restatement of your original thesis. It is often helpful to outline your major points before you begin to write. Be sure you answer all parts of the question. Write clearly and directly. All of this is hard to do, but you will get better at it as the course moves along.

6. *Enhance your understanding* of important historical questions by undertaking additional reading and/or a research project as suggested in the "Understanding History Through Reading and the Arts" and "Problems for Further Investigation" sections in the *Study Guide*. Note also that each textbook chapter has an excellent bibliography. Many of the books suggested are available in paperback editions, and all of the music suggested is available in most record-lending libraries and record stores.

7. *Know why you are studying history*. Nothing is worse than having to study a subject that appears to have no practical value. And indeed, it is unlikely that by itself this history course will land you a job. What, then, is its value, and how can it enrich your life? Although many students like history simply because it is interesting, there are a number of solid, old-fashioned reasons for studying it. It is often said that we need to understand our past in order to live in the present and build the future. This is true on a number of levels. On the psychological level, identification with the past gives us a badly needed sense of continuity and order in the face of ever more rapid change. We see how change has occurred in the past and are therefore better prepared to deal with it in our own lives. On another level, it is important for us to know how differing political, economic, and social systems work and what benefits and disadvantages accrue from them. As the good craftsperson uses a lifetime of experience to make a masterpiece, so an understanding of the accumulated experiences of the past enables us to construct a better society. Further, we need to understand how the historical experiences of peoples and nations have differed, and how these differences have shaped their respective visions. Only then can we come to understand how others view the world differently from the ways in which we do. Thus, history breaks down the barriers erected by provincialism and ignorance.

The strongest argument for the study of history, though, is that it re-creates the big picture at a time when it is fashionable and seemingly prudent to be highly specialized and narrowly focused. We live in the Age of Specialization. Even our universities often appear as giant trade schools, where we are asked to learn a lot about a little. As a result, it is easy to miss what is happening to the forest because we have become obsessed with a few of the trees. While specialization has undeniable benefits, both societies and individuals also need the generalist perspective and the ability to see how the entire system works. History is the queen of the generalist disciplines. Looking at change over time, history shows us how to take all the parts of the puzzle—politics, war, science, economics, architecture, sex, demography, music, philosophy, and much more—and put them together so that we can understand the whole. It is through a study of the interrelationships of the parts over a long expanse of time that we can develop a vision of society. By promoting the generalist perspective, history plays an important part on today's college campus.

Finally, the study of history has a more personal and surprisingly practical application. It is becoming increasingly apparent to many employers and educators that neglect of the liberal arts and humanities by well-meaning students has left them unable to think and reason analytically and to write and speak effectively. Overspecialized, narrowly focused education has left these students seriously deficient in basic verbal skills, placing them at a serious disadvantage in the job market. Here is where this course can help. It is universally recognized that studying history is an excellent way to develop the ability to reason and write. And the moving pageant of centuries of human experience you are about to witness will surely spark your interest and develop your aptitude if you give it the chance.

CHAPTER 1

NEAR EASTERN ORIGINS

CHAPTER OBJECTIVES

After reading and studying this chapter you should be able to answer the following questions:

Q-1. How did wild hunters become urban dwellers?
Q-2. What caused Mesopotamian culture to take root and become predominant in the ancient Near East?
Q-3. What contributions to Western culture did the Egyptians make?
Q-4. What impact did the Hittites have on Near Eastern culture?

CHAPTER SYNOPSIS

This first chapter of the book explores how civilization in the Western world began in the Near East in the area that became modern-day Israel, Iraq, Iran, and Egypt. It was here that agriculture and the first cities emerged. Here is where writing was invented, where law, science, and mathematics developed, and where the religious standards of the modern West evolved. The chapter begins by describing two prehistoric periods, the Paleolithic, or Old Stone, Age, and the Neolithic, or New Stone, Age, which set the stage for early civilization. Although the invention of tools, the control of fire, and the discovery of the uses of language and art by the Paleolithic people were remarkable achievements, it was the Neolithic people's use of systematic agriculture and settled life that was one of the most important events in world history.

As these early people gave up the nomadic life for the settled life of towns and agriculture, civilization, which meant law, government, economic growth, and religion, became possible. By around 3000 B.C., the first urban-agricultural societies had

1

emerged in Mesopotamia—the fertile land between the Tigris and Euphrates rivers. The most important of these early communities of farmers and city builders were the southern Mesopotamians, called the Sumerians. Sumerian society was a mixture of religious ritual war, slavery, and individual freedom. The Sumerians' greatest achievement was their system of writing, a system called cuneiform. The conquerors of Sumer, people called Semites from the northern part of Mesopotamia, spread Sumerian-Mesopotamian culture throughout the Near East. They were followed by the more important Babylonians, a people whose city, Babylon, dominated the trade of the Tigris and Euphrates. The Babylonians united Mesopotamia and gave the world one of its most important law codes, the code of Hammurabi. This code tells us how Mesopotamian people lived: how husbands treated their wives, how society dealt with crime, how consumer protection evolved, and so forth.

Egyptian society grew alongside the Nile River, which sheltered and isolated its people more effectively than the rivers of Mesopotamia. Egypt was first united into a single kingdom in about 3100 B.C. The focal point of all life in ancient Egypt was the pharaoh. His tomb, the pyramid, provided him with everything that he would need in the afterlife. Egyptian society was a curious mixture of freedom and constraint. Slavery existed, and life was void of modern Western concepts of freedom and human rights.

Between 2000 and 1200 B.C., Egypt and the entire Near East were greatly influenced by two migrations of Indo-Europeans which disturbed and remolded existing states. While all of Mesopotamia became unified under the Hittites, Egypt was first influenced by Hyksos and then by the introduction of monotheism by the pharaoh Akhenaten. During one of the resulting periods of political disintegration a number of petty kingdoms grew up, although the old culture of the Near East —especially that of Mesopotamia—lived on in the kingdoms of the newcomers.

STUDY OUTLINE
(see pp. vii-xii in this guide for suggestions on studying and preparing for exams)

I. The Paleolithic and Neolithic ages
    A. The Paleolithic, or Old Stone, Age (ca 400,000 B.C.-7000 B.C.)
        1. Human survival depended on the hunt; people did not farm
        2. Paleolithic people learned to control fire and make tools from stone and clothes from animal skins
            a. Social organization allowed them to overpower animals
            b. They had some knowledge of plants and agriculture
            c. Kinship and tribe ties were crucial
        3. The greatest accomplishments of Paleolithic peoples were intellectual: thought and language
        4. The first art—cave paintings and small clay statues—dates from this time

B. The Neolithic, or New Stone, Age (7000 B.C.-3000 B.C.)
1. The planting of crops and the domestication of animals—the "Agricultural Revolution"—was the age's greatest achievement
   a. Systematic agriculture ended people's dependence on hunting and allowed people to settle in towns and eventually cities
   b. Agriculture began in four areas (the Near East, western Africa, northeastern China, and Central and South America) at roughly the same time
2. Systematic agriculture led to population increase, trade, and the division of labor
3. The settled lifestyle allowed time to develop new tools and techniques
4. Systematic agriculture gave rise to towns and, eventually, urban life
5. In arid regions, irrigation was undertaken—resulting in the need for a central government

II. Mesopotamian civilization
A. The first cities were built in Mesopotamia (ca 3500-1700 B.C.)
1. The Sumerians and the Semites turned to an agricultural-urban way of life
2. The Sumerians made Mesopotamia the "cradle of civilization"
B. Environment and Mesopotamian culture
1. Geography greatly affected the political life and mental outlook of people in Mesopotamia
   a. The land is desert: only irrigation made farming possible
   b. Rivers isolated cities from one another, making them independent and willing to fight to remain so
   c. Floods and droughts made life difficult and people pessimistic

III. Sumerian society
A. Religion-centered life
1. The Sumerians tried to please the gods, especially the patron deity of the city
2. Monumental architecture—the ziggurat, or temple—evolved from religion
3. Recent discoveries indicate that a king (*lugal*) ruled and that most property was held privately
B. Varieties of freedom and dependence
1. The temple priests were wealthy and powerful but did not govern the city
2. The nobility—the king and his family, the chief priests, and the high palace officials—controlled most of the wealth and held most of the power
3. The commoners were free and had a political voice
4. Individual citizens owned much of the city's land
5. Slavery existed in Sumerian society

IV. The spread of Mesopotamian culture
    A. The short-lived empire of Sargon
        1. In 2331 B.C., Sargon, a Semitic chieftain, conquered Sumer and spread Mesopotamian culture throughout and beyond the Fertile Crescent
        2. The Ebla tablets reveal much about Sargon's work and the Mesopotamian influence, but they have added very little to biblical scholarship
    B. The triumph of Babylon
        1. Babylon's economic potential helped Hammurabi unify Mesopotamia
        2. War and Hammurabi's genius enabled Babylon to become the cultural center of Mesopotamia
    C. The invention of writing and the first schools
        1. Pictograph writing—the forerunner of cuneiform writing—existed long before Sumerian society
        2. Sumerian cuneiform evolved from a pictographic system to a phonetic system
        3. The Sumerian educational system was widely copied
    D. Mesopotamian thought and religion
        1. Mathematics
            a. The Mesopotamian numerical system was based on units of sixty
            b. Mesopotamians developed the concept of *place value*
            c. They emphasized practical uses—for example, construction—rather than theorizing
        2. Medicine
            a. Demons and evil spirits were believed to cause sickness
            b. Treatment was by magic, prescription, and surgery
        3. Theology, religion, and mythology
            a. The Mesopotamians believed in a hierarchy of anthropomorphic, all-powerful gods
            b. The aim of worship was to appease the gods
            c. The Mesopotamians created myths and an epic poem—the *Epic of Gilgamesh*—to learn of life and immortality
            d. Their myths about the creation of the universe and of human beings later influenced Jewish, Christian, and Muslim thought
    E. Daily life in Mesopotamia
        1. Hammurabi's code was based on several principles
            a. Equality before the law did not exist: there were milder penalties for members of the nobility than for commoners and slaves
            b. When criminal and victim were social equals, punishment fit the crime
            c. Individuals represented themselves, fair trials were guaranteed, and officials who failed to protect the innocent were penalized
        2. Hammurabi's law code reflects what life was like

    a. The law provided for consumer protection and for preventing crime

    b. The code contains many laws about farming, irrigation, crops, and animals

    c. Marriage was a business arrangement between the groom-to-be and his future father-in-law

    d. Women had little power within the family while husbands had absolute power

V. The land of the pharaohs (3100-1800 B.C.)

  A. Geography

    1. Egypt was known as the gift of the Nile: annual flooding made crop-raising easy and Egypt prosperous

    2. The Nile unified Egypt

    3. Egypt was nearly self-sufficient in raw materials

    4. Geography shielded Egypt from invasion and immigration

  B. The god-king of Egypt

    1. Egypt was politically unified under a pharaoh, or king, who was considered to be a god in human form

    2. The greatness of the pharaohs is reflected in their tombs, the pyramids

      a. The pyramid was believed to help preserve the pharaoh's body so that his *ka* would live on

      b. Tomb paintings, originally designed for the *ka*, give a vivid picture of everyday life

  C. The pharaoh's people

    1. Social mobility existed, but most people were tied to the land and subject to forced labor

    2. Peasants could be forced to work on pyramids and canals and to serve in the pharaoh's army

    3. The pharaoh existed to prevent internal chaos, which could lead to war and invasion

VI. Hyksos in Egypt (1640-1570 B.C.)

  A. About 1800 B.C., Semites (Hyksos) began to push into Egypt, Mesopotamia, and Syria from the Arabian peninsula

  B. Their "invasion" of Egypt was probably gradual and peaceful

  C. The Hyksos brought new ideas and techniques to Egyptian life

VII. The New Kingdom in Egypt (1570-1200 B.C.)

  A. A period of wealth, imperialism, and slavery

    1. The eighteenth-dynasty warrior-pharaohs Ahmose, Tutmose I, and Tutmose III created the first Egyptian empire and inaugurated the New Kingdom

    2. Warrior-pharaohs built huge granite monuments and created an empire

  B. Akhenaten and monotheism

    1. The pharaoh Akhenaten was interested in religion, not conquests

    a. His monotheistic religion was unpopular

    b. Akhenaten and his wife, Nefertiti, attempted to impose mono-
     theism on Egypt

   2. Akhenaten's attack on the traditional gods was seen by some as dan-
    gerous

   3. Akhenaten built a new capital and used art to convey his ideas

   4. In the end monotheism did not take hold

VIII. The Hittite Empire

  A. Migration of new groups

   1. Hittites were a part of the Indo-European migrations at the time the
    Hyksos entered Egypt

    a. The term *Indo-European* refers to a large family of languages,
     spoken throughout most of Europe and much of the Near East

    b. The original home of the Indo-Europeans may have been Central
     Europe

  B. The rise of the Hittites and Hittite society

   1. Hattusilis I led the Hittites to conquer Anatolia and then moved east-
    ward as far as Babylon

   2. The Hittite society was headed by a royal family and an often rebellious
    aristocracy

   3. The Hittites adopted the Mesopotamian culture

  C. The era of Hittite greatness (ca 1475-1200 B.C.)

   1. Through wise diplomacy and war, the Hittites came to control much
    of the Near East

    a. The Hittites defeated the Egyptians at the battle of Kadesh

    b. The Hittites often ruled through vassal-kingdoms and protectorates

    c. Along with Egyptians, the Hittites provided the Near East with an
     interlude of peace

  D. The fall of empires

   1. The fall of Egypt and the Hittites in the thirteenth century B.C. allowed
    for the growth of small kingdoms

    a. Both Egypt and the Hittite Empire were destroyed by invaders

    b. The old cultures of Mesopotamia, however, lived on through a dark
     age

REVIEW QUESTIONS

Q-1. What were the major accomplishments of the Paleolithic peoples? Why were
their lives so precarious?

Q-2. Why are the artistic creations of Paleolithic and Neolithic people so important
to the historian?

Q-3. Explain the impact that systematic agriculture had on the lives of these early peoples. Why did farming and the domestication of animals constitute a revolution in human life?

Q-4. What effect did the geography of Mesopotamia have on the lives of the people who lived between the Tigris and Euphrates rivers?

Q-5. What importance did the Nile River have in the economic and political development of Egypt?

Q-6. What was the role of the pharaoh in Egyptian society?

Q-7. Why were artistic works placed in the pharaoh's tomb?

Q-8. How much freedom existed in Egyptian society? Was Egypt an oriental slave state?

Q-9. Who unified Mesopotamia and how was it accomplished? Was it inevitable that Mesopotamia became unified?

Q-10. Describe the evolution of Sumerian writing.

Q-11. Describe the Mesopotamian religion. How did the Mesopotamians explain life and the universe?

Q-12. What role has myth played in Western culture? Does society live by myths today?

Q-13. What does the code of Hammurabi tell us about social and business relationships in Mesopotamia?

Q-14. Describe Mesopotamian family and marriage practices. How were women treated in Mesopotamian society? How do you account for their powerlessness?

Q-15. What were the religious beliefs of Akhenaten and his wife, Nefertiti? Why were their ideas seen as a threat by some Egyptians?

Q-16. Who were the Indo-Europeans and what impact did they have on the history of the Near East?

Q-17. Who were the Hyksos and what changes did they bring to Egypt? What was the Egyptian response?

Q-18. What were the contributions of the Hittites to Near Eastern history?

Q-19. What was the cause of the coming of the "dark age" in the thirteenth century B.C.?

STUDY-REVIEW EXERCISES

Define the following key concepts and terms.

pankus

anthropomorphic gods

monotheism

cuneiform

systematic agriculture

ziggurat

the Battle of Kadesh

place value

pharaoh

Identify each of the following and give its significance.

Mursilis I

Amon-Re

ka

Ebla tablets

Epic of Gilgamesh

Akhenaten

Nefertiti

Neanderthal Man

Homo sapiens

Sumer

Indo-European

code of Hammurabi

Hattusilis I

eighteenth-dynasty pharaohs

Explain who the following groups of people were and why they were important.

Sumerians

Semites

Amorites

Hittites

Hyksos

Explain and describe how (a) agriculture and (b) writing evolved.

Test your understanding of the chapter by answering the following questions.

1. The author of *On the Origin of Species* (1859). _____
2. His law code demanded that the punishment fit the crime.

    _____

3. A term meaning "king" or "great house." _____
4. The people whom the Egyptians called the "Rulers of the Uplands" were the

    _____

5. The pharaoh who advocated monotheism was _____
6. The two empires that fell in the thirteenth century B.C. were

    _____ and _____

7. The capital city of Mesopotamia under Hammurabi was _____
8. Most ordinary people in ancient Egypt *were/were not* tied to the land and subject to forced labor.
9. Under Hammurabi's code, the husband *could/could not* sell his wife and children into slavery.
10. The Agricultural Revolution is the chief event of the *Paleolithic/Neolithic* Age.

11. Mesopotamia was the land between the _____

    and _____ rivers.
12. The code of Hammurabi indicates that burglary *was/was not* a serious problem in Babylon.

Number the following events in correct chronological order.

1. _____   The rise of the Hittite Empire

2. _____   The unification of Mesopotamia under Babylon

3. _____   The reign of Akhenaten

4. _____   The establishment of Sumer

5. _____   The Hyksos invasion of Egypt

6. _____   The establishment of systematic agriculture

MULTIPLE-CHOICE QUESTIONS

1. Which of the following was not a characteristic of Paleolithic society?
   a. Violence
   b. Hunting technology and primitive art
   c. Written language
   d. The use of reason to govern actions

2. The most influential ancient Near Eastern culture was the
   a. Egyptian culture.
   b. Mesopotamian culture.
   c. Assyrian culture.
   d. Hittite culture.

3. Amon-Re was the Egyptian god (king) of
   a. the dead.
   b. fertility.
   c. the gods.
   d. agriculture.

4. The ziggurat, the world's first monumental architecture, was a monument to the
   a. pharaoh.
   b. Sumerian gods.
   c. Battle of Nineveh.
   d. Great Flood.

5. According to the code of Hammurabi, tavern keepers who watered down drinks were

   a. sent to jail.
   b. sold into slavery.
   c. drowned.
   d. dragged through a field.

6. The Ebla tablets, discovered in 1976, prove
   a. the close connection between Mesopotamia and Syria, plus the presence of a written language.
   b. that there was no Mesopotamian influence on the Bible.
   c. that Mesopotamian culture remained *only* in Mesopotamia.
   d. that no link existed between Mesopotamian literature and religion and Old Testament theology.

7. Which of the following was *not* a goal of King Hammurabi of Babylon?
   a. To make Babylon secure
   b. To unify Mesopotamia
   c. To win a place in Mesopotamian civilization for the Babylonians
   d. To live at peace with his neighbors, regardless of the cost

8. Which of the following groups did *not* participate in the mass migration of 2000-1200 B.C.?
   a. The Sumerians
   b. The Hittites
   c. The Hyksos
   d. Indo-European peoples

9. The law code of King Hammurabi in Mesopotamia
   a. included a great deal of legislation on agriculture and irrigation canals.
   b. handed down mild punishments for almost all crimes.
   c. treated all social classes equally.
   d. did not protect the consumer.

10. Irrigation is a special feature of
   a. Egypt.
   b. Anatolia.
   c. Syria.
   d. Assyria.

11. Geography influenced Sumerian society by
   a. making communications within the region easy.

    b. making communications within the region difficult.
    c. providing the inhabitants with everything they needed.
    d. providing an abundance of precious metals.

12. Rivers in Mesopotamia were important because they
    a. were a unifying factor.
    b. drained off excess water.
    c. kept out invaders.
    d. made irrigation possible.

13. The Sumerians responded to their environment by
    a. achieving rapid political unification.
    b. developing a pessimistic view of life.
    c. appreciating the value of floods.
    d. developing an appreciation of nature.

14. The ziggurat was
    a. an agricultural community.
    b. a temple to the gods.
    c. the king's palace.
    d. a military camp.

15. The *lugal* in Mesopotamia was the
    a. secular war-leader and administrator.
    b. chief priest of the temple.
    c. council of elders.
    d. legal owner of a slave.

16. Marduk was the chief god of the
    a. Sumerians.
    b. Egyptians.
    c. Amorites.
    d. Hittites.

17. The common people of Egypt were
    a. completely without legal rights.
    b. at the bottom of the social scale.
    c. divided on the basis of color.
    d. related to the Mesopotamians.

18. The most influential ancient Near Eastern culture was the
    a. Hittite.

　　b.　Mesopotamian.
　　c.　Egyptian.
　　d.　Assyrian.

19.　The Hittites were
　　a.　Persians.
　　b.　Semites.
　　c.　Akkadians.
　　d.　Indo-Europeans.

20.　The Egyptian god Osiris was closely associated with
　　a.　Isis.
　　b.　Aton.
　　c.　Amon-Re.
　　d.　Serapis.

21.　Akhenaten was interested in fostering
　　a.　military expansion.
　　b.　worship of Aton.
　　c.　agricultural improvements.
　　d.　a return to traditional values.

GEOGRAPHY

1.　Referring to Map 1.1, use the following space to describe the geographical features that had a major impact on Egypt's economic and political development.

2.　Referring to Map 1.1, use the space below to describe the geographical features that account for Mesopotamia's economic and political development.

UNDERSTANDING HISTORY THROUGH READING AND THE ARTS

The life and times of the great pharaohs make interesting reading. Two excellent books are L. Cottrell, *Life Under the Pharaohs* (1964) and C. Desroches-Noblecourt, *Tutankhamen* (1965). Desroches-Noblecourt has also written an account of Egyptian art entitled *Egyptian Wall Paintings from Tombs and Temples* (1962) that is richly illustrated and informative, while C. Aldred's *Egyptian Art in the Days of the Pharaohs** (1985) examines nearly 3000 years of Egyptian art in terms of the religious, historical, and environmental forces of Egypt. The early cave paintings, pottery, and gold ornaments of the Neolithic and Bronze Age artists and the metalwork of the Iron Age artists and others are examined in T. Powell, *Prehistoric Art** (1985).

The importance of the Sumerians in the origins of civilization is the subject of S. H. Kramer's excellent survey, *The Sumerians: Their History, Culture and Character** (1984), and among the best introductions to Egyptian civilization is C. Aldred's *The Egyptians* (1984). Everyday life in the Egyptian village during the New Kingdom is interestingly evoked by J. Romer in *Ancient Lives: Daily Life in Egypt of the Pharaohs* (1984).

PROBLEMS FOR FURTHER INVESTIGATION

Precisely who were the Sumerians, and what were their contributions to the origins of civilization in Mesopotamia? The history of the discovery and study of the Sumerians is described in Tom B. Jones, ed., *The Sumerian Problem** (1969).

The origins and early development of agriculture, urban life, trade, and writing in the Near East have raised questions still hotly debated among historians and archaeologists. One can find excellent introductions to these issues in a volume of readings from *Scientific American* titled *Hunters, Farmers, and Civilizations: Old World Archeology** (1979).

*Available in paperback.

READING WITH UNDERSTANDING
EXERCISE 1

LEARNING HOW TO UNDERLINE OR HIGHLIGHT THE MAJOR POINTS

Underlining (or highlighting with a felt-tipped pen, as many students prefer) plays an important part in the learning process in college courses. Underlining provides you with a permanent record of what you want to learn. It helps you in your efforts to master the material and prepare for exams.

The introductory essay (pp. vii-xii) provides some good guidelines for learning how to underline effectively, and you should review it carefully before continuing.

Further Suggestions

1. In addition to underlining selectively, *consider numbering the main points* to help you remember them. Numbering helps make the main points stand out clearly, which is a major purpose of all underlining or highlighting.

2. *Read an entire section through before you underline or highlight it.* Then, as you read it a second time, you will be better able to pick out and underline key facts, main points, and sentences or paragraphs that summarize and interpret the information.

3. *Avoid false economies.* Some students do not mark their books because they are afraid that the bookstores will not buy them back. This is a foolish way to try to save money for two reasons. First, students must of necessity invest a great deal of time and money in their college education. By refusing to mark their books, they are reducing their chances of doing their best and thus endangering their whole college investment. Probably the only alternative to marking your books is making detailed written notes, which is more difficult and much more time consuming.

Second, carefully underlined books are *a permanent yet personal record of what you study and learn*. Such books become valuable reference works, helping you recall important learning experiences and forming the core of your library in future years.

Exercise

Read the following passage once as a whole. Read it a second time to underline or highlight it. Consider numbering the points. On completion, compare your underlining with the model on the next page, which is an example of reasonable and useful underlining. Finally, compare the underlined section with the chapter outline in the *Study Guide*. You will see how the outline summary is an aid in learning how to underline major points.

EGYPT, THE LAND OF THE PHARAOHS
(3100-1200 B.C.)

The Greek historian and traveler Herodotus in the fifth century B.C. called Egypt the "gift of the Nile." No other single geographical factor had such a fundamental and profound impact on the shaping of Egyptian life, society, and history as the Nile. Unlike the rivers of Mesopotamia it rarely brought death and destruction. The river was primarily a creative force. The Egyptians never feared the relatively calm Nile in the way the Mesopotamians feared their rivers. Instead they sang its praises:

Hail to thee, O Nile, that issues from the earth and comes to
  keep Egypt alive! . . .
He that waters the meadows which Re created,
He that makes to drink the desert . . .
He who makes barley and brings emmer [wheat] into being . . .
He who brings grass into being for the cattle.
He who makes every beloved tree to grow . . .
O Nile, verdant art thou, who makest man and cattle to live.[15]

In the minds of the Egyptians, the Nile was the supreme fertilizer and renewer of the land. Each September the Nile floods its valley, transforming it into a huge area of marsh or lagoon. By the end of November the water retreats, leaving behind a thin covering of fertile mud ready to be planted with crops.

The annual flood made the growing of abundant crops almost effortless, especially in southern Egypt. Herodotus, used to the rigors of Greek agriculture, was amazed by the ease with which the Egyptians raised their crops:

For indeed without trouble they obtain crops from the land more easily than all other men. . . . They do not labor to dig furrows with the plough or hoe or do the work which other men do to raise grain. But when the river by itself inundates the fields and the water recedes, then each man, having sown his field, sends pigs into it. When the pigs trample down the seed, he waits for the harvest. Then when the pigs thresh the grain, he gets his crop.[16]

As late as 1822, John Burckhardt, an English traveler, watched nomads sowing grain by digging large holes in the mud and throwing in seeds. The extraordinary fertility of the Nile valley made it easy to produce an annual agricultural surplus, which in turn sustained a growing and prosperous population.

Whereas the Tigris and Euphrates and their many tributaries carved up Mesopotamia into isolated areas, the Nile served to unify Egypt. The river was the principal highway and promoted easy communication throughout the valley. As individual bands of settlers moved into the Nile valley, they created stable agricultural communities. By about 3100 B.C. there were some forty of these communities in constant contact with one another. This contact, encouraged and facilitated by the Nile, virtually ensured the early political unification of the country.

Egypt was fortunate in that it was nearly self-sufficient. Besides the fertility of its soil, Egypt possessed enormous quantities of stone, which served as the raw material of architecture and sculpture. Abundant clay was available for pottery, as was gold for jewelry and ornaments. The raw materials that Egypt lacked were close at hand. The Egyptians could obtain copper from Sinai and timber from Lebanon. They had little cause to look to the outside world for their essential needs, which helps to explain the insular quality of Egyptian life.

Geography further encouraged isolation by closing Egypt off from the outside world. To the east and west of the Nile valley stretch grim deserts. The Nubian Desert and the cataracts of the Nile discourage penetration from the south. Only in the north did the Mediterranean Sea leave Egypt exposed. Thus, geography shielded Egypt from invasion and from extensive immigration. Unlike the Mesopotamians, the Egyptians enjoyed centuries of peace and tranquillity, during which they could devote most of their resources to peaceful development of their distinctive civilization.

Yet Egypt was not completely sealed off. As early as 3250 B.C. Mesopotamian influences, notably architectural techniques and materials and perhaps even writing, made themselves felt in Egyptian life. Still later, from 1680 to 1580 B.C., northern Egypt was ruled by foreign invaders, the Hyksos. Infrequent though they were, such periods of foreign influence fertilized Egyptian culture without changing it in any fundamental way.

The God-King of Egypt

The geographic unity of Egypt quickly gave rise to political unification of the country under the authority of a king whom the Egyptians called "pharaoh." The details of this process have been lost. The Egyptians themselves told of a great king, Menes, who united Egypt into a single kingdom around 3100 B.C. Thereafter the Egyptians divided their history into *dynasties*, or families of kings. For modern historical purposes, however, it is more useful to divide Egyptian history into periods. The political unification of Egypt ushered in the period known as the Old Kingdom, an era remarkable for its prosperity and artistic flowering, and for the evolution of religious beliefs.

EGYPT, THE LAND OF THE PHARAOHS
(3100-1200 B.C.)

Geography

1

The Greek historian and traveler Herodotus in the fifth century B.C. called Egypt the "gift of the Nile." No other single geographical factor had such a fundamental and profound impact on the shaping of Egyptian life, society, and history as the Nile. Unlike the rivers of Mesopotamia it rarely brought death and destruction. The river was primarily a creative force. The Egyptians never feared the relatively calm Nile in the way the Mesopotamians feared their rivers. Instead they sang its praises:

> Hail to thee, O Nile, that issues from the earth and comes to
>   keep Egypt alive! . . .
> He that waters the meadows which Re created,
> He that makes to drink the desert . . .
> He who makes barley and brings emmer [wheat] into being . . .
> He who brings grass into being for the cattle.
> He who makes every beloved tree to grow . . .
> O Nile, verdant art thou, who makest man and cattle to live.[15]

In the minds of the Egyptians, the Nile was the supreme fertilizer and renewer of the land. Each September the Nile floods its valley, transforming it into a huge area of marsh or lagoon. By the end of November the water retreats, leaving behind a thin covering of fertile mud ready to be planted with crops.

1a

The annual flood made the growing of abundant crops almost effortless, especially in southern Egypt. Herodotus, used to the rigors of Greek agriculture, was amazed by the ease with which the Egyptians raised their crops:

> For indeed without trouble they obtain crops from the land
> more easily than all other men. . . . They do not labor to dig
> furrows with the plough or hoe or do the work which other
> men do to raise grain. But when the river by itself inundates
> the fields and the water recedes, then each man, having sown
> his field, sends pigs into it. When the pigs trample down the

5   Yet Egypt was not completely sealed off. As early as 3250 B.C. Mesopotamian influences, notably architectural techniques and materials and perhaps even writing, made themselves felt in Egyptian life. Still later, from 1680 to 1580 B.C., northern Egypt was ruled by foreign invaders, the Hyksos. Infrequent though

6   they were, such periods of foreign influence fertilized Egyptian culture without changing it in any fundamental way.

The God-King of Egypt

The geographic unity of Egypt quickly gave rise to political unification of the country under the authority of a king whom the Egyptians called "pharaoh." The details of this process have been lost. The Egyptians themselves told of a great king, Menes, who united Egypt into a single kingdom around 3100 B.C. Thereafter the Egyptians divided their history into *dynasties*, or families of kings. For modern historical purposes, however, it is more useful to divide Egyptian history into periods. The political unification of Egypt ushered in the period known as the Old Kingdom, an era remarkable for its prosperity and artistic flowering, and for the evolution of religious beliefs.

CHAPTER 2

SMALL KINGDOMS AND MIGHTY
EMPIRES IN THE NEAR EAST

CHAPTER OBJECTIVES

After reading and studying this chapter you should be able to answer the following questions:

Q-1. How did Egypt pass on its cultural heritage to its African neighbors?
Q-2. How did the Hebrew state evolve, and what are the distinguishing features of Hebrew life and religious thought?
Q-3. What enabled the Assyrians to overrun their neighbors, and how did their cruelty finally cause their undoing?
Q-4. How did Iranian nomads create the Persian Empire?

CHAPTER SYNOPSIS

From about the thirteenth century B.C., when the empires of the Hittites and the Egyptians were destroyed by invaders, until the ninth century B.C., when Assyrian rule was imposed on the area, the Near East existed as a patchwork of small, independent kingdoms. This chapter opens with a description of how a weakened Egypt was overrun by its African neighbors, the Nubians and the Libyans, who gave Egypt a new vibrancy while assimilating themselves to Egyptian culture. By 700 B.C., Egypt was reunited, and although it did not re-emerge as an empire, its cultural influence remained paramount, particularly in northern Africa.

The power vacuum that followed the fall of the great empires was significant because it allowed less powerful peoples to settle and propser independently and, as a result, make particularly important contributions to Western society. Foremost among these peoples were the Phoenicians, who used their freedom to sail in the

Mediterranean Sea and build a prosperous commercial network, and the even smaller kingdom of the Hebrews. Modern archaeology tends to confirm the Old Testament account of the Hebrews' movement from Mesopotamia into Canaan, enslavement in Egypt, and subsequent liberation and establishment of a homeland in Palestine. Important in this process was the Hebrews' vision of their god, Yahweh. A covenant with Yahweh—centering on the Ten Commandments—formed the basis of Hebrew life and law and provided the energy with which the kings Saul, David, and Solomon, along with the great prophets, unified the Hebrews into a prosperous society based on high standards of mercy and justice. Their unique monotheism, combined with settled agriculture and urban life, provided the framework for the Hebrews' daily life. A chief feature of this life was its ability to change, best seen in the evolution of the family from a strong patriarchy based on the extended family to a more liberated urban nuclear family.

The power vacuum in the Near East evaporated in the ninth century with the rise of the Assyrians, the most warlike peoples the Near East had yet known. For two hundred years the Assyrians ruled an empire that stretched from the Persian Gulf across the Fertile Crescent and westward through northern Egypt. Despite their brutality, the Assyrians owed their success less to calculated terrorism than to efficient military organization. The Assyrian empire fell swiftly in 612 B.C., and had it not been for modern archaeological work may have continued to be unknown.

The Persian Empire, which grew out of the unique geographic position of what is now Iran, was the most tolerant and humane empire to date. The empire began in 550 B.C. with the first conquests of Cyrus the Great. The next two hundred years of Persian rule in the Near East were marked by efficient administration and respect for the diverse cultures of conquered states. Out of this benevolent rule came an important new religion, Zoroastrianism, which gave to Western society the idea of individual choice in the struggle between goodness and evil. All in all, these seven hundred years were marked by chaos, order, diversity, and unity, as the Near East forged some of its most important achievements.

STUDY OUTLINE

I.   Eygpt, a shattered kingdom
   A.   The invasion of the sea people
      1.   These invasions brought 400 years of dark ages to Egypt
      2.   The Third Intermediate Period (eleventh to seventh centuries B.C.) meant the end of Egypt's greatness in the Near East
      3.   From 950 to 730 B.C. northern Egypt was ruled by Libyans, while southern Egypt came under the control of the Africans of Nubia
      4.   Both Nubians and Libyans adopted the Egyptian culture

5. Egypt was reunified by the African Kingdom of Kush
   a. The king of Kush, Piankhy, brought unity and peace to Egypt—but not a revival of empire
   b. These Africans adopted Egyptian culture and continued to carry it south into northeastern Africa

II. The children of Israel
   A. The power vacuum created by the fall of the Hittite and Egyptian states allowed lesser states to thrive
      1. The Phoenicians were outstanding seafarers, merchants, and explorers
      2. Among their achievements were the building of Carthage and the development of a new alphabet that related one letter to one sound
   B. The collapse of Egypt and the Hittites and the growth of small kingdoms
      1. According to the Old Testament, the Hebrews followed Abraham out of Mesopotamia into Canaan, and from there migrated into the Nile delta, where eventually they were enslaved
      2. Moses then led the Hebrews out of Egypt and into Canaan, where they built a political confederation
      3. Under Saul and David, the Hebrews built the Kingdom of Judah, with its capital at Jerusalem
      4. King Solomon built a great temple and extended Hebrew power
         a. The temple was the symbol of Hebrew unity
         b. At his death the kingdom was divided in two
         c. The northern half became Israel while the southern half was Judah
   C. The evolution of Hebrew religion
      1. The Hebrew religion was monotheistic, centered on the covenant with the god Yahweh
      2. Jewish law and ethics, with their stress on justice and mercy, evolved from the Ten Commandments of Yahweh and the words of the prophets
   D. Daily life in Israel
      1. The end of nomadic life and coming of urban life changed family and marriage customs
         a. Communal land ownership gave way to family ownership
         b. The extended tribal family gave way to the *nuclear* family, although urbanization weakened family ties and the power of the father
         c. The end of nomadic life led to monogamous marriages
         d. Most marriages were legal contracts arranged by the parents
         e. Divorce was available only to the husband
      2. Jewish society places strong emphasis on rearing children
         a. Children, particularly sons, were important for economic reasons
         b. Both parents played a role in the child's education
         c. Children worked in agriculture with their parents

   3. Peace and prosperity brought about a decline of the small family farm
      and a rise of large estates and slave labor
   4. The rise of urban life brought new job opportunities and increased trade
      a. Craft and trade specialization thrived
      b. At first commerce was dominated by the king and/or foreigners
III. Assyria, the military monarchy
   A. Growth of militarism and political cohesion among the Assyrians
      1. King Shalmaneser unleashed the first of the Assyrian attacks on Syria
         and Palestine
      2. Under Tiglath-pileser III and Sargon II, the Assyrians created an empire
         that extended from Mesopotamia to central Egypt
      3. Conquest bred revolt, which in turn led to brutal Assyrian retaliation
   B. Sources of Assyrian success
      1. Effective military organization and new military techniques and equip-
         ment were developed
      2. Assyrians set up a flexible system of rule over their conquered land
   C. Assyrian rule
      1. The Assyrians organized an empire with provinces and dependent states
      2. A good communication system was established, and calculated terrorism
         was practiced
      3. The Assyrians disappeared from history until A. H. Layard discovered
         Nineveh in 1939
      4. Layard found that Assyrian art was brutal yet sophisticated
      5. Assyrian art, like its military and political innovations, influenced the
         Persians
IV. The empire of the Persian kings
   A. The Persians were Indo-European Iranians who unified many cultures into
      a tolerant and humane empire
   B. Iran's chief geographical feature
      1. This is a great central plateau between the Tigris-Euphrates valley and
         the Indus valley
   C. The first Iranians—the coming of the Medes and Persians
      1. The first Iranians were nomadic Medes and Persians with great horse-
         manship skills
      2. They established a patchwork of small kingdoms centered on agricultural
         towns
      3. These towns became centers for agriculture, mineral extraction, and
         horse-breeding
      4. The Iranians of the north, the Medes, grew strong enough to help over-
         throw the Assyrian Empire
   D. The creation of the Persian Empire

1. The founder of the Persian Empire, Cyrus the Great (559-530 B.C.) held enlightened views
    a. He viewed Persia and Medea as the state of Iran
    b. His empire gave respect, toleration, and protection to its conquered people
    c. His first act was to unify the Persians and the Medes
2. Next Cyrus won control of the west as far as the Greek coast of Anatolia
3. Then Cyrus marched to eastern Iran (Parthia, Bactria) to strengthen Iran from warring nomads
4. He conquered Babylonia and gave protection to the Jews

E. Thus Spake Zarathustra, the religion of Iran
1. At first Iranian religion was polytheistic, simple, and primitive
2. Zoroaster gave Iranian religion new ideas
    a. Most information about this unique new religion comes from the hymns and poems called *Zend Avesta*
    b. Life is a battleground between good and evil, and each individual can decide between the two
    c. Eternal fate (the Last Judgment) will be decided on the basis of one's deeds in life
    d. The conversion of King Darius to Zoroastrianism led to its spread throughout the empire

F. Persia's world empire
1. Cyrus's successors rounded out the empire to India in the east and Anatolia, Egypt, and Libya in the west
    a. The empire was divided into twenty satrapies
    b. Roads were built so that royal couriers could enable the king to rule effectively
    c. The conquered people, left free to enjoy their traditional ways of life, were grateful for Persian rule
    d. For over two hundred years the Persians gave the Near East a period of peace which allowed people to enjoy their native traditions

REVIEW QUESTIONS

Q-1. Explain how the peoples of Nubia, Libya, and the Kingdom of Kush interacted with Egypt and its culture. What were the results?

Q-2. Why is the Old Testament such an important source for historians in reconstructing Hebrew society?

Q-3. What are the main features of the Hebrew religion? How important was religion in the daily life of the people?

Q-4. What effect did the end of nomadic life have on Hebrew property and marriage practices?

Q-5. Describe Hebrew attitudes toward children. What was childhood like for Hebrew sons and daughters?

Q-6. What changes did prosperity and urbanization bring to Hebrew life?

Q-7. What impact did Assyria have on the Near Eastern world? Was its influence long-lasting?

Q-8. Describe the extent of the Assyrian Empire. What were the secrets of Assyrian success?

Q-9. How did the discoveries of A. H. Layard shed "remarkable new light" on Assyrian history?

Q-10. Iran has been described as the "highway between East and West." Explain.

Q-11. Describe the accomplishments of Cyrus the Great. Why was this conqueror regarded by many non-Persians as a liberator and benefactor?

Q-12. Zoroaster gave the Near East some novel ideas about divinity and human life. What were these ideas?

Q-13. Describe the Persian system of imperial rule. In what ways is it different from or similar to that of the Assyrians?

STUDY-REVIEW EXERCISES

Define the following key concepts and terms.

nuclear family

monotheism

polygamy

monogamy

Yahweh

the Hebrew Covenant

Zoroastrianism

satrapy

the Torah

Identify and give the significance of the following.

Sargon II

Nubians

Solomon's Jerusalem temple

Libyans

Phoenicians

the Ten Commandments

Moses

Zend Avesta

kingdom of Kush

Jeremiah

Ark of the Covenant

the Old Testament

Nineveh

Cyrus the Great

Siyalk

Ahura

Medes

Persians

Explain each of the following and give its significance by noting the basic ideas of *each and the ways in which they were unique: (a) the Hebrew religion and (b) Zoro-astrianism.*

<u>*Test*</u> *your understanding of the chapter by answering the following questions.*

1. With the coming of peace and prosperity, the tendency in Hebrew society was toward (a) greater concentration of landholding, (b) more small family farms,

    (c) a decline in slavery. _____
2. As opposed to the early Hebrew law, the Torah, later legal tradition in Hebrew society tended to be *more/less* humanitarian.
3. The Hebrew religion was based on a personal covenant with one god,

    _____.
4. The African invaders of Egypt in the thirteenth century *did/did not* admire and adopt Egyptian culture.
5. The two groups of Iranian peoples united by Cyrus the Great were the

    _____ and the _____.
6. With the rise of the Persian Empire, the balance of power in the Near East shifted to the *east/west* of Mesopotamia.
7. For administrative purposes, the Persians divided their empire into twenty

    _____, or provinces.

MULTIPLE-CHOICE QUESTIONS

1. Which one of the following is not true with regard to marriage in early Hebrew society?
    a. Divorce was available to the husband.
    b. Restrictions against mixed marriages existed.
    c. Marriages were usually undertaken as a result of affection and physical attraction of the partners.

2. King Solomon is important in Hebrew history because of all but which one of the following?
    a. He fostered Hebrew unity and economic growth.
    b. He encouraged the division of Israel in its old tribal system.
    c. He built a religious temple to stand as the symbol of Hebrew unity.

3. The most brutal and militaristic of all the Near Eastern cultures was that of the
    a. Persians.
    b. Assyrians.
    c. Phoenicians.

4. The Persian king Cyrus the Great carried out a foreign policy based on
    a. torture and submission to Persian traditions.
    b. tolerance of other cultures.
    c. universal acceptance of the Zoroastrian religion.

5. The Zoroastrian religion stressed all but which one of the following?
    a. Individual free will
    b. The eventual triumph of evil over good
    c. The possibility of eternal life

6. Egypt was reunified in the eighth century by the African Kingdom of
    a. the Nile.
    b. Phoenicia.
    c. Kush.
    d. Ethiopia.

7. The power vacuum that followed the fall of the empires of the Hittites and the Egyptians from about the thirteenth century was important because
    a. it resulted in the end of Egypt as an influential culture in the Near East and Africa.
    b. it led to the unification of the Near East under Hebrew rule.
    c. it allowed less powerful peoples, such as the Phoenicians and the Hebrews, to settle and prosper independently.
    d. it led to four centuries of backwardness and cultural regression.

8. The Hebrew family pattern evolved
    a. from an extended family to an urban nuclear family.
    b. from a nuclear family to an extended family.
    c. from a strong emphasis on monogamy to an emphasis on polygamy.
    d. from a matriarchy to a patriarchy.

9. Peace and prosperity in Israel brought about
   a. increased landholding for small farmers.
   b. a breakup of the large estates.
   c. the end to slave labor.
   d. the decline of the small family farm.

10. Zoroaster stressed all but which one of the following ideas?
    a. the individual has free choice
    b. life is a struggle between good and evil
    c. each individual will face a last judgment
    d. life ends with death

11. The successors of Cyrus the Great divided his empire into
    a. three separate kingdoms.
    b. twenty satrapies.
    c. an east and a west province.
    d. six military districts.

12. The founder of the Persian empire was
    a. King Darius.
    b. Zoroaster.
    c. Cyrus the Great.
    d. Siyalk.

13. All but one of the following is true with regard to marriage in early Hebrew society:
    a. Divorce was available to the husband only.
    b. Marriage was most often arranged for family and economic reasons.
    c. Restrictions against mixed marriages existed.
    d. Children were not seen as an important reason for marriage.

14. Iran's chief geographical feature is
    a. a great central plateau between the Tigris-Euphrates and the Indus valleys.
    b. a thick mountainous region.
    c. a dense tropical coastal area as its western edge.
    d. the eastern portion of the fertile crescent.

15. The wealth of Iran was based on
    a. iron production.
    b. horse-breeding and overland trade.
    c. small-farm agriculture.
    d. all of the above.

16. The Persians acquired many of their military and political practices and organizational genius from
    a. the Hebrews.
    b. the Sumerians.
    c. the Assyrians.
    d. the Philistines.

17. The most brutal and militaristic of the Near Eastern peoples were
    a. the Medes.
    b. the Persians.
    c. the Phoenicians.
    d. the Assyrians.

18. The Phoenicians are best known as
    a. great militarists.
    b. prosperous urban merchants and sea traders.
    c. religious innovators.
    d. rulers of the entire Near East after the fall of Persia.

19. The Phoenicians
    a. overthrew the Egyptian kingdom.
    b. developed a thriving agricultural community.
    c. waged large-scale wars against the Hebrews.
    d. became merchants and explorers.

GEOGRAPHY

1. Describe the geographic features of Iran and explain how they have influenced the course of Near Eastern history. How does the economic development of early Iran reflect its geography?

2. Referring to Maps 2.2 and 2.3 in the text, describe the extent of the Assyrian and Persian empires. How did the two differ in terms of its attitude toward other peoples and cultures?

PROBLEMS FOR FURTHER INVESTIGATION

Students interested in ancient Near Eastern religion and the idea of one god should start with R. J. Christen and H. E. Hazelton, eds., *Monotheism and Moses** (1969), or, the more general work, *A History of Religious Ideas,** 3 vols. (1978-1985), by M. Eliade. Problems of interpretation and investigation in the history of the ancient Near East are set forth, along with an excellent bibliography, in M. Covensky, *The Ancient Near Eastern Tradition** (1966). The impact of infectious diseases on ancient civilization is considered in W. McNeill, *Plagues and Peoples* (1976).

There are many interesting research topics related to archaeological study and the Old Testament. For instance, the biblical flood story did not originate with the Hebrews, and Hammurabi's law code is not the oldest. The sources of the story and the code and other lively subjects relating to the ancient Near East are considered in S. N. Kramer, *History Begins at Sumer, Twenty-seven "Firsts" in Man's Recorded History** (1959). Hebrew law and morality are dealt with in G. Mendenhall, *Law and Covenant in Israel and the Ancient Near East* (1955), and J. Goldwin, *The Living Talmud: The Wisdom of the Fathers and Its Classical Commentaries** (1954), is an interesting essay on Jewish life and religion.

How are the Old Testament's accounts of the early history of the Hebrews corroborated by the findings of archaeologists who have excavated in the Middle East? In fact, archaeological data do not always agree with the Biblical accounts. For a good introduction, read K. Kenyon, *Archaeology in the Holy Land** (1979). Also informative is D. J. Wiseman, ed., *Peoples of Old Testament Times* (1973).

UNDERSTANDING HISTORY THROUGH READING AND THE ARTS

Reading the Old Testament is one of the best sources for learning the history and culture of the Near East. See especially the major history books of the Old Testament: Joshua, Judges, Ruth, I and II Samuel, I and II Kings, Nehemiah, and Esther.

*Available in paperback.

Michael Grant, *The History of Ancient Israel* (1984), provides an eminently readable discussion of early Hebrew society and the rise of the Hebrew monarchy. A briefer summary is Harry M. Orlinsky, *Ancient Israel** (1960). Hebrew law and morality are described in G. Mendenhall, *Law and Covenant in Israel and the Ancient Near East* (1955); and J. Goldwin, *The Living Talmud: The Wisdom of the Fathers and its Classical Commentaries** (1954), offers an interesting essay on Jewish life and religion.

*Available in paperback.

CHAPTER 3

THE LEGACY OF GREECE

CHAPTER OBJECTIVES

After reading and studying this chapter you should be able to answer the following questions:

Q-1. What geographical factors helped to mold the city-state?
Q-2. How and why did the Greeks develop different political forms, such as tyranny and democracy?
Q-3. What did the Greek intellectual triumph entail?
Q-4. How and why did the Greek experiment fail?

CHAPTER SYNOPSIS

Ancient Greece made an invaluable contribution to human progress and the development of Western civilization. Greek society explored a remarkable range of the problems that beset men and women of all ages: the nature of God and the universe, the dimensions of human sexuality, the challenges of war and imperialism, the proper relationship between the individual and the state. The Greeks were also great thinkers and actors. They have become an example of both human excellence and human frailty, for the Greeks eventually destroyed themselves through war and imperialism. An important question this chapter seeks to answer is why the Greek experiment failed.

The chapter stresses the importance of geographical isolation and proximity to the sea in the political and economic development of the city-state, or polis. It also describes how Greek (Hellenic) religion, art, and life were intimately interwoven. Though believed to be immortal, the Greek gods were attributed with human qualities. In honoring their gods the Greeks honored the human spirit and sought human excellence.

For the Greeks, the search for truth and meaning in life was pursued not only through mythology and religious experience but through rational philosophy—by great thinkers such as Socrates, Plato, and Aristotle—and the arts as well. The plays of the great dramatists Aeschylus, Sophocles, and Euripides have led generations of people to examine life's basic conflicts. The Greeks saw drama, comedy, sculpture, and philosophy as ways to relate to their gods and discover the truth about life. Bisexuality and homosexuality were taken for granted in Greek society.

The reasons for Greek aggression in the Aegean world are explored, as are the reasons for the war between the two Greek superpowers, Sparta and Athens. These two states represented opposing political systems and different philosophies of life. Daily life in Athens included sophisticated art and great literature, but the economic system was simple and based on slavery to a large extent. Although it was war that saved Greece (and the West) from the oriental monarchy of the Persians, it was also war within Greece—especially among Sparta, Athens, and Thebes—that destroyed the freedom of the Greeks and brought on their conquest by the ambitious Philip II of Macedonia.

STUDY OUTLINE

I. Hellas: the land
   A. The effects of the topography of Greece and the Aegean archipelago
      1. The mountains both inspired the Greeks and isolated them from one another, hindering unity, while good harbors encouraged interest in Asia Minor and Egypt
II. The Minoans and Mycenaeans (ca 1650-ca 1100 B.C.)
   A. The Greeks had established themselves in Greece by ca 1650 B.C.
      1. The first and most important Greek-speaking culture was probably at the city of Mycenae
      2. In addition, an early Greek culture, called Minoan, grew up on the island of Crete
         a. The head of Crete was a king; its political-economic centers were a series of palaces
         b. The Minoan culture was wealthy and had bronze implements
      3. From its center at Cnossus, Mycenaeans built cities at Thebes, Athens, Tiryns, and Pylos
         a. The king and his warrior-aristocracy exercised political and economic control
         b. Scribes kept records, but little is known of the ordinary people except that an extensive division of labor existed

      4. Minoan-Mycenaean contacts turned from peace to war ca 1450 B.C.
- a. The Minoan capital of Cnossus was destroyed for unknown reasons
- b. Thereafter the Mycenaeans grew rich, but eventually were destroyed, probably because of internecine war

      5. The fall of the Mycenaean kingdoms ushered in a "Dark Age" of Greece from 1100-800 B.C.

B. Homer, Hesiod, and the heroic past (1100-800 B.C.)
1. Bronze Age and Dark Age epic poems idealized the past
2. The *Iliad*, the *Odyssey*, and the *Theogony* contributed to the rebirth of literacy
   - a. The *Iliad* by Homer points to the flaws in the human character and the whims of the gods
   - b. The *Odyssey* is also about human nature and unpredictable gods
   - c. Hesiod, the poet, centered his works on ethics and divine justice
3. The great poets taught men and women how to live

III. The polis

A. The polis, or city-state
1. Athens, Sparta, and Thebes were the chief city-states
2. The acropolis was the religious center of the polis, and the agora was its marketplace and political center
3. The polis was both an agricultural and an urban center
4. The polis was an intimate community of citizens that tended to exclude outsiders and maintain its independence jealously
5. The polis could be governed as a monarchy, aristocracy, oligarchy, or democracy

B. The exclusiveness and individualism of each polis led to constant war and the eventual decline of Greece

IV. The Lyric Age (800-500 B.C.)

A. Overseas expansion following the breakdown of the Mycenaean world
1. The expansion of Greeks throughout the Mediterranean was due to land shortage and the desire for adventure
2. Greek communities extended from the Black Sea to North Africa and into Spain
3. The Greek poet Archilochus exemplifies the energy and adventure of this period of growth

B. The Lyric Poets encouraged individualism, patriotism, and justice
1. Erotic love and adventure are portrayed in the lives and work of the poets Sappho and Archilochus
2. Homosexuality was not considered abnormal by the Greeks

C. The growth of Sparta into a powerful polis
1. Sparta's victory in the Messenian wars extended its boundaries and enslaved the Messenians

      2. The warriors, or "hoplites," demanded and received political rights

      3. The Lycurgan regime brought about military tyranny in Sparta

      4. The Spartans disdained wealth and luxury and glorified war

  D. Evolution of Athens

      1. Athens moved from aristocracy to democracy

         a. Poor peasants demanded legal reforms

         b. Draco's code—Athen's first law—established the fact that the law belonged to all citizens

         c. Peasants looked to "tyrants" for land reform

      2. Solon's reforms benefited the common man

      3. Pisistratus reduced the power of the aristocracy

      4. The rule by tyrants was followed by Cleisthenes' reorganization of the state and the creation of democracy

         a. *Demes* were the basis of political citizenship

         b. *Ostracism* was a way to get rid of dangerous politicians

      5. Athenian democracy proved that a large number of people could run the affairs of state and enjoy equal rights

V. The Classical Period (500-338 B.C.)

  A. The deadly conflicts—war between the Greeks and the Persians

      1. Greek victory in war guaranteed and protected the flowering of Greek culture and freedom

      2. Xerxes invaded Greece in 480 B.C., but the Persian forces were eventually defeated

  B. The growth of the Athenian Empire (478-431 B.C.)

      1. The Athenians established the Delian League to continue the fight against Persia

         a. Led by Cimon, the Athenians drove the Persians out of the Aegean

         b. The Athenians turned the League and its resources to promote their own empire

         c. Athenian aggressiveness alarmed Sparta and its allies

      2. Athens' conflict with Corinth led to war with Sparta

  C. The Peloponnesian War (431-404 B.C.)

      1. War between 430 and 421 B.C. led to death, destruction, stalemate, and a new breed of self-serving Athenian politicians

      2. The Peace of Nicias (421 B.C.) led to a cold war

      3. The opportunist Alcibiades led to Athens in an invasion of Syracuse in Sicily—only to be defeated (413 B.C.)

      4. A final phase was marked by renewed war between Athens and Sparta, Persian intervention, and revolt by many Athenian subjects

      5. Under Lysander, the Spartans defeated Athens in 405 B.C.

  D. The birth of historical awareness

1. The upheaval of war gave birth to the writing of history by men such as Herodotus
2. Herodotus claimed that the greatness of the Greeks lay in their stress on simplicity of life rather than luxury
3. The historian Thucydides claimed that war was due to the foolishness of man, not the intervention of the gods

E. Athenian arts in the age of Pericles
   1. Pericles turned Athens into the showplace of Greece
   2. The Athenian Acropolis became the center of Greek religion and art
   3. The art and architecture of the Acropolis served to praise both the gods and human life
   4. To the Greeks, drama aided in the understanding of basic truths about life and society
   5. Aeschylus, Sophocles, and Euripides were the three greatest dramatists of Athens
      a. Aeschylus wrote a triology of plays about humans in conflict, stressing the themes of betrayal, reconciliation, reason, and justice
      b. Sophocles' masterpieces (the three *Oedipus* plays) deal with the interplay of human matters, justice, and the will of the gods
      c. Euripides' plays focus on humans who face disaster because they allow their passions to overwhelm them

F. Daily life in Periclean Athens
   1. Material life was simple, and home production of goods was common
   2. Slavery was common
   3. Agriculture and small crafts were the major types of labor
   4. Women were protected by law but did not have equal rights with men
   5. Both family life and homosexuality were important parts of Greek life
   6. Greek religion was individual and lacked organized creeds or central authorities
      a. Religion was a matter of ritual and a way to honor the polis
      b. The Olympic games were held for the glory of Zeus and were a unifying factor in Greek life

G. The flowering of philosophy
   1. The Greeks of the Classical Period viewed the universe in terms of natural law, not mythology
   2. Thales, Anaximander, and Heraclitus made important contributions to the sciences
   3. Hippocrates was the founder of modern medicine
   4. The Sophists taught excellence and believed that nothing is absolute
   5. Socrates attempted to discover truth by continuous questioning

   6. Plato's philosophy is based on the idea that reality exists only in the immaterial world
   7. Plato sought to define the perfect society
   8. Aristotle's ideas about the universe lasted for thousands of years
H. The final act: the fall of Greece (403-338 B.C.)
   1. With Athens defeated in the Peloponnesian War, Sparta strove for empire
   2. Thebes then destroyed Spartan power
   3. Finally, conquest by Philip of Macedonia meant an end to Greek freedom

REVIEW QUESTIONS

Q-1. Describe the early Greek Minoan and Mycenaean cultures. What caused their eventual destruction?

Q-2. Describe the function of the acropolis and the agora in the Greek polis.

Q-3. What impact did climate and population size have on polis life?

Q-4. Define and explain the significance of (a) monarchy, (b) aristocracy, (c) oligarchy, and (d) democracy.

Q-5. Describe the relationship between religion and civic duty in the polis.

Q-6. Discuss the nature of Mycenaean culture. What were the repercussions of the fall of the Mycenaean kingdoms?

Q-7. "The Greeks used the gods to help explain the makeup of the universe and how man should live." Explain this statement by referring to specific Greek legends and gods.

Q-8. Why are Homer and Hesiod important sources for us in attempting to understand ancient Greek society?

Q-9. Describe the causes of Greek expansion from ca. 750 to 550 B.C.

Q-10. In what ways does Archilochus represent the spirit of Greek colonization?

Q-11. How did the Spartans settle the problems of overpopulation and land hunger?

Q-12. Discuss life in Sparta in terms of (a) the military, (b) the family, and (c) economic needs.

Q-13. In what ways did Athenian democracy differ from modern democracy?

Q-14. Describe the accomplishments of Draco, Solon, Pisistratus, and Cleisthenes.

Q-15. What were the causes of the conflict between Athens and Sparta? The outcome? Are there any parallels to the world of today?

Q-16. What was the purpose of the acropolis? What role did architecture and building play in the age of Pericles?

Q-17. What role did drama and comedy play in the life of the polis and the people?

Q-18. What was the position of women in Greek society? Were women completely powerless?

Q-19. How widespread and important was homosexuality in Greek society? Did the Greeks regard homosexuality as deviant behavior?

Q-20. How would you judge Hippocrates' ideas? What were the strengths and deficiencies of his views on illness?

Q-21. What were the causes and the outcome of the Theban-Spartan conflict?

STUDY-REVIEW EXERCISES

Define the following key concepts and terms.

polis

rationalism in art and architecture

natural laws versus mythological explanation of the universe

deme

Sophist relativism

Hippocrates' theory of four humors

empirical knowledge

Identify each of the following and give its significance.

Mycenaeans

Minoans

Cnossus

Messenian wars

Helot

Parthenon

Draco's law code

Marathon

Delian League

Peloponnesian War

ostracism

hoplites

Identify the following people and explain their importance.

Homer

Thucydides

Hippocrates

Socrates

Sappho

Solon

Lysander

Plato

Zeus

Aristotle

Cimon

Sophocles

Xerxes

Pericles

Odysseus

Aspasia

Explain the following forms of government.

monarchy

aristocracy

tyranny

Fill in the following blank lines with the letter of the correct answer.

_____ 1.	He thought that the basic element of the universe is water.	a. Hippocrates
_____ 2.	This Pre-Socratic thinker was the first to use general concepts.	b. Democritus
_____ 3.	He theorized that the earth is made of invisible, indestructible atoms.	c. Socrates
_____ 4.	He is known as the father of medicine.	d. Anaximander
_____ 5.	He thought that excellence and happiness could be learned through continuous questioning.	e. Plato
		f. Sappho
_____ 6.	He believed that visible things are merely copies of ideas.	g. Thales
_____ 7.	He claimed that the universe revolves and is spherical.	h. Pericles
_____ 8.	She is best known for erotic poetry.	i. Aristotle

Test your understanding of the chapter by answering the following questions.

1. The three major Greek city-states were _____,

    _____, and _____ .
2. The Olympian gods *were/were not* seen as having human qualities.
3. The democratic Athenians *did/did not* conquer other people and force them to submit to their rule.

4. He defeated a Theban-Athenian army in 338 B.C. to win control of Greece.

_____

5. Sophocles' character Antigone supports the idea of the presence of *divine law/ the state* in human conduct.
6. The hoplites of Sparta *were/were not* successful in gaining political rights.
7. In general, the peasants of Athens *supported/opposed* rule by the tyrants.

MULTIPLE-CHOICE QUESTIONS

1. The two main historians of ancient Greece were
   a. Homer and Hesiod.
   b. Herodotus and Thucydides.
   c. Sophocles and Aristotle.

2. Mycenaean Greece was most probably destroyed by
   a. foreign invaders.
   b. famine.
   c. internecine war.

3. The Delian League was transformed into a means of imperialistic expansion by which of the following city-states?
   a. Sparta.
   b. Thebes.
   c. Athens.

4. Which of the following statements about the Mycenaeans is *false*?
   a. They were the ancestors of the ancient Greeks.
   b. Their political unit was the polis.
   c. The king and his warrior-aristocracy stood at the top of society.
   d. The symbol of the king's power and wealth was the palace.

5. The two main historians of ancient Greece were
   a. Homer and Hesiod.
   b. Pliny and Sappho.
   c. Sophocles and Aristotle.
   d. Herodotus and Thucydides.

6. The polis included all of the following *except*
   a. a public square or marketplace.
   b. a citadel or acropolos.

    c. agricultural land and pastureland.
    d. land reserved for the king and priesthood.

7. The polis can be best described as
    a. a community of citizens.
    b. a religious community.
    c. a community of merchants.
    d. a community of warriors.

8. Mycenaean Greece was destroyed by
    a. internecine warfare.
    b. social unrest.
    c. foreign invaders.
    d. famine and plague.

9. The *Iliad* and *Odyssey* were
    a. sacred writings.
    b. collections of laws.
    c. historical records.
    d. epic poems.

10. Sappho was
    a. a politician.
    b. a prostitute.
    c. a priestess.
    d. a poet and lesbian.

11. Solon was an Athenian
    a. tyrant.
    b. reformer.
    c. king.
    d. priest.

12. Greeks at first used the word *tyrant* to denote a
    a. leader who ruled without legal right.
    b. cruel leader who oppressed the poor.
    c. champion of the commercial classes.
    d. dictator who suppressed democracy.

13. Cleisthenes was famous because
    a. he made Athens a major commercial center.
    b. he suppressed popular unrest.

c. he was the most successful Athenian tyrant.
d. he created the Athenian democracy.

14. Athens used the Delian League
a. to colonize the Mediterranean.
b. to fight the Persians.
c. to promote Mediterranean trade.
d. to spread Greek culture.

15. Thucydides wrote in order to
a. analyze the Peloponnesian War.
b. describe the Athenian democracy.
c. record events in the Persian wars.
d. defend Athenian foreign policy.

16. All except one of the following is a description of the drama *Oresteia* by Aeschylus:
a. The trilogy deals with the themes of betrayal, murder, and reconciliation.
b. Reason and justice are urged to reconcile fundamental conflicts.
c. The trilogy ends with a plea that civil dissension not be allowed to destroy societal stability.
d. The trilogy's major theme was the societal taboo of incest.

17. Aristophanes was popular because
a. the government tried to censure his plays.
b. he was the most religious Athenian poet.
c. he justified Athenian imperialism.
d. he was a critic of political and social life.

18. Most Greeks supported themselves by
a. fishing.
b. trading.
c. warfare.
d. farming.

19. Athenian women
a. had the status of slaves.
b. had full citizens' rights.
c. had protection under the law.
d. had greater rights than men.

20. Greek homosexuality was considered
    a. the curse of the lower classes.
    b. a threat to family life.
    c. an insult to religion.
    d. for many a normal practice.

GEOGRAPHY

1. Show on the outline map of the Aegean basin the approximate location of the following places.

Athens	Crete	Asia Minor	Mount Olympus
Sparta	Mediterranean Sea	Lesbos	Marathon
Thebes	Aegean Sea	Peloponnesus	Mycenae
Troy	Ionian Sea	Ionia	

2. The geography of Greece encouraged political fragmentation. Explain.

3. Using Map 3.2 as a reference, describe the area that came under Greek control as a result of its overseas expansion. What were the causes of this expansion?

UNDERSTANDING HISTORY THROUGH READING AND THE ARTS

The best short introduction to Greek society—including the polis, religion, war, and the Greek mind—is H. D. F. Kitto, *The Greeks** (1951). Students interested in the development of Greek thought and the Greek way of thinking should read W. K. C. Guthrie, *The Greek Philosophers** (1950, 1960). The two best books on Greek sexuality are H. Licht, *Sexual Life in Ancient Greece* (trans., J. H. Freese, 1932), and K. Dover, *Greek Homosexuality* (1978).

Nothing can be of more value in understanding the Greeks than to go directly to their great literature. The two dialogues of Plato, *Protagoras* and *Meno,** W. K. C. Guthrie (trans., 1956), are among the best of Greek prose. *Protagoras*, his dramatic masterpiece, deals with the problem of teaching the art of successful living, while *Meno* considers the immortality of the soul and the idea that learning is knowledge acquired before birth.

*Available in paperback.

The elegance and excellence of Greek sculpture and architecture are explored in Chapter 5, "Greek Art," in H. W. Jansen, *History of Art* (1962), and Greek mythology is interestingly told in E. Hamilton, *Mythology* (1942).

Gore Vidal's historical novel, *Creation** (1981)—much of which is based on the accounts of Herodotus—imparts a lively, well-informed impression of the size and cultural complexity of the Persian empire (and the intrigues in the Persian royal court) during the days of Darius, Xerxes, and the Persian invasions of Greece.

PROBLEMS FOR FURTHER INVESTIGATION

Why did Greek democracy eventually fail? Was Greek society truly democratic? Students interested in pursuing the subject of Greek politics and political theory should begin with J. N. Claster, ed., *Athenian Democracy** (1967), which is a collection of interpretations by various historians, and B. Tierney, et al., *Periclean Athens— Was It a Democracy?** (1967).

Did the Trojan War actually take place? If so, when? What did Heinrich Schliemann actually find at Troy? All these problems are taken up in an engaging work by Michael Wood, *In Search of the Trojan War* (1985), a well-illustrated companion volume to a six-part BBC television series with the same title.

*Available in paperback.

CHAPTER 4

HELLENISTIC DIFFUSION

CHAPTER OBJECTIVES

After reading and studying this chapter you should be able to answer the following questions:

Q-1. How was the development of philosophy, religion, science, medicine, and economics affected by the meeting of East and West?

Q-2. What did the spread of Hellenism mean to the Greeks and the peoples of the Near East?

Q-3. Did the spread of the Greek spirit by Philip and Alexander lay the groundwork for later cultures?

CHAPTER SYNOPSIS

This chapter shows how the ancient Near Eastern cultures such as Egypt and Persia, which were discussed in Chapter 2, and the Greek, or Hellenic, culture discussed in Chapter 3 came together to form a new, Hellenistic culture during the time of Alexander the Great. The Hellenistic age created throughout the Near Eastern and Mediterranean world both the political confusion and cultural unity that prepared the way for the triumph of Roman imperialism.

Alexander the Great, who was given a Greek education by Aristotle, conquered most of the known world by 324 B.C. He defeated and conquered Persia and then marched on to India, part of which was incorporated into his Macedonian state. Along the way he founded new cities and military colonies, all of which became agencies by which Greek (Hellenistic) culture spread throughout most of the Mediterraenean and Near Eastern world. When he died, his empire was divided into four kingdoms, which became frontiers of opportunity for large numbers of Greeks in search of jobs,

wealth, and power. Thus, Greek men and women settled throughout the East, forming an elite class of professionals and administrators. These Greek settlers also carried
Greek literature, law, engineering, architecture, and philosophy into every corner of
the Near East and the Mediterranean.

Important new discoveries in science and medicine were made in the Hellenistic
period. Philosophy became extremely creative, led by the competing doctrines of the
Cynics, the Epicureans, and the Stoics. There were also important advances in food
production, trade, and mining. Thus, while the Hellenistic age is often regarded as a
period of stagnation, it was actually a time of change and accomplishment.

STUDY OUTLINE

I. Alexander the Great and the crusade to conquer Asia Minor
   A. Alexander's invasion of Persia
      1. The son of King Philip, Alexander received a Greek education
      2. Alexander became king in 336 B.C. and invaded Asia in 334 B.C.
      3. By 324 B.C., he had defeated the Persians to avenge the Persian invasion
        of Greece and pushed into India
      4. He built a huge Macedonian-Greek empire
   B. Alexander's political legacy
      1. After his death his empire was divided into four monarchies
      2. In Greece the polis system was replaced by leagues of city-states
      3. The Hellenistic (Alexander and post-Alexander) world was fragmented
        and constantly at war
   C. Alexander's cultural legacy
      1. Alexander's 250 colonies brought many Greeks into Asia, thereby bring-
        ing east and west together
      2. His empire spread Greek culture as far east as India
II. The spread of Hellenism
   A. Cities and kingdoms of the Hellenistic age
      1. The new polis was not politically free but rather a part of a kingdom
        a. The polis was not self-governing, but subject to interference from
          the king
        b. Legal and social inequality existed in the Hellenistic polis; Greeks
          had greater rights
      2. The Hellenistic kingdoms were frequently at war as they attempted to
        solidify their kingdoms and gain the loyalty of subjects
      3. These Hellenistic cities formed the cultural foundation on which Roman
        and Christian cultures were to spread and flourish
   B. The Greeks open the East

    1. The Hellenistic kingdoms in Asia and Egypt provided Greeks with lucrative jobs
    2. Greeks dominated the administrative and military branches of the kingdoms
    3. But the Hellenistic kings could not gain the complete loyalty of their soldiers and professionals, and thus their kingdoms were weakened

III. Greeks and Easterners: the spread of Hellenism
    A. The uneven spread of Greek culture
        1. A Greco-Egyptian culture evolved slowly in Egypt
        2. Under the Seleucid kings, Greek and Eastern culture merged in Asia Minor
        3. For most Easterners only the externals, such as language, were Greek
    B. Hellenism and the Jews
        1. The Greeks allowed the Jews political and religious freedom
        2. Despite adoption of some Hellenistic culture, Jews remained Hebrew at heart

IV. Economic scope of Hellenism
    A. Commerce
        1. Alexander's conquests brought the East and the West together for trade
        2. Overland trade to India and a sea route to Italy were established
        3. Eastern grain was essential to Greece and the Aegean Sea area; in return Greece exported oil, wine, and fish
        4. The slave trade flourished because slavery was important to the Hellenistic economy
    B. Industry
        1. Cheap labor left no incentive to invest machinery
        2. The only change in mining was the introduction of the Archimedean screw for pumping water out of the mines
        3. Labor in the mines was harsh; many of the workers were political prisoners
        4. Gold, silver, and iron were mined; pottery production was widespread
        5. Important changes in pottery style took place, but production methods remained unchanged
    C. Agriculture
        1. Advances were made in seed and in improving and writing handbooks on farming
        2. The Ptolemys of Egypt made great strides in irrigating the land, partly because of their strong central government

V. Religion and philosophy in the Hellenistic world
    A. Religion in the Hellenistic world
        1. The Greek religious cults centered on the Olympian gods

2. The cults, consisting mainly of rituals, did not fill the religious needs of the people
3. Many people turned to a belief in *Tyche*, which meant fate or chance
4. There was a growth in mystery religions to fill emotional and ethical needs
5. Isis, who promised life after death, was the most important goddess of the new mystery cults
6. The most important development was a growing belief in one god who ruled over all people

B. Philosophy and the common man
1. Common people became interested in philosophy
2. The new philosophies rejected the idea that people cannot change their lives
3. The Cynics believed in the rejection of the material life
4. Diogenes, the greatest of the Cynics, stressed living according to nature and without allegiance to a particular city or monarchy
5. The Epicureans taught that pleasure was the chief good
6. The Stoics stressed the unity of man and universe and resignation to one's duty
   a. Zeno, the Stoic, made Stoicism the most popular Hellenistic philosophy
   b. Participation in worldly affairs was encouraged, but leading a virtuous life was most important

VI. Hellenistic women
A. Women during the Hellenistic period
1. The Hellenistic period brought royal women back into politics
2. Women became important in art, literature, and medicine
3. While the Stoics regarded women as inferior, the Cynics treated them as equals
4. Women became economically more important and as a result had more opportunities than in Hellenic times

VII. Hellenistic science and medicine
A. Aristarchus developed the heliocentric theory; Euclid compiled a text on geometry
B. Archimedes, an inventor and theoretician, sketched out basic principles of mechanics
C. Eratosthenes made advances in mathematics and geography
D. Theophrastos founded the study of botany
E. The Dogmatic school of medicine, under Herophilus and Erasistratus used vivisection and dissection to gain knowledge of the body—including the nervous system

F. The Empiric school stressed observation and use of medicine and drugs, including opium

G. Many quacks did untold harm, but were popular

REVIEW QUESTIONS

Q-1. What were the major achievements of Alexander? Does he deserve to be called "the Great"?

Q-2. Trace the expansion of the Macedonian kingdom into Asia. What were the reasons for this movement?

Q-3. Explain why Alexander's empire began disintegrating at the time of his death. Why could the empire not remain intact?

Q-4. How did the Hellenistic polis differ from the earlier Greek polis? Why?

Q-5. What did the new Hellenistic kingdoms offer the Greeks? Why couldn't these kingdoms gain the loyalty of the Greek immigrants?

Q-6. How successful was Greek culture in penetrating the cultures of Egypt and the East?

Q-7. What was the impact of Hellenistic politics and culture on the Jews who resided in Hellenic areas?

Q-8. Trace the developments in agriculture and industry in Hellenistic society. Why was there so little invention of machinery?

Q-9. Explain the interregional trade patterns of the Hellenistic world. What products did the various parts of the Hellenistic world specialize in?

Q-10. What kinds of commodities would one find in the cargo of the Eastern caravans?

Q-11. Did the position and power of women in Hellenistic society change from those of earlier periods? Explain.

Q-12. Discuss the religious and philosophical trends in the Hellenistic world. Why did the common person become interested in philosophy?

Q-13. Compare and contrast Cynicism, Epicureanism, and Stoicism.

Q-14. Define "natural law." Why is this an important idea?

Q-15. Trace the development of medical science in the Hellenistic era. What advances were made over the previous, Hellenic period?

STUDY-REVIEW EXERCISES

Define the following key concepts and terms.

Hellenism

politeuma

Tyche

natural law

heliocentric theory

the empirical tradition

Explain the major ideas and accomplishments of the following Hellenistic people.

Aristarchos of Samos

Euclid

Archimedes

Eratosthenes

Theophrastos

Herophilos

Explain the ideas and beliefs of three new Hellenistic schools of philosophy.

Philosophical School	*Founder*	*Principal Ideas and Beliefs*
The Cynics		
The Epicureans		
The Stoics		

Identify the following and give its significance.

Hellenistic period

Aetolian League

Ptolemy

koine

Alexander the Great

Zero

Isis

dogmatic school of medicine

empiric school of medicine

Test your understanding of the chapter by answering the following questions.

1. Epicurus taught that the gods had *no/great* effect on human life.
2. The most popular philosophy of the Hellenistic world was

   _____ .

3. The Cynics advised men and women to *accept/discard* the traditional customs and conventions.

4. The founder of the Cynics was _____, who believed that nothing natural was dirty or shameful.
5. The Hellenistic world *did/did not* see much trade in manufactured goods.
6. Alexander the Great's conquest of Persia was completed by about the year

   _____ .

7. The Greek immigrants in the Hellenistic kingdoms generally *did/did not* develop a strong loyalty to the state.
8. After Alexander's death the empire was broken into four parts,

   the _____, _____, _____, and

   _____ kingdoms.

9. The political and economic power of women tended to *increase/decrease* during the Hellenistic period.

10. *Tyche* was the common Hellenistic belief in _____ .

11. Generally, the Greeks tended to be *tolerant/intolerant* toward other religions.

12. _____ was the goddess of marriage, conception, and childbirth.

MULTIPLE-CHOICE QUESTIONS

1. The Epicureans believed that one could find happiness
   a. by becoming involved in politics.
   b. through pain.
   c. by retiring within oneself.
   d. by pleasing the gods.

2. The most important achievement of the Stoics was the
   a. idea of rejecting the state.
   b. cult of Isis.
   c. education of Alexander.
   d. concept of natural law.

3. Which of the following statements about Hellenized Easterners is true?
   a. They rejected everything Greek except Greek religion.
   b. They adopted much but retained the essentials of their own culture.
   c. They became thoroughly assimilated into Greek culture.
   d. They had no culture of their own.

4. Within the Hellenistic world Greeks formed the
   a. middle class of merchants.
   b. favored class.
   c. slave class.
   d. priest class.

5. Alexander's troops refused to proceed farther after they reached
   a. Persia.
   b. India.
   c. Bactria.
   d. China.

6. Alexander made his greatest contribution toward understanding between West and East when he
   a. forced Greeks to marry barbarians.
   b. established the Greek church in India.
   c. established colonies for Greek emigration.
   d. encouraged the adoption of barbarian food and dress.

7. Women's position improved during the Hellenistic age because of
   a. the Greeks' belief that women were equal.
   b. full citizenship rights conferred by law.
   c. their increased activity in economic affairs.
   d. their noble and self-sacrificing deeds.

8. Of all the post-Alexander empires, the greatest strides in agriculture were made by the
   a. Ptolemies in Egypt.
   b. Macedonians.
   c. Seleucids.
   d. Athenians.

9. The Greek word *tyche* means
   a. revelation.
   b. honor.
   c. to be strong.
   d. fate.

10. The author of the still-influential book *The Elements of Geometry* was
    a. Euclid.
    b. Archimedes.
    c. Aristarchus of Samos.
    d. Eratosthenes.

11. After his death, Alexander's empire was divided and controlled in part by each of the following *except*
    a. the Seleucid monarchy.
    b. the Ptolemaic monarchy.
    c. the Antigonid monarchy.
    d. the Partian monarchy.

12. In the Hellenistic period philosophy was
    a. the pastime of the wealthy.
    b. the profession of specialists.
    c. a propaganda tool of kings.
    d. an outlet for common people.

13. The Cynics thought that
    a. people should avoid pain.
    b. people should live according to nature.
    c. people should uphold the norms of society.
    d. people should enjoy luxury in moderation.

14. Epicurean philosophy taught
    a. the overthrow of monarchies.
    b. the virtue of self-discipline.
    c. the value of religion.
    d. the value of pleasure.

15. The Stoics evolved the idea of
    a. might makes right.
    b. pain against pleasure.
    c. the unity of mankind and the universe.
    d. the unity of mankind and the state.

16. Aristarchus of Samos is important because he thought that
    a. the sun revolved around the earth.
    b. the moon revolved around the earth.
    c. the earth revolved around the sun.
    d. the sun and moon were fixed bodies.

17. Which of the following sciences got its start in the Hellenistic period?
    a. economics
    b. physics
    c. botany
    d. geology

18. The discoverer of the nervous system was
    a. Herophilus.
    b. Erasistratus.
    c. Heraclides.
    d. Serapion.

19. The Empiric school of medicine emphasized
    a. the study of anatomy.
    b. the study of physiology.
    c. the use of vivisection and dissection.
    d. the cure of sickness through observation and drugs.

20. Hellenistic industry relied chiefly on
    a. labor-saving machines.
    b. new techniques of production.
    c. increased use of animal power.
    d. use of manual labor.

GEOGRAPHY

1. Show on the outline map the location of the following places of importance in the Hellenistic world.

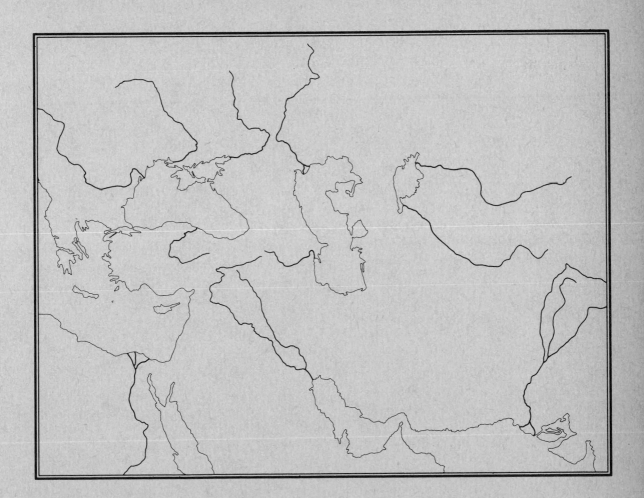

India	Mesopotamia	Mediterranean Sea	Asia Minor
Persia	Nile River	Black Sea	Alexandria
Macedonia	Persepolis	Egypt	Arabian Desert

2. Shade in the area conquered by Alexander the Great.
3. Draw in the boundaries of the four kingdoms that came into being after Alexander's death and label each kingdom.
4. Show with a dotted line a route by which goods might have moved between Greece, Asia Minor, Egypt, and the Far East.

UNDERSTANDING HISTORY THROUGH READING AND THE ARTS

Alexander the Great is the subject of two recent biographies: R. L. Fox, *Alexander the Great* (1974) and P. Green, *Alexander of Macedon, 356-323 B.C.** (1973). A fascinating historical novel about life, love, and adventure with Alexander is M. Renault, *The Persian Boy** (1972). The Jewish war of liberation against their Hellenistic Syrian overlords is one of a number of subjects dealt with in V. Tcherikover, *Hellenistic Civilization and the Jews* (trans., S. Applebaum, 1959). Many of the remarkable personages of the Hellenistic Age—including Cleopatra and Ptolemy of Egypt—are featured in N. Davis and C. Kraay, *The Hellenistic Kingdoms: Portrait Coins and History* (1973). This fascinating book is also of value for anyone interested in the use of ancient coins in understanding the past.

For developments in architecture see T. Fyfe, *Hellenistic Architecture* (1963), and for painting and sculpture see C. Havelock, *Hellenistic Art* (1970). The traditions of Hellenistic literature and culture are explored in T. Webster, *Hellenistic Poetry and Art* (1964).

PROBLEMS FOR FURTHER INVESTIGATION

Did the Hellenists make any significant contributions to science and medicine? To pursue this question begin with E. Hamilton, *The Greek Way to Western Civilization** (1943).

What were the reasons for Alexander the Great's conquest of the Near Eastern world? Begin your research with A. R. Burn, *Alexander the Great and the Hellenistic World** (1964).

*Available in paperback.

How did Greek philosophy change in this period? What are Stoicism and Cynicism? Those interested in Greek thought should see a book of essays, interpretations, and source material entitled *The Greek Mind** (1957) by W. R. Agard and A. Long, *Hellenistic Philosophy* (1974).

*Available in paperback.

CHAPTER 5

THE RISE OF ROME

CHAPTER OBJECTIVES

After reading and studying this chapter you should be able to answer the following questions:

Q-1. How did Rome rise to greatness?
Q-2. What effects did the conquest of the Mediterranean have on the Romans?
Q-3. Why did the Roman Republic collapse?

CHAPTER SYNOPSIS

Whereas the Greeks gave the Mediterranean world cultural unity, Rome gave it political unity and a political heritage. The *pax Romana*, or peace of Rome, allowed the spread of Roman law, justice, and administration as well as the further diffusion of Greek culture—especially into the European world. This chapter traces the origins of that legacy from the Etruscans in the eighth century B.C. through the troubled but dynamic days of the republic in the first century B.C. Between these two periods the Romans built an enormous empire, gave the world important lessons in politics, and established some new concepts in law.

There are three major themes in this chapter. The first is assimilation. The Romans, like the Macedonians before them, readily adopted the culture of Hellenic Greece. Earlier, the Romans had copied many of the customs of the ancient Etruscans. Conquest and imperialism is the second theme. The Romans became empire builders almost by accident. A conflict in southern Italy led to foreign involvement, first in Sicily and then in North Africa during the Punic wars between Rome and Carthage. The third theme is the impact of imperialism on Rome. Did imperialism bring more harm than blessings? The chapter evaluates the economic and political changes that military victory brought, noting how the coming of empire meant a change in life-style and, according to some Romans, such as Cato, a general moral deterioration. Certainly, foreign conquests created large standing armies and veterans who played a growing role in Roman politics. Once this happened, government by constitution was doomed.

STUDY OUTLINE

I.   The land and the sea: the geography and early settlement of Rome
  A. The land and the sea
    1. Italy's lack of rivers for transportation and of harbors discouraged trade, but the land was fertile and productive and the mountains not as divisive as those of Greece
    2. The two great fertile plains of Italy are Latium and Campania
    3. The Romans established their city on seven hills along the Tiber River in Latium
  B. The Etruscans and Rome (750-500 B.C.)
    1. Between 1200 and 750 B.C., many peoples moved into Italy from the north
    2. Etruscan urban life came to dominate much of Italy
    3. According to legend, Romulus and Remus founded Rome in 753 B.C.
    4. The Etruscans passed many customs and practices on to the Romans
    5. The Etruscans turned Rome into an important city and brought it into contact with the Mediterranean world
  C. The Roman conquest of Italy (509-290 B.C.)
    1. Much of early Roman history is based on legends and tales, brought together by Livy
    2. According to tradition, the Romans expelled the harsh Etruscan rulers and founded a republic in 509 B.C.
    3. The Romans fought continually against their neighbors and became adept at the arts of war and diplomacy
    4. In 390 B.C., invading Gauls destroyed Rome but also eliminated the Etruscans, so a rebuilt Rome was able to expand
    5. Between 390 and 290 B.C., the Romans conquered much of Italy and stood unchallenged
  D. The Roman state
    1. In the early republic power resided in the hands of the members of the aristocracy, called the patricians; commoners were called plebeians
    2. Rome was ruled by people's assemblies, elected magistrates, and—most important—the senate

      a. The senate advised the consuls and magistrates, and its advice had the force of law

      b. The senate provided stability and continuity to the republic

      c. The assembly *comitia centuriata* was dominated by the patricians

      d. In 471 B.C. the plebeians gained their own assembly, the *concilium plebis*

      e. In effect the two consuls and the senate ran the state

   3. Rome's greatest achievement was its development of the concept of law

      a. Civil law developed to protect people and property

      b. Gradually, the concept of universal law applicable to all societies developed

  E. Social conflict in Rome

   1. The plebeians' desire for equality and justice led to a struggle with the patricians

   2. A general strike led to concessions being granted to the plebeians—partly because of patrician fears of hostile neighbors

   3. The plebeians won legal and land reforms

      a. The *lex canuleia* allowed for intermarriage

      b. The Law of the Twelve Tables—a codification of previously unpublished laws—was a result of plebeian legal reform

      c. Later, the patricians were forced to publish legal procedures, too, so plebeians could enjoy full protection under the law

   4. Licinius and Sextus brought about further reform for the plebeians, but the struggle did not end until the passage of *lex Hortens*

II. The age of overseas conquest (282-146 B.C.)

  A. Roman imperialism

   1. The Romans did not have a pre-existing strategy for world conquest

   2. Roman imperialism took two forms: aggression in the West and patronage in the East

   3. Rome's need to control Sicily for its own protection meant it needed to control the sea

      a. The historian Polybius claimed that Rome feared Carthage expansion

   4. Rome's conquest of Spain was not complete until 133 B.C.

   5. By 146 B.C., Rome had conquered the eastern Mediterranean and turned it into Roman provinces

  B. The Punic wars

   1. The First Punic War, fought over Sicily, was won by Rome

   2. The Second Punic War found Carthage attacking Rome by way of Spain, with a major victory at Canne in 216 B.C.

   3. Hannibal of Carthage led Carthage forces over the Alps into Italy

   4. But Rome's commander, Scipio, took Spain in 207 B.C.

5. Then a Roman victory at Zama in 202 B.C. meant that the western Mediterranean would be Roman—but a Third Punic War meant further conflict with Carthage

III. Old values and Greek culture
  A. Consequences of empire
    1. The building of empire brought about the end of traditional values and encouraged a new materialism
  B. The "traditional ideal" of a simple and virtuous life, represented by Marcus Cato
    1. In traditional Rome the paterfamilias held immense power within the family
    2. The virtues of chastity and modesty among women were valued
    3. Infants and children were often left to servants' care
    4. The Romans developed an agricultural system to adjust to the seasons and the soil
    5. Slavery was common; relations between master and slave were often good
    6. Religion played an important role in Roman life; Romans believed that the gods could give divine favor to them
  C. The new spirit of wealth and leisure, represented by Scipio Aemilianus
    1. For the new Romans victory in war meant materialism and the pursuit of pleasure
    2. Greek culture—Hellenism—came to dominate Roman life
    3. Scipio Aemilianus introduced to Rome the art of personal politics
    4. He was the center of a circle of Hellenists
    5. Hellenism stimulated the growth of Roman art, literature, and leisure activities such as bathing and dinner parties
    6. Despite this hedonism, Rome prospered for six more centuries

IV. The late republic (133-27 B.C.)
  A. War and the demands of the new empire created serious political problems
    1. The republican constitution no longer suited Rome's needs
    2. The army became a threat
    3. Rome's Italian allies agitated for the rights of citizenship
  B. War and the new empire also caused economic problems
    1. Many veterans sold their war-ruined farms to the big landowners and migrated to the cities
    2. A large number of urban poor emerged
    3. The Gracchus brothers sought a solution to the problem of the veterans and the urban poor
      a. Tiberius Gracchus angered aristocrats and the senate by proposing land reform

      b. The murder of Tiberius Gracchus by the senators initiated an era of political violence

      c. Gaius Gracchus demanded further land reform and citizenship for all Italians

      d. Gaius was killed by the senate while new foreign threats emerged

   4. Marius reformed the army by promising land to recruits

   5. Social war in Italy and factional chaos in Rome continued

C. Social war and political struggles led to the end of the republican constitution

   1. Sulla became dictator of Rome, and civil war followed

   2. Cicero urged a balance of political interests

   3. The First Triumvirate (Pompey, Caesar, and Crassus) controlled Rome after Sulla, but Caesar dominated

   4. Conflict between Caesar and Pompey resulted in more civil war

   5. The Second Triumvirate (Augustus, Antony, and Lepidus) followed Caesar's rule

   6. In 31 B.C., Augustus put an end to civil war by defeating Antony at the battle of Actium

REVIEW QUESTIONS

Q-1. Who were the Etruscans and of what importance were they to the early Romans?

Q-2. What do the early Roman legends reveal about Roman values and ideas? Are legends valid sources for the historian?

Q-3. How did Rome differ from Greece with regard to ideas about the state, citizenship, and participation in the state?

Q-4. Define *ius civile, ius gentium, ius naturae.* Where did political power lie in republican Rome?

Q-5. What were the causes and the outcome of the Struggle of the Orders?

Q-6. What were the motives and events that caused Rome to become an expansionist state?

Q-7. What were the causes and results of the Punic wars?

Q-8. Why did Sicily and Spain become battlegrounds for the Punic wars? What was Hannibal's military strategy?

Q-9. Trace the territorial expansion of Rome that came about as a result of war. By what year could the Romans declare the Mediterranean to be *mare nostrum?*

Q-10. Describe the role of the paterfamilias in Roman life.

Q-11. How were women and children treated in Roman society? How does the status of Roman women compare to that of women of the Hellenistic period?

Q-12. Discuss the institution of slavery in Roman society. Is slavery ever a humane institution?

Q-13.   How did the Romans regard their gods? Was religion important to the Romans? Did Christianity completely replace Roman religion? Explain.

Q-14.   Contrast the interests and lifestyles of Marcus Cato and Scipio Aemilianus. Do you believe that Greek culture corrupted the Romans? What causes certain elements within society to break with their past?

Q-15.   What impact did the imperial expansion of Rome have on the economic and political condition of the republic? Who were the winners and the losers?

Q-16.   What did the Gracchus brothers intend to do for Rome? Why was there so much opposition? What were the results?

Q-17.   What were the reasons for instability in Rome from about the time of Gaius Marius in 107 B.C. to Augustus in 31 B.C.? Was dictatorship the only answer?

STUDY-REVIEW EXERCISES

Define the following key concepts and terms.

Pyrrhic victory

ius naturae

mare nostrum

paterfamilias

pax Romana

latifundia

senatus populusque Romanus

imperialism

Identify each of the following and give its significance.

Punic wars

First Triumvirate

the *comitia centuriata*

the *concilium plebis*

Law of the Twelve Tables

lex Hortensia

plebeians

Roman senate

Hannibal

Cincinnatus

Marcus Cato

Scipio Africanus

Gauls

Etruscans

<u>Explain</u> *who the following people were and the role each played in the troubled years of the late republic.*

Gracchus brothers

Cicero

Sulla

Pompey

Julius Caesar

<u>Test</u> *your understanding of the chapter by answering the following questions.*

1. The Punic wars were between Rome and _____ .
2. The general strike of the plebeians in 494 B.C. *did/did not* gain them rights.

3. Once the Romans had conquered southern Italy, they found themselves in need

   of controlling _____ and then

   _____ .

4. The Romans *did/did not* hold racist attitudes toward their slaves.
5. After the wars of conquest the Romans began to express *more/less* interest in Hellenism.

6. The Roman sky god _____ became the equivalent of the Greek Zeus.
7. Roman art tended to be more *idealistic/realistic* than Greek Art.
8. Prior to 90 B.C., all Italians *did/did not* hold Roman citizenship.
9. The wealthy landowning aristocracy in Rome was known as the

   _____ class.

Number the following events in correct chronological order.

1. _____ The end of the First Punic War

2. _____ The Roman conquest of Spain

3. _____ The invasion of Italy by the Gauls

4. _____ The defeat of Hannibal at Zama

5. _____ The completion of the Roman conquest of the eastern Mediterranean

6. _____ The invasion of Italy by Pyrrhus

MULTIPLE-CHOICE QUESTIONS

1. Which of the following statements about the paterfamilias is *false*?
   a. He was the oldest male in the family.
   b. He could legally kill his wife.
   c. His sons could not own property until he died.
   d. He never consulted the other family members.

2. As a result of the wars of conquest, the small, independent Roman farmers
   a. gained vast new markets for their grain.
   b. found their farms in ruins.
   c. became an important political power.
   d. got rich.

3. Overall, the Romans' greatest achievements were in the field of
   a. empire building.
   b. agriculture and trade.
   c. the arts.
   d. literature.

4. Rome's greatest achievement was to
   a. conquer peoples and let them govern themselves.
   b. always live peacefully with its neighbors.
   c. always peacefully incorporate peoples into the Roman system.
   d. conquer peoples and incorporate them into the Roman system.

5. Which of the following was *not* a Roman republican office?
   a. emperor
   b. quaestor
   c. praetor
   d. consul

6. The Struggle of the Orders resulted in all but
   a. the office of the tribune.
   b. the ascendancy of the patricians.
   c. the Law of the Twelve Tables.
   d. a stronger and more unified Rome.

7. The goal of the Gracchi was to
   a. exploit the urban poor and the peasant farmers.
   b. join the patricians.
   c. aid the urban poor and the peasant farmers.
   d. deny citizenship to certain Romans.

8. All but one of the following are principal geographical characteristics of Italy.
   a. few good harbors except in the south
   b. the Appenine mountain range running east/west and cutting the peninsula in half
   c. few navigable rivers
   d. two large fertile plains

9. According to Roman legend, the founders of Rome were
    a. the Greeks.
    b. the tribe of Autun.
    c. Livy and his family.
    d. Romulus and Remus.

10. The Roman citizen who returned to his farming after defeating his country's enemy was
    a. Augustus of Spoleto.
    b. Cincinnatus.
    c. Lycurgus.
    d. Sulla.

11. The chief magistrates of republican Rome—the officials who administered the state and commanded the army—were known as
    a. consuls.
    b. quaestors.
    c. Praetors.
    d. senators.

12. During the Second Punic War the Carthaginian leader who attempted to conquer Rome was
    a. Philip of Carthage.
    b. Hannibal.
    c. Alexander.
    d. Meneius Agrippa.

13. Most ordinary Roman women
    a. had little influence in family affairs.
    b. spent most of their time performing religious rituals.
    c. had considerable influence and responsibility in the family economy.
    d. exercised total control of the children's upbringing.

14. Which of the following best represents the status of Roman slaves?
    a. The Romans thought slaves were inferior human beings.
    b. The Romans thought of slavery in racial terms.
    c. The Romans thought of slavery primarily as a byproduct of Rome's military victories.
    d. Freedom was often granted to slaves by their masters.

15. The father of Latin poetry was
    a. Eilliam.
    b. Ennius.
    c. Scipio Aemilianus.
    d. Cato.

16. The conservative and traditionalist elements of Rome regarded the public baths as
    a. the only way to encourage reform in public health.
    b. a good way of using Greek culture for the benefit of Rome.
    c. a waste of time and an encouragement to idleness.
    d. important as places for political discussion.

17. The wars during the time of republican Rome
    a. left Rome a strong and prosperous agriculture.
    b. left Roman farms in a state of decay.
    c. caused Rome to look elsewhere for its food supply
    d. caused a decentralization of land ownership.

18. The Roman leader who was murdered because he proposed that public land be given to the poor in small lots was
    a. Sulla
    b. Tiberius Gracchus
    c. Cato
    d. Caesar

19. The consul who reorganized the Roman army and introduced the use of the sword and javelin as standard weapons of the legionaries was
    a. Cincinnatus.
    b. Tiberius.
    c. Sulla
    d. Marius.

20. By the time of the late republican period in Rome, most industry and small manufacturing was in the hands of
    a. plebeians.
    b. slaves.
    c. Christians.
    d. the army.

GEOGRAPHY

Study the text on pages 130 to 132 and Map 5.1 and then answer the following questions:

1. How did geography encourage Italy to "look to the Mediterranean"?
2. What geographic features of Italy encouraged her growth and development? What was special about the area where Rome was established?

UNDERSTANDING HISTORY THROUGH READING AND THE ARTS

Much of the culture and beliefs of the peoples of the Italian peninsula can be understood through a study of Etruscan and Roman art. For an interestingly written and illustrated beginning source see Chapters 6 and 7 of H. W. Janson, *History of Art* (1962). The best of Roman literature includes Cicero's essay *On Moral Obligation* (trans., J. Higgenbotham, 1967). Other works by Cicero can be found in J. and A. Raubitschek, trans., *Selected Works of Cicero* (1948). A revised and modernized version of Caesar's own story of his conquest of Gaul is found in S. Brady, *Caesar's Gallic Campaigns* (1967). If you are interested in Roman mythology see J. Lindsay, *Men and Gods on the Roman Nile* (1968) and M. Grant, *Myths of the Greeks and Romans* (1965), and for Roman accomplishments in sculpture, town planning, painting, and the like see M. Wheeler, *Roman Art and Architecture** (1985).

PROBLEMS FOR FURTHER INVESTIGATION

Students interested in doing research or writing a report on the origins of the Roman Empire may get some ideas from D. Hood, ed., *The Rise of Rome** (1970).

Two books for students wanting to pursue the subject of religion in ancient Rome are M. Grant, *The Jews in the Ancient World* (1973), and T. R. Glover, *The Conflict of Religions in the Early Roman Empire* (1960).

*Available in paperback.

CHAPTER 6

THE PAX ROMANA

CHAPTER OBJECTIVES

After reading and studying this chapter you should be able to answer the following questions:

Q-1. How did the Roman emperors govern the empire and spread Roman influence into northern Europe?

Q-2. What was the effect of the *pax Romana* on the Mediterranean and European world?

Q-3. How did the empire meet the grim challenges of barbarian invasion and economic decline?

Q-4. Why did Christianity sweep across the Roman world to change it fundamentally?

CHAPTER SYNOPSIS

When Julius Caesar's nephew Augustus became "the First Citizen of the State" in 31 B.C., Rome began a new era called the Augustan Age. This was the "golden age" of Rome in terms of economy, literature, and imperial expansion. Under the Roman Empire the Mediterranean and European peoples enjoyed a long tradition of firmly established personal freedom. The *pax Romana*, or peace of Rome, encouraged the spread of Roman law, justice, and administration as well as the further diffusion of Greek culture, especially into the European world. This era of peace occurred in part because of the constitutional monarchy Augustus established, which lasted until the third decade, when once again Rome became wracked by civil war. The emperor's power, however, rested mainly with the army, which he controlled. Indeed, control of the army became a growing problem for Augustus and his successors, many of whom owed their power to some military rebellion in the provinces. Thus, in the long run, Augustus's settlement was not successful. Nevertheless, his contributions were many.

Augustus's treatment of the imperial subjects in the conquered provinces was just, and his expansion of the empire north and east into Europe was of enormous importance for subsequent European history. His reign also ushered in a great age of Latin literature. And it is through reading the works of Virgil, Livy, and Horace, all of whom are discussed in this chapter, that we are able to gain a sense of what Roman people were like and what they expected of life.

The development and spread of Christianity also occurred during this era. Paul of Tarsus turned the Jewish cult of Jesus into a universal religion based on the ethics of love and forgiveness. Many Romans misunderstood the early Christians and regarded them as atheists because they refused to worship Roman gods. Finally, in the fourth century A.D., Christianity was made the official religion of Rome. Oddly, what had begun as a Judaean hope for salvation from Rome became Rome's state religion.

In the third century A.D., the breakdown of government and order ushered in an age of civil war and barbaric invasion from which Rome never fully recovered. The reforming emperors Diocletian and Constantine were able to restore the old system only partially. They were not able to turn around the depression and decline in trade and agriculture.

Why did Rome "fall"? Certainly, economic and political explanations are important, but they do not tell the entire story. In a real sense there is no answer because the Roman Empire did not actually fall at all but instead slowly merged into a new medieval world. It was Rome and Christianity that provided Europe with the framework for a new age.

STUDY OUTLINE

I.   Augustus's settlement (31 B.C.-A.D. 14)
   A.   Augustus's goal was to reestablish the republic after years of civil war, to demobilize the army, and to meet the danger of barbarians
   B.   The principate and the restored republic
      1.   Augustus re-established the republic but did not give the senate power equal to his own
      2.   Augustus became *princeps civitatis*, "the First Citizen of the State" and held other political, religious, and military titles
      3.   His control of the army was the main source of his power
         a.   New colonies were founded by the soldiers, thus spreading Roman culture further
         b.   The colonies were important in unifying the Mediterranean world
      4.   Overall, the system was a new "constitutional monarchy"

      5. Augustus eventually established the practice of dynastic inheritance of the principate
- C. Augustus's administration of the provinces
  1. He saw no reason to interfere with the colonies' traditions
  2. The cult of Roma et Augustus gave the empire unity
- D. Roman expansion into northern and western Europe
  1. Augustus continued Caesar's push into Europe
  2. In Gaul he founded towns and built roads
  3. He pushed into Spain, Germany, and eastern Europe
- E. Literary flowering
  1. The Augustan Age was a productive age of Latin literature
  2. Virgil wrote about the greatness and virtue of Rome in his masterpiece the Aeneid, thus spreading Roman culture and building Roman camps
  3. Livy's history was one of Rome's gifts to the modern world
  4. Horace praised the simple life and Rome's greatness

II. The coming of Christianity
- A. The colony of Judaea suffered during the Roman civil wars, and hence Jewish resentment of Rome arose
- B. Hatred of King Herod and the Romans led to civil war in Judaea
- C. Two anti-Roman movements existed: the Zealot extremists who fought Rome and the militants who believed that the coming of the Messiah would end Roman rule
- D. Pagan religious cults were numerous, but it was particularly the new mystery cults which met the needs of the people for security and emotional release
- E. Jesus was a teacher who claimed to be the Messiah of a spiritual kingdom
  1. His teachings were in the orthodox Jewish tradition
  2. He taught his followers not to revolt against Rome
- F. Pontius Pilate, the Roman prefect, was worried about maintaining civil order, so he condemned Jesus to death
- G. Peter continued the Jesus cult in accord with Jewish law
- H. Paul of Tarsus transformed the Jesus cult and made it applicable to all people—particularly those who were attracted to the mystery religions
- I. Christianity was attractive for many reasons
  1. It was open to all, including non-Jews, women, and common people
  2. It held out the promise of salvation and forgiveness
  3. It gave each person a role and a sense of community

III. The Julio-Claudians, the Flavians, and the "five good emperors" (27 B.C.-A.D. 180)
- A. The Julio-Claudians and the Flavians
  1. Augustus's dynasty was known as the Julio-Claudians
  2. Claudius created a system of imperial bureaucracy and extended Roman frontiers, including the conquest of Britain in A.D. 43

        3. The army began to interfere in politics
        4. Civil war proved the Augustan settlement a failure
    B. The Flavian dynasty
        1. Vespasian created a monarchy and suppressed rebellion, such as that of
            the Jews
        2. He also expanded the bureaucracy to increase the emperor's power
IV. The Age of the Five Good Emperors
    A. The age of Five Antonies was one of prosperity
    B. The Antonine monarchy
        1. The principate became an emperorship
        2. The emperors were the source of all authority
        3. Hadrian reformed the bureaucracy
    C. Changes in the army
        1. Under the Flavians the boundaries of the empire became fixed
        2. The army was a source of economic stability and a Romanizing agent
 V. Life in the "golden age"
    A. Rome
        1. The government provided the citizens of Rome with free grain, oil, and
            wine
        2. Free, often brutal, entertainment was provided, but the most popular
            was chariot racing
        3. Most Romans worked hard and lived average lives
    B. The provinces prospered under the Antonines
        1. From Augustus onward, free farming and immigration thrived
        2. The army brought farming and towns to new areas
        3. Under the Romans, eastern Mediterranean trade expanded and grain
            production in northern Europe increased as the provinces became
            linked in a vast economic network
        4. Manufacturing, such as glass and pottery making, tended to move from
            Italy to the provinces, especially to northern Europe
        5. Northern and Western European cities enjoyed growth and peace under
            Roman rule
VI. Civil wars and invasion in the third century
    A. Commodus's reign led to civil war; over twenty emperors ascended the
        throne between 235 and 284
    B. Civil war left the empire open to invasion
    C. Barbarians on the frontiers found gaps in the Roman defenses
        1. In A.D. 258, the Goths burst into Europe
        2. The Alamanni, Franks, Saxons, and other tribes invaded the empire
    D. Invasion brought turmoil and impoverishment to farm and village life
        1. The breakdown of the system led to crime and disorder
        2. Much of the damage was done by officials and soldiers

VII. Reconstruction under Diocletian and Constantine (A.D. 284-337)
   A. The end of political turmoil under Diocletian's reign
      1. Diocletian claimed the gods had chosen him to rule; his power became absolute
      2. Because the empire was too big for one person to govern well, Diocletian reorganized it
         a. Imperial authority was split between two emperors—Diocletian in the east and an *augustus* in the west
         b. Each emperor was assisted by a *caesar*
         c. The power of the provincial governors was reduced
         d. Diocletian's division between east and west became permanent
   B. Inflation and taxes
      1. The monetary system was in ruins and highly inflated
      2. Diocletian attempted to curb inflation through wage and price controls
      3. The new imperial taxation system led to a loss of freedom as people became locked into their jobs
   C. The decline of small farms
      1. Worsening conditions fostered the growth of self-sufficient villas
      2. Freemen turned to big landlords for protection
   D. The legalization of Christianity
      1. Constantine realized that Christianity could serve his empire
      2. Many Romans misunderstood Christianity
         a. The pagans accused the Christians of atheism
         b. Overall, persecutions were minor and limited even during the third-century turmoil
         c. Christianity was legalized by Constantine, and in 380 it was made Rome's official religion
   E. The construction of Constantinople
      1. Constantine built a new capital for the empire at the site of Byzantium
      2. The focus of the empire shifted to the east
VIII. The Awful Revolution
   A. Reasons for the "decline and fall" of Rome
      1. Gibbon and others blamed Christianity, the size of the empire, and inevitability but Gibbon was wrong—as Christianity's influence was small
      2. Likewise, the biological analogies and the theories of racial corruption are wrong
      3. Population decline, lead poisoning, and—in Lot's view—slavery and economic depression are still other reasons given by some historians
      4. Rome's many political problems offer yet another set of possible reasons

B. Continuity and change: did Rome really "fall"?
   1. The concept of change and development may be more valid than that of the collapse
   2. Many aspects of the Roman world still survive—particularly its tradition of law and freedom

REVIEW QUESTIONS

Q-1. What were the sources of Augustus's power? Was Augustus a "dictator" in the modern sense?

Q-2. What were Augustus's accomplishments with regard to the administration and expansion of the empire?

Q-3. What does the work of the writers during Rome's Augustan age of literature tell us about Roman life and what the Romans thought important?

Q-4. Why was the relationship between Rome and its colony Judaea so strained in the age of Augustus? What were the motives and responses of both Jews and Romans?

Q-5. Did Jesus intend to found a new religion? Explain by evaluating the work of this teacher.

Q-6. What role did Paul of Tarsus play in the evolution of Christianity, and what might have happened if Peter of Jerusalem had kept control over the cult?

Q-7. Why was Christianity so attractive? How was this religion unlike that of the Greeks and Romans?

Q-8. What was the system of picking the *princeps civitatis* after the death of Augustus? Did the system work?

Q-9. Under what circumstances did the Flavian dynasty come about and what were its contributions?

Q-10. What features of the Roman army made it a source of both strength and weakness for the empire?

Q-11. What is meant by the terms "barracks emperors"?

Q-12. What was the pattern of immigration and what were the reasons for the increase in free farming after the time of Augustus?

Q-13. What were the causes and the results of the civil wars between A.D. 235 and 284?

Q-14. Discuss the impact the barbarians had on the empire. Were the invasions the cause or the result of a political breakdown?

Q-15. Explain the changes in the concept and power of the emperor under Diocletian and Constantine. Why did these changes occur?

Q-16. Why did the number of small farmers and the amount of personal freedom decrease during and after the period of civil war?

Q-17. What did Diocletian and Constantine do to restore and strengthen the empire?

Q-18. Describe the political climate in Judaea within which Jesus of Nazareth emerged. Did this influence the course of "religious" history?
Q-19. Why were many Romans distrustful of Christianity?
Q-20. What do you believe to have been the cause of the "decline and fall" of Rome? How valid do you consider the various explanations given?

STUDY-REVIEW EXERCISES

Define the following key concepts and terms.

Messiah

princeps civitatis

pax Romana

imperator

the Julio-Claudian dynasty

apocalypse

villa

"The Awful Revolution"

Identify each of the following and give its significance.

Goths

Jesus

Paul of Tarsus

the Antonines

King Herod of Judaea

Zealots

gladiatorial fighting

the Five Good Emperors

Mithraism

Commodus

barracks emperors

Constantine

Edward Gibbon

Virgil

Ferdinand Lot

Explain the contributions of each of the following to Rome and the Roman Empire.

Augustus

Claudius

Hadrian

Vespas

Diocletian

Constantine

Explain the subject matter and the central theme of each of the following books.

Virgil, *Georgics*

Virgil, *Aeneid*

Livy, *Ab Urbe Condita*

<u>Test</u> *your understanding of the chapter by answering the following questions.*

1. Augustus *did/did not* believe that the colonies should be self-governing and culturally independent.
2. The capital of the Roman Empire was eventually moved to the new eastern city

   of _____.
3. The great Roman historian-writer who believed that history should be applied to

   the present was _____.
4. From the time of Augustus, the power of the principate tended to *increase/de-
   crease.*

5. Christianity was made the official religion of Rome in the year _____.
6. The Roman government *did/did not* provide free food and entertainment for the
   citizens of Rome.
7. With the reign of Augustus, free farming tended to *increase/decrease.*
8. For the most part, the Roman persecutions of Christians were *minor/widespread.*
9. Under the Five Good Emperors the areas of northern and western Europe underwent a period of economic *expansion/decline.*

<u>Number</u> *the following events in correct chronological order.*

1. _____ The first barbarian invasion

2. _____ The "Year of the Four Emperors"

3. _____ The execution of Jesus of Nazareth

4. _____ The ending of the republican civil wars by Augustus

5. _____ The golden age of Rome under the "five good emperors"

6. _____ The building of Constantinople

MULTIPLE-CHOICE QUESTIONS

1. Which of the following statements about Jesus of Nazareth is *false*?
    a. Jesus was a Jewish teacher.
    b. Jesus sought to lead a rebellion against the hated Romans.
    c. Jesus revealed himself as the Messiah.
    d. Jesus's teachings and cult were basically Jewish.

2. According to Edward Gibbon, the major cause of the decline and fall of Rome was
    a. the invasions.
    b. lead poisoning.
    c. civil war.
    d. Christianity.

3. The government-constitutional settlement which came about under Augustus is best described as a
    a. dictatorship.
    b. constitutional monarchy.
    c. republic.
    d. democracy.

4. The man most responsible for the spread of Christianity to non-Jews was
    a. emperor Diocletian.
    b. St. Peter.
    c. Livy.
    d. Paul of Tarsus.

5. Which of the following statements about farm and village life during the turmoil of the third century is *false*?
    a. Crime increased.
    b. Corruption increased.
    c. The villas disintegrated.
    d. Small landholdings declined.

6. In 31 B.C., Augustus established a new government for Rome that was a
    a. republic.
    b. constitutional monarchy.
    c. democracy.
    d. dictatorship.

7. Augustus's attitude toward the provinces was one of
   a. neglect.
   b. oppression.
   c. prejudice toward minorities.
   d. respect for local customs.

8. Which of the following was an anti-Roman group in Judaea?
   a. Zealots
   b. Baruchs
   c. Essenes
   d. Hittites

9. The Roman world was attracted to Christianity for all but which one of the following reasons?
   a. Christianity didn't discriminate by class or sex.
   b. Christianity offered a sense of community.
   c. Christianity was passive.
   d. Christianity offered salvation and forgiveness of sin.

10. The backbone of Roman agriculture in the Augustan Age was
    a. slave labor.
    b. imported foods from the empire.
    c. captured barbarian labor.
    d. small free farmers.

11. Before Constantine legalized Christianity, the Romans demanded that the Christians
    a. worship the Roman gods.
    b. observe the ritual of sacrifice to the gods.
    c. deny Christ as a god.
    d. go back to their Jewish beliefs.

12. The city that Constantine made the capital of the Eastern Roman Empire was
    a. Kiev.
    b. Constantinople.
    c. Alexandria.
    d. Athens.

13. The *History of the Decline and Fall of the Roman Empire* was written by
    a. Constantine
    b. Livy

    c. Gibbon

    d. Paul of Tarsus

14. During the reign of Augustus, the direction of Roman conquest was toward
    a. Judaea.
    b. northern Europe.
    c. Britain.
    d. the Black Sea.

15. Above all, Virgil's *Aeneid* is
    a. a plea for Christianity.
    b. an argument against Roman imperialism and war.
    c. a vision of Rome as the protector of good in the world.
    d. the history of the fall of Athens.

16. The Roman-appointed king of Judaea was
    a. Herod.
    b. Jesus.
    c. Philip Augustus.
    d. Cato.

17. All except one of the following were characteristic of the third century period of the so-called barracks emperors.
    a. civil war
    b. barbarian invasions
    c. severe economic decline
    d. expansion of the empire into northern and western Europe

18. A villa was
    a. a Jewish military district.
    b. the Roman banking system.
    c. a Roman civil service district.
    d. none of the above

19. In order to avert starvation and unrest, the government of Rome provided free grain, oil, and wine to
    a. the military only.
    b. the poor only.
    c. all citizens.
    d. no one.

20. The man most important in the spread of Christianity to non-Jews was
    a. Paul of Tarsus.
    b. St. Peter.
    c. the emperor Diocletian.
    d. the writer Adolphus.

21. The Flavian period came about largely because of
    a. military interference in the selection of the emperor.
    b. the Flavian control of the banking system.
    c. military defeat of Rome by the Goths.
    d. revolution in Judaea.

GEOGRAPHY

1. Using Map 6.1 in the text as a guide, show on the outline map on page 84 the boundaries of the Roman Empire under Augustus; then use Map 6.2 to show the empire's division under Diocletian.
2. Locate and label on the outline map the following places.

Rome	Sicily	Britain	Rhine River
Byzantium	Crete	Danube River	Carthage
Jerusalem	Teutoburger forest		

3. Describe the Roman penetration into northern and western Europe. What kinds of problems did the Romans face, and what techniques did they use in their successful conquests?

UNDERSTANDING HISTORY THROUGH READING AND THE ARTS

Reading biography can be an interesting and rewarding way of discovering the past. A. Schweitzer's *The Quest of the Historical Jesus* (1948) is a superb work, and A. D. Nock's *St. Paul* (1938) is an interesting study of one of the most important men in

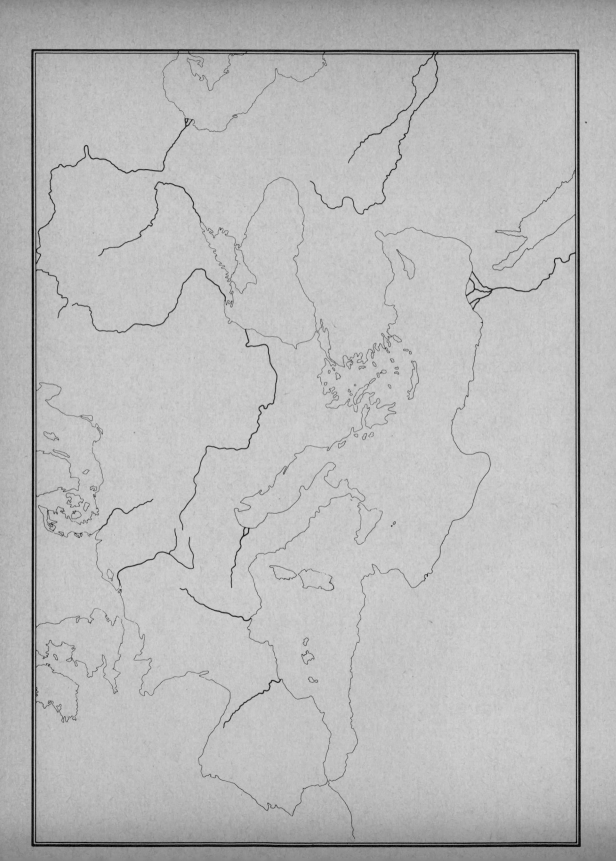

world history. *Rome in the Augustan Age* (1962) by H. Rowell is about Augustus, the man whose imprint on the empire was immense. Also recommended is R. Warner, *The Young Caesar* (1958). R. Graves's *I, Claudius** (1934) is an exciting account of the families, the work, and the loves of the emperors from Augustus to Claudius.

Since the source of most Roman art was Greece, there is hardly such a thing as a "Roman" style. Only in architecture were the Romans truly original. The arch and vault and construction projects such as sewers, bridges, roads, and aqueducts were among Rome's great enterprises. Chapter 7, "Roman Art," in H. W. Janson's *History of Art* (1962) is an excellent review. A more detailed account is G. Rivoira, *Roman Architecture* (1930).

The Romans produced some of the world's greatest literature. Virgil's *The Aeneid* is twelve books of some of mankind's most-read poetry. For an insight into the working of this poetic genius see W. Knight, *Roman Virgil** (1966). Of interest to students in science and philosophy would be the essay *On the Nature of the Universe** (trans., R. Latham, 1967) by the Roman Lucretius, a poet and Epicurean, and Ovid's *The Love Poems of Ovid** (trans., H. Gregory, 1964) can be enjoyed by all.

PROBLEMS FOR FURTHER INVESTIGATION

The reasons for the decline of Roman civilization have interested scholars for hundreds of years. Even the people of Rome were obsessed with the feeling of deterioration. Many prophecies, including the biblical Book of Revelation, foretold the end of the empire. The problems of decline and identification of its causes are the subjects of a scholarly book, *The Awful Revolution* (1969), by F. W. Walbank. The subject is also dealt with in the Problems in European Civilization series' *Decline and Fall of the Roman Empire** (1962) by D. Kagan. These can be supplemented by G. Milner, *The Problem of Decadence* (1931).

*Available in paperback.

CHAPTER 7

THE MAKING OF EUROPE

CHAPTER OBJECTIVES

After reading and studying this chapter you should be able to answer the following questions:

Q-1. How did the Greco-Roman heritage, the Germanic traditions, and Christianity act upon one another and contribute to the making of a new Europe?

Q-2. What influence did Byzantine and Islamic cultures have on the making of European civilization?

CHAPTER SYNOPSIS

Between 400 and 900 a distinctly European society evolved. The basic ingredients of this new European civilization were the Greco-Roman culture, the customs and traditions of the Germanic peoples, and Christianity. Most of the creation and development of the new society took place in the centuries between 400 and 900.

Diocletian had divided the Roman Empire into two major parts. The capital of the western half was Rome; the capital of the eastern half was Constantinople. The eastern (Byzantine) empire lasted for nearly a thousand years after the disintegration of the western empire in the fifth century. Imperial administration in the West had, by 476, given way to massive Germanic invasions. Within Europe the strongest power and the only stabilizing force was the Roman church, which, largely by default, came to be the major political as well as spiritual power. In the eastern empire the emperor held supreme authority over the church. In Rome, however, the bishops formulated the theory of the church's ultimate power over the state. The church in the West assimilated much of the Greco-Roman culture and used its intellectual passion and administrative talent to tame and transform the Germanic tribes. Of equal importance

in the making of Europe were the monastic orders, which after about 529 were unified under the *Rule* set forth by Saint Benedict.

While Germans were being baptized and were consolidating themselves into great
kingdoms, the new threat of Islam pushed into Europe. Founded by Mohammed in
the early seventh century, the religion of Islam united the Arabs and in a short period
produced one of the most expansionist cultures the world has ever witnessed. By the
early eighth century, Muslims had conquered Spain and were pushing into France.

Both the Byzantine and the Islamic empires were important for European development. Both preserved much Greco-Roman knowledge, a great deal of which was
not rediscovered in the West until much later, and they made important contributions to law, science, and medicine. Germanic tradition and custom were also important in that development. But above all, it was Christianity that gave Europe its
strength and unity.

STUDY OUTLINE

I.   The growth of the Christian church
   A.   The word "church" can mean several things, but at this time it was often
        applied to the officials—or *papa*—who presided over all Christians
   B.   The church and the Roman emperors
      1.   Constantine supported and legalized Christianity in 312
      2.   Theodosius increased the power of the church and made Christianity the
           official religion of the Roman Empire
      3.   The emperors were important in enforcing theological uniformity in the
           church
         a.   Constantine summoned the Council of Nicaea in 325 to combat
              Arianism
         b.   The council supported the doctrine that Christ was of the same sub-
              stance as God, and this became the orthodox position, supported by
              the state
      4.   Bishop Ambrose formulated the theory that the church was supreme over
           the state
   C.   Inspired leadership in the early church
      1.   Many talented Romans, such as Ambrose, became administrators and
           workers in the church
         a.   The church adopted the Empire's system of dioceses
         b.   Bishops came to preside over dioceses
      2.   The bishop of Rome eventually became the supreme head (the pope) of
           the church in Europe
      3.   Because the position of emperor disappeared in the West, the Roman
           bishop became the chief civil authority in Italy

        a. It was said that Pope Leo I saved Rome from Attila

        b. Pope Gregory acted as civil authority

    D. The missionary activity of the early Christians

      1. The Roman soldier Martin of Tours brought Christianity to Gaul while Saint Patrick brought Christianity and Roman culture to Ireland

        a. Under Saint Columba, Iona in Scotland became an important Christian center

      2. Augustine and other missionaries carried Christianity to the Germans

      3. Two forms of Christianity—Roman and Celtic—clashed, but the Roman form won out at the Synod of Whitby in 664

      4. Because of the Germans' warlike customs and different culture their assimilation into Christianity was slow

        a. The Christian emphasis on poverty, universal brotherhood, and love of enemies was difficult for German warriors to accept

        b. The Christian concepts of sin and repentance were also hard for them to understand

    E. Conversion and assimilation

      1. The missionaries pursued a policy of assimilating pagan customs and beliefs into Christianity

      2. Penitentials—manuals used to examine one's conscience—were used by priests to teach people Christian virtue, as was preaching

II. Christian attitudes toward classical culture and the rise of monasticism

    A. The early Christians were hostile toward pagan Roman culture

      1. Early Christians believed that Roman culture was useless and immoral

      2. They hated the Romans because they had crucified Christ and persecuted his followers

    B. Christianity's compromise and adjustment to Roman culture

      1. Most early Christians had pagan backgrounds

      2. Early Christians had no objections to homosexuality

      3. Saint Paul and Saint Jerome incorporated pagan thought into Christianity

    C. Saint Augustine and the synthesis of pagan and Christian thought

      1. Augustine is the most important Christian thinker since his time

        a. His book, *The Confessions*, is one of the most influential in Europe

        b. Contrary to Donatism, Augustine believed that Christians should change society

        c. He believed that human beings are basically weak and evil

        d. He believed that the state is a necessary evil to protect people, and that ultimate authority in society lies with the church

      2. Augustine assimilated Roman-pagan history and culture into Christianity

    D. Christian monasticism and the *Rule* of Saint Benedict

      1. Early eremitical life was at first viewed as dangerous by the church

   2. There were many experiments in communal monasticism in the fifth
      and sixth centuries
   3. Benedict of Nursia's *Rule* became the guide for all Christian monastic
      life
   4. The Benedictine *Rule* was flexible and encouraged all kinds of labor
      and participants
   5. The Christian monastic orders played an important role—including eco-
      nomic and educational—in European life
III. The migration of the Germanic peoples
   A. The migrations or volkerwanderugen
      1. Germanic tribes had been pushing against the Roman Empire's frontiers
         since 250
         a. The Huns who moved Westward from China to the east drove the
            Goths into the empire
         b. In 378, the Visigoths defeated the Romans, and full-scale Germanic
            invasions began
      2. The Germans migrated into Europe possibly because they were over-
         populated, had food shortages, and were attracted to Roman wealth
      3. Except for the Lombards, their conquests on the continent ended
         around 600
      4. They replaced Rome as rulers of Europe and established a number of
         kingdoms, the most important being the Frankish kingdom under the
         chieftain Clovis
IV. Germanic society
   A. Germanic kinship, customs, and class
      1. The basic social and political unit was the tribe
         a. The tribe was united by kinship
         b. Every tribe had its own customs, and these customs were its
            law
      2. The tribes were led by a king, or chieftain
      3. The *comitatus* or "warband" was the beginning of a warrior nobility
   B. Germanic law
      1. Under Salic Law each person had a wergeld, or monetary value, and each
         offense had a fine
      2. German law—as shown by the Salic Law—aimed not at justice but at the
         reduction of violence
   C. German life
      1. The pagan Germans believed that gods inhabited the forests, so they
         would not cut trees or clear the land for farming
      2. Germanic peoples lived in cooperative agricultural villages
      3. The end of their animistic beliefs encouraged them to exercise greater
         control over their environment

        4. They often lived in *wattle* huts
        5. They adopted Roman taste and practices
    D. Anglo-Saxon England
        1. The exit of the Romans in 407 led to the establishment of seven Germanic kingdoms in England
        2. Alfred, king of Wessex, unified England in the ninth century
V. The Byzantine East
    A. The Roman Empire divided
        1. The western part was controlled by the Germans
        2. The eastern part continued the traditions and institutions of the old empire
    B. Differences between the Byzantine East and the Germanic West
        1. Because imperial protection of the western empire disappeared in the fifth century, the Roman church assumed much civil authority
        2. In the eastern part of the empire, Roman culture was preserved
        3. In the West there were conflicts between church and state leaders, while in the East the state was supreme over the church
            a. In the West the spiritual ideals of confessor, martyr, and virgin were seen to exist in "Saints" who were socially prominent persons
            b. In the East the Saints were seen to avoid society
        4. The Byzantine Empire was an important geographic buffer in protecting the West from invasions
        5. The Byzantines civilized the Slavic people and converted them to Christianity
    C. The law code of Justinian
        1. The law codes of the emperors Theodosius and Justinian are among the most important contributions of the Byzantine Empire
        2. The *corpus juris civilis*—the civil law—is the foundation of European law
    D. Byzantine intellectual life
        1. The Byzantines kept scholarship alive, especially history
        2. They passed Greco-Roman culture on to the Arabs
        3. They were not creative in science or mathematics
        4. They made advances in the art of war and in medicine
VI. The Arabs and Islam
    A. The Arabs
        1. The Hejaz Arabs were urban and commercial, while the Bedouin Arabs were nomadic and rural
        2. All Arabs, however, were tribal and practiced certain similar religious rules
    B. Islam
        1. Mohammed, the founder of Islam, claimed to be the successor to Abraham and Christ

2. Islam is a monotheistic religion that looks to the Day of Judgment, when the saved and the damned will be separated
3. The Koran—the holy book—outlines the strict code of behavior required of the believer
4. The strict codes of the Koran were more fair to women than the codes of the Christian West
5. Islam is in many ways similar to Judaism and Christianity

C. Muslim expansion
1. The Hegira, or flight from Medina to Mecca in 622, was the beginning of the Muslim era
2. Mohammed destroyed traditional Arab communal and tribal customs and thus unified the Arabs
3. United by their religion, the Muslims pushed into the old Roman world as far north as Tours in France in 733, into Africa, and across Asia to India
4. They established a kingdom in Spain, and Toledo became a center of Arab learning
5. The Arabs made great advances in science, mathematics, and medicine

REVIEW QUESTIONS

Q-1. Describe the role of the Roman emperors and the empire in the growth of Christianity from an outlawed movement to the most important power in Rome.

Q-2. Why did Rome become the capital of the Christian church in the West?

Q-3. Using the kingdom of Kent as an example, explain how the Christian missionaries converted the pagans. What devices and techniques did they use in the assimilation of Germanic peoples into Christianity?

Q-4. Why and how did the Christian rejection of paganism turn to compromise?

Q-5. What ideas did Saint Augustine contribute to Christian thought?

Q-6. What was happening to Rome at the time Saint Augustine wrote the *City of God*? How could this have influenced his philosophy that the City of God is more important than the city of man?

Q-7. What was the purpose of monasticism? Why is Benedict of Nursia one of the most important figures in the history of Christian monasticism?

Q-8. Describe the Benedictine *Rule*. Why was it the most successful monastic rule?

Q-9. The monasteries were completely isolated from European life and played no role in European society. Agree or disagree with the preceding statement. Explain the reasons for your decision.

Q-10. In 378, a Visigothic army defeated the Roman army. Why was this a turning point in European history? Who were the Germans and what were their motives and interests?

Q-11. What patterns of social and political life existed in German society and what was the economy like?

Q-12. How and why did Germanic law evolve and how did it work?

Q-13. Why did Christianity dramatically change the way Germans viewed and used their environment?

Q-14. Name the kingdoms of the English Heptarchy. What were their origins and what role did King Alfred of Wessex play in this development?

Q-15. Compare and contrast the Byzantine and western European societies in terms of (a) political development, and (b) religion.

Q-16. Describe and give examples of the church-state conflict in the West. Why was this conflict not a problem in the eastern part of the empire?

Q-17. The Byzantine civilization is often pictured as decadent and unproductive. Is this a correct evaluation? Explain.

Q-18. Explain: "Byzantine served the West as both a protector from the East and a preserver of ancient culture."

Q-19. Describe the historical evolution of Islam and its major beliefs. What kind of lifestyle does it demand of its followers?

Q-20. Three of the world's great religions—Judaism, Christianity, and Islam—originated in the same part of the world. Why? What are the similarities among them?

Q-21. Mohammed was a prophet. What was his message?

Q-22. What impact did the Muslims have on the politics and culture of the Mediterranean world?

STUDY-REVIEW EXERCISES

Define the following key concepts and terms.

ekklesia

Justinian's *Code*

catholic

penitentials

Salic Law

City of God

Rule of Saint Benedict

Arianism

Islamic Day of Judgment

wergeld

heresy

dioceses

Identify each of the following and give its significance.

Dooms of Ethelbert

Theodosius

Byzantine Empire

King Alfred of Wessex

Augustine the missionary

Mohammed

Bishop Ambrose

Pope Leo I

Saint Martin of Tours/Saint Patrick

Saint Augustine

Saint Jerome

Clovis

Saint Benedict

Koran

Toledo

Explain the following events and tell why they are important.

Synod of Whitby, 664

Battle of Tours, 733

The Hegira, 622

The Council of Nicaea, 325

The Theodosius-Ambrose dispute

Test your understanding of the chapter by answering the following questions.

1. Overall, the Benedictine monastic movement *did/did not* result in economic and material benefits to Europe.

2. This emperor legalized Christianity in the year 312. _____
3. In Germanic society each person's monetary value to the tribe was called the

   _____ .

4. Of the two parts of the old Roman empire—east and west—it was the

   _____ that was politically and culturally more stable and progressive.
5. The early church fathers believed that the church *was/was not* ultimately superior to the state.
6. The author of *The Confessions* and an important Christian philosopher.

   _____

7. After the year 476 it was _____, not emperors, who held power in the western Roman world.
8. The Germanic people's pre-Christian view of their environment *aided/retarded* their material standard of living.

9. The beginning of the Muslim religion dates from the _____ , or flight of Mohammed from Mecca to Medina in 622.

10. This book, written at the time of Rome's destruction, argues that humanity is divided between those who live the earthly life of selfishness and those who live according to the spirit of God.

    _____

11. The head of the Byzantine Church was the *emperor/pope*.

MULTIPLE-CHOICE QUESTIONS

1. At the Council of Nicaea in 325 it was decided that
    a. the Arians were correct.
    b. emperors should not participate in theological disputes.
    c. Christ was of the same substance as God.
    d. God and Christ were of different substances.

2. Writers of penitentials tended to be most concerned about the people's
    a. faith in God.
    b. rejection of Roman authority.
    c. baptism and the end of fighting.
    d. sexual behavior.

3. Which of the following statements about the Benedictine *Rule* is *false*?
    a. It applied to both men and women.
    b. It was quite flexible.
    c. It emphasized love of self.
    d. It encouraged nonintellectual labor.

4. The greatest intellectual contribution of Islam to the West is in the area of
    a. literature.
    b. mathematics and medicine.
    c. law.
    d. music.

5. The major accomplishment of Alfred the Great was
    a. the unification of the Anglo-Saxon kingdoms.
    b. the conversion of Britain to Christianity.
    c. the defeat of Rome's last emperor.
    d. a new law code.

6. Which of the following statements about the Muslim religion is *false*?
   a. It is strictly monotheistic.
   b. Its adherents believe that Mohammed is the successor to Abraham and Christ.
   c. It professes the coming of a Day of Judgment.
   d. It states that good behavior can bring salvation.

7. Which of the following statements about the Germanic peoples in post-Roman Europe is *false*?
   a. They held animistic beliefs.
   b. They seldom engaged in agriculture.
   c. Their war bands swore loyalty to the king.
   d. Their law was aimed at the reduction of violence.

8. Saint Augustine is important in European history because he
   a. worked out the theory of papal supremacy.
   b. compiled the writings of Jesus into a new testament.
   c. assimilated Greco-Roman thought into Christianity.
   d. was the first bishop of Rome.

9. The Benedictine *Rule* was primarily designed to
   a. spread Christianity to the Germans.
   b. draw the individual away from love of self.
   c. encourage new economic ventures.
   d. train officials for government.

10. The Koran is the
    a. sacred book of Islam.
    b. Germanic practice of infanticide.
    c. Islamic religious center at Mecca.
    d. leading Muslim official.

11. Collections of early Germanic laws dealt primarily with
    a. sex.
    b. civil rights.
    c. property rights.
    d. fines for criminal offenses, such as theft, murder, rape, and so forth.

12. The Germanic peoples held animistic beliefs. This means that
    a. the flesh meat of animals should not be eaten.
    b. gods or spiritual forces live in natural objects such as rivers.

    c. bulls or cattle are sacred.

    d. animals, like human beings, have souls.

13. The most important ecclesiastical statement about church-state relations was formulated by

    a. Arius of Alexandria.

    b. the emperor Theodosius.

    c. the emperor Diocletian.

    d. Ambrose of Milan.

14. Which of the following did *not* provide political and social leadership in the early Christian era?

    a. Giaseric

    b. St. Paul

    c. Leo I (440-461)

    d. Gregory I (590-604)

15. Religious conversion means

    a. baptism.

    b. a turning of the heart and mind to God.

    c. confession.

    d. confirmation.

16. Missionaries got pagan peoples to accept Christianity through which of the following?

    a. preaching and teaching

    b. living exemplary lives

    c. the adaptation of pagan places and practices to Christian use

    d. all of the above

17. Unlike elsewhere, church organization was closely associated with local monastic life in

    a. Germany

    b. Scotland

    c. Ireland

    d. Italy

18. Cassiodorus identified monasticism entirely with

    a. prayer and mortification.

    b. study and learning.

    c. manual labor.

    d. all of the above

19. The monastic vows in the *Rule* of St. Benedict were
    a. poverty, chastity, and obedience.
    b. the Work of God.
    c. stability, conversion of manners, and obedience.
    d. none of the above

20. Benedictine monasticism replaced other forms of early Christian monasticism largely because
    a. of its moderation, flexibility, and balanced life.
    b. the emperors encouraged it.
    c. Benedictine monks were cleverer.
    d. Europeans were especially suited to the eremitical life.

21. The Byzantine emperor Justinian secured a permanent place in European history for his
    a. defeat of the Slavs and Turks.
    b. production of the *corpus juris civilis*.
    c. marriage to the naughty lady, Theodora.
    d. invention of the cyrillic alphabet.

22. The *corpus juris civilis* was
    a. snippets of the works of Herodotus, Procopius, and Aristotle.
    b. Russian, Roman, and Greek laws.
    c. Roman law and Greek practices.
    d. the body of civil law of Justinian.

23. "Islam" literally means
    a. the day of judgment is at hand.
    b. submission to the word of God.
    c. the Koran is a sacred book.
    d. Mohammed is Allah's prophet.

24. The Western intellectual debt to Islam is primarily in the area of
    a. law.
    b. mathematics and medicine.
    c. a code of ethical behavior.
    d. literature.

GEOGRAPHY

1. Using Map 6.1 in the text as a guide, show on the outline map the boundaries of the Roman Empire at the time of Hadrian.

2. Using Map 7.1 in the text as a guide, draw in the invasion routes of the seven invasion groups.
3. Locate and label the battle site of Tours. Why was this battle significant?

4. Locate and label the following places.

   Constantinople   Mecca   Red Sea   Paris

   Rome   Jerusalem   Black Sea   Egypt

   Arabian Desert

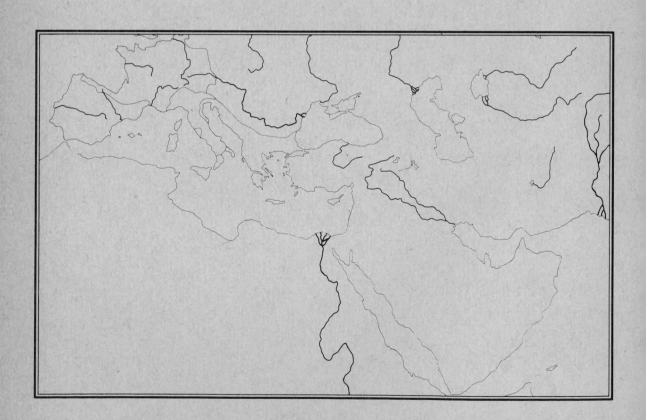

5. Who were the Anglo-Saxons, and what impact did they have on the peoples of Britain?

6. Using Map 7.3 in the text as a guide, (a) show the extent of Muslim expansion by 733, and (b) locate and give the significance of the following Muslin cities: Damascus, Cordova, Toledo.

UNDERSTANDING HISTORY THROUGH READING AND THE ARTS

The best architectural statement of the Byzantine age is the Hagia Sophia (Church of Holy Wisdom) built between 532 and 637 in Constantinople in the age of Justinian. After the Turkish conquest it became a mosque and the minarets were added. See E. H. Swift, *Hagia Sophia* (1940) and N. Pevsner, *An Outline of European Architecture* (7th ed., 1963), Chapters 1 and 2.

PROBLEMS FOR FURTHER INVESTIGATION

Reading biographies is an excellent way to further your understanding of this period of expansion and change. P. Brown, *Augustine of Hippo* (1967) and T. Andrae, *Mohammed: The Man and His Faith* (1970) are biographies of two important men of the post-Roman world. If you are interested in the Germanic invaders, see C. D. Gordon, *The Age of Attila* (1961). P. H. Blair, *Anglo-Saxon England* (1956) is about the establishment of Germanic kingdoms in England, and E. S. Duckett, *Alfred the Great* (1956) is about the life and times of that warrior and scholar and is filled with drama and action.

*Available in paperback.

Scholarship on women in the Middle Ages is just underway. Highly acclaimed by undergraduates is a collection of essays by R. Reuther and E. McLaughlin, eds., *Women of Spirit: Female Leadership in the Jewish and Christian Tradition* (1979). It includes women from the first century to modern times. See also M. Rose, ed., *Women in the Middle Ages and the Renaissance: Literary and Historical Perspectives* (1986).

Challenging but rewarding for undergraduates, especially those interested in psychology or interdisciplinary history is C. Redding, *A World Made by Men: Cognition and Society, 400-1200* (1985). It applies Piaget's theories to the Middle Ages.

*Available in paperback.

READING WITH UNDERSTANDING
EXERCISE 2

LEARNING TO IMPROVE YOUR UNDERLINING SKILLS

Read the following paragraphs, in which some words are printed in italic type to help you find the major points. Read the passage a second time and underline or highlight one or two sentences in each paragraph that best summarize the paragraph's major point. Now study and review these points. Finally, close the book and on a piece of notepaper summarize the major points *with a few words* under the heading "The Success of Benedictine Monasticism." Compare your summary with that found at the end of the exercise.

The Success of Benedictine Monasticism

Why was the Benedictine form of monasticism so successful? Why did it eventually replace other forms of Western monasticism? The answer lies partly in its *spirit of flexibility and moderation,* and partly in the *balanced life* it provided. Early Benedictine monks and nuns spent part of the day in prayer, part in study or some other form of intellectual activity, and part in manual labor. The monastic life as conceived by Saint Benedict did not lean too heavily in any one direction; it struck a balance between asceticism and idleness. It thus provided opportunities for persons of entirely different abilities and talents—from mechanics to gardeners to literary scholars. Benedict's *Rule* contrasts sharply with Cassiodorus's narrow concept of the monastery as a place for aristocratic scholars and bibliophiles.

Benedictine monasticism also *suited the social circumstances of early medieval society.* The German invasions had fragmented European life: the self-sufficient rural estate replaced the city as the basic unit of civilization. A monastery too had to be *economically self-sufficient.* It was supposed to produce from its lands and properties all that was needed for food, clothing, buildings, and the liturgical service of the altar. The monastery fit in—indeed, represented—the trend toward localism.

Benedictine monasticism also succeeded partly because it was so *materially successful*. In the seventh and eighth centuries, monasteries pushed back forest and wasteland, drained swamps, and experimented with crop rotation. For example, the abbey of Saint Wandrille, founded in 645 near Rouen in northwestern Gaul, sent squads of monks to clear the forests that surrounded it. Within seventy-five years, the abbey was immensely wealthy. The abbey of Jumièges, also in the diocese of Rouen, followed much the same pattern. Such Benedictine houses made *a significant contribution to the agricultural development* of Europe. The socialistic nature of their organization, whereby property was held in common and profits pooled and reinvested, made this contribution possible.

Finally, *monasteries conducted schools* for local young people. Some learned about prescriptions and herbal remedies and went on to provide medical treatment for their localities. A few copied manuscripts and wrote books. This training did not go unappreciated in a society desperately in need of it. Local and royal governments drew on the services of *the literate men and able administrators* the monasteries produced. This was not what Saint Benedict had intended, but the effectiveness of the institution he designed made it perhaps inevitable.

ANSWER

The Success of Benedictine Monasticism

1. A flexible and balanced life

2. Economically self-sufficient

3. Economically successful, especially in agriculture

4. Provided education for young and able administrators for governments

CHAPTER 8

THE CAROLINGIAN WORLD: EUROPE
IN THE EARLY MIDDLE AGES

CHAPTER OBJECTIVES

After reading and studying this chapter you should be able to answer the following questions:

Q-1. How did Charlemagne acquire and govern his empire?
Q-2. What were the relations between Carolingian rulers and the church?
Q-3. What was the Carolingian Renaissance and in what sense was it the first European civilization?
Q-4. What was feudalism and how did it come about?
Q-5. What factors contributed to the disintegration of the Carolingian Empire?

CHAPTER SYNOPSIS

For about a century after the Franks defeated the Muslims at the battle of Tours in 733, Europe enjoyed a period of political and economic regeneration and unity. The chief benefactor of this regeneration was the Frankish Carolingian family. It was the Carolingian Charles Martel who won at Tours, and it was his son Pippin III and grandson Charlemagne who molded western Europe into a unified Christian empire—the Carolingian Empire.

The Carolingian era was a high point of stability and creativity in the early Middle Ages, which was generally a precarious time. The Carolingians struck up a mutually beneficial relationship with the church. They supported church missionaries and enforced Christian moral codes. In return, the pope recognized and strengthened Carolingian political authority. Charlemagne extended the boundaries of his empire and brought peace to Europe. Within this climate of peace a meaningful renaissance in learning and the arts took place. The center for both the intellectual renaissance and the Carolingian Empire was northern Europe, not Italy. The very fact that this Carolingian Empire and culture developed in the north, or even at all, was due to the forced isolation of Europe from the Islamic-Mediterranean world, as the great historian Henri Pirenne first argued.

While these changes related to the Carolingian era were taking place, Europe continued to experience the economic-political transformation that historians call feudalism. Beginning as a natural response of insecure people to the disappearance of the protection which the strong Roman government had provided, feudalism became a means for communities to defend themselves. Over time, as we have already seen in Chapter 6 (pp. 203-204), freemen gave up their personal rights and their property to local lords. These lords provided protection, in return, and built their own little empires. Essential to the feudal system was the fief—the land a lord received from the monarch. Charlemagne was able to manage the feudal lords, but his grandsons could not keep control of the feudal system. When they divided Charlemagne's empire into three parts in 843, it was already soaked in blood because of the ambitions of petty lords. The division was an invitation to invasion from the outside. The Vikings, Magyars, and Muslims then threw Europe back into a period of violence and fear.

STUDY OUTLINE

I. The Frankish aristocracy and the rise of the Carolingian dynasty
    A. The Frankish kingdom under the Merovingians included most of France and the south-west of Germany
        1. Clovis, the Merovingian leader, made the Franks, with their capital at Paris, the most powerful people of Europe
        2. After Clovis's death in 511, the Merovingians fell into a long period of civil war
        3. Civil war was accompanied by the rise of a wealthy and powerful aristocracy
        4. Reconstruction of the Frankish kingdom began with Pippin of Landen who was mayor of the East Frankish palace
    B. The rise of the Carolingian dynasty
        1. The Carolingian family under Martel and Pippin III built a vast power base in France, aided by the church
        2. Bishop Boniface organized the church and spread Christianity in central Europe
            a. He made Mainz the center of the German church and founded the abbey of Fulda
            b. He reformed the Frankish church

        3. Boniface and the Carolingians attacked pagan sexual customs and promoted respect for civil authority

   C. Monarchy and papacy

        1. Pippin III's acquisition of the kingship was aided by the pope

        2. Pippin created strong ties between the church and the Carolingian dynasty

II. The empire of Charlemagne and the Carolingian renaissance

   A. The warrior-ruler Charlemagne is described in Einhard's biography as both an intellectual and a strong, brutal man of Christian virtue

   B. Territorial expansion

        1. Charlemagne continued the Carolingian tradition by building a large European kingdom

        2. He checked the Muslim expansion and conquered the Saxon German tribes

        3. His need for children (and wives and concubines) was partly a result of political and diplomatic considerations

        4. He added northern Italy to his Frankish kingdom, but his Spanish campaign had only literary significance

   C. The government of the Carolingian Empire

        1. The empire of Charlemagne was mainly a collection of agricultural estates —the *villae* of the aristocracy

        2. He made the *missi dominici*, or agents of the king, the link between the country and king

        3. Charles's empire was not a state in the modern sense

        4. The Carolingians sought a single, unified Christian society presided over by a Christian king

   D. The imperial coronation of Charlemagne in 800

        1. The church supported Charlemagne, and in 800 the pope crowned Charles the Roman Emperor

        2. Charles unified old Rome, Christianity, and Frankish practices

        3. The motives of both Charles and the pope are unclear; it is possible that each planned the coronation in order to increase his own power

        4. The coronation gave rise to theories of both imperial and papal supremacy

III. The Carolingian intellectual revival

   A. The revival of learning began with Irish-Celtic influence in Anglo-Saxon Britain

   B. Northumbrian culture in Britain

        1. Irish-Celtic culture permeated Roman Britain and Europe, partly by way of monastic missals, or books

        2. The Lindisfarne book is a high point in the Northumbrian artistic renaissance

        3. The monk Bede was one of the greatest scholars of the Middle Ages

    4. Bede wrote a history of early Britain—*The Ecclesiastical History of the English Nation*—that is the chief source of information about early Britain

    5. The poem *Beowulf* illustrates the complexities and contradictions within people and society and the importance of loyalty, fame, and warfare in medieval society

    6. Anglo-Saxon and Carolingian riddles were intended to instruct and entertain and today tell us much about how medieval people thought

C. The Carolingian renaissance

    1. Charlemagne fostered an intellectual revival which centered on his court at Aachen

    2. His scholars (the most important being Alcuin) encouraged interest in and preserved Greek and Roman knowledge

    3. Basic literacy was established among the clergy and Christianity was spread

D. Health and medical care in the early Middle Ages

    1. No rational understanding of disease existed

    2. Drug and prescription therapy was common

    3. "Physicians" knew little about disease, and their treatments were primitive and often harmful

    4. Christianity contributed to a better understanding of health, and later secular schools were founded for the study of medicine

    5. The Italian school at Salerno was an important medical center and several women physicians played a key role in medical writings

IV. Feudalism

A. Early feudalism served the needs of medieval society

B. The two levels of feudalism were retainers (knights) and counts

    1. Feudalism was a type of government in which power was considered private and was divided among many lords

    2. Its two levels were armed knights at the bottom and great counts on a higher level

    3. Stirruped cavalry made the Carolingian use of armed retainers (knights) possible

    4. Retainers, or *vassals*, took an oath of *fealty*, and some were given estates by their lords

    5. Counts held power at the local level and came to rule independently

C. Because of the premium placed on physical strength, women were subordinate to men, although they occasionally held positions of power

D. Manorialism was the economic and social side of feudalism, which centered on the relationship between peasant (or serf) and the lord's estate

E. Over time the free farmer (peasant) became a serf

V. The division and disintegration of the Carolingian Empire and the great invasions
   A. The empire divided
      1. Without the unifying force of Charlemagne's personality, the empire began to fall apart
      2. Charlemagne's grandsons, Lothair, Louis, and Charles, agreed to divide the empire in 843 in the Treaty of Verdun
      3. The "middle kingdom" of Lothair became a disputed territory
      4. War among the Carolingians meant the growth of the feudal military system and disorder
   B. The great invasions of the ninth century
      1. Disunity in Europe after Charlemagne's death was an invitation to aggression from the outside
      2. The Vikings from the north overran northwest France, Britain, parts of Russia, and elsewhere
      3. The Magyars, or Hungarians, pushed into Europe from the east
      4. The Muslims pushed up from the south
      5. These invasions also accelerated the growth of feudalism

REVIEW QUESTIONS

Q-1. "Without Mohammed, Charlemagne would have been inconceivable." Explain and evaluate this statement.

Q-2. Define feudalism and describe its origins. What impact did it have on the peasants?

Q-3. Describe Germanic marriage and sexual practices. What impact did Christianity have on these customs? Who was responsible for the change?

Q-4. It has been said that Saint Boniface carried on the "Romanization of Europe." Explain this statement in the light of the missionary activities of this important figure.

Q-5. What was the relationship between the Carolingians and the pope? How did both sides benefit from the relationship?

Q-6. How successful was Charlemagne in expanding the power of the Frankish state?

Q-7. What techniques and methods did Charlemagne use to govern his vast empire? How well did his empire function?

Q-8. What was the church's attitude toward Charlemagne and the political value of the "state"?

Q-9. What were the probable reasons for Charlemagne's quest for the title of emperor? The results?

Q-10. Describe the Northumbrian cultural revival. What were its sources of inspiration and its goals?

Q-11. What was the "Carolingian renaissance"? Who were its participants and what did they accomplish?

Q-12. In this early medieval period, a person of forty was considered old. Why did people die so young? How much did people understand about disease, and what kind of health care existed?

Q-13. Who were the Vikings? What were their motives and why were they able to terrorize Europe so well after 814?

Q-14. Describe the Magyar and Muslim invasions in terms of motives, areas terrorized, methods, and impact.

Q-15. Was feudalism a blessing or a disaster for Europe? Did it bring order and stability or merely chaos and exploitation?

STUDY-REVIEW EXERCISES

Define the following key concepts and terms.

fief

feud

rex et sacerdos

missi dominici

Papal States

vassal

polygamy

ecclesiastical

Carolingian renaissance

Pirenne thesis

Charlemagne's *marks*

Identify the following people and explain their importance.

The Venerable Bede

Pippin of Landen

Pippin III

Saint Boniface

Charles Martel

Willibrord

Charlemagne

Alcuin

Louis the Pious

Pope Leo

Benet Biscop

Louis the German

Charles the Bald

Lothair

Explain *what the following events were, who participated in them, and why they were important.*

Northumbrian cultural renaissance

coronation of Charlemagne

Battle of Tours

Treaty of Verdun

Explain the subject matter and historical significance of the following books.

Bede, *The Ecclesiastical History of the English Nation*

Abbess Hildegard, *On the Physical Elements*

Beowulf

Paul the Deacon, *History of the Lombards*

Test your understanding of the chapter by answering the following questions.

1. The author of the *City of God.* _____
2. The author of *The Ecclesiastical History of the English Nation.*

_____

3. In general, the economic and political power and status of aristocratic women in the early Middle Ages tended to *increase/decrease.*
4. In the eighth and ninth centuries, the population of western Europe tended to become *more/less* free.
5. In general, the relationship between the Carolingian emperor Charles and the Christian church was *good/warlike.*
6. This Northumbrian was an important scholar and educator and the major advisor

to Charlemagne. _____

7. The foundation of a medical school at _____ in the ninth century gave tremendous impetus to medical study.

MULTIPLE-CHOICE QUESTIONS

1. Saint Boniface, the missionary monk
    a. refused to support the Carolingian kings.
    b. took the *Rule* of Saint Benedict to many monasteries.
    c. attacked Germanic sexual and marriage customs.
    d. was a staunch enemy of Roman ideas and Roman traditions.

2. The most important source of Northumbrian (and then Carolingian) cultural revival was

   a. Muslim society.
   b. Jewish society.
   c. Irish-Celtic society.
   d. Frankish society.

3. The *missi dominici* of Charlemagne were
   a. missionaries.
   b. peasant farmers.
   c. royal legal officials.
   d. military outposts.

4. Charlemagne was crowned emperor by
   a. himself.
   b. his father Pippin.
   c. the pope.
   d. the Frankish council.

5. Only one of the following peoples was not a part of the great invasions of the ninth century.
   a. The Vikings
   b. The Franks
   c. The Byzantines
   d. The Muslims

6. Which of the following was *not* an accomplishment of Charlemagne?
   a. the establishment of the *missi dominici*
   b. the creation of marks
   c. the encouragement of literature and art
   d. the destruction of papal power

7. The Northumbrian period of creativity was centered in
   a. Charlemagne's court.
   b. the monasteries of Britain
   c. the courts of feudal lords
   d. Pavia in Lombardy

8. When Charlemagne's son, Louis the Pious, died, the empire
   a. was divided three ways.
   b. remained intact under Charles Martel.
   c. was united with the Anglo-Saxon kingdoms.
   d. remained a unified but weak state.

9. The monk-historian who wrote *The Ecclesiastical History of the English Nation* was
   a. Louis the German.
   b. Pippin III.
   c. Bede.
   d. Augustine.

10. The fundamental importance of the battle of Tours (733) was that it
    a. aided the spread of Christianity in the Frankish kingdom.
    b. checked the advance of the Muslims in Europe.
    c. made Pippin II mayor of the palace.
    d. ended the Viking attacks.

11. St. Boniface is famous as
    a. the biographer of Charlemagne.
    b. the author of *Beowulf*.
    c. the Apostle of Germany.
    d. the author of a great medical treatise.

12. Historians consider the narrative poem *Beowulf* useful for
    a. an illustration of early Germanic marriage laws.
    b. its information on eighth-century monastic life.
    c. an early example of Germanic fairy tales.
    d. the picture it provides of Anglo-Saxon society and ideals.

13. The Carolingian Empire collapsed because
    a. it was too large and lacked effective machinery of government.
    b. it was overrun by Arabs and Turks.
    c. Charlemagne's grandsons were lazy and incompetent.
    d. Charlemagne failed to make a will.

14. The first major medical center in Europe was at
    a. Aix-la-Chapelle.
    b. Bologna.
    c. Salerno.
    d. Strasbourg.

15. Constantine the African advanced medical knowledge by
    a. founding hospitals.
    b. researching gynecological problems.
    c. recommending heroin as an anesthetic.
    d. translating Arabic medical treatises.

16. Viking expansion in the eighth century was probably due to
    a. overpopulation.
    b. the search for a warmer climate.
    c. the search for new trade and commercial outlets.
    d. all of the above

17. The word *feud* used in connection with feudalism refers to
    a. a bitter struggle.
    b. the land given by a lord to his vassal.
    c. the economic aspects of the system.
    d. a lazy serf.

18. A feudal lord exercised which of the following rights?
    a. judicial
    b. economic
    c. political
    d. all of the above

GEOGRAPHY

With Maps 8.1, 8.2, and 8.3 as a guide, use the outline map on the following page to complete the following questions.

1. Describe the geographic boundaries of Charlemagne's empire and explain why it disintegrated after his death.

UNDERSTANDING HISTORY THOUGH READING AND THE ARTS

For a closer look at the architectural achievements of this age see K. Conant, *Carolingian and Romanesque Architecture, 800-1200** (1978), and a good general introduction to the illuminated manuscripts and religious treasures of the period is J. Beckwith, *Early Medieval Art** (1979).

*Available in paperback.

Going directly to the sources can be an interesting and rewarding enterprise. Paperback editions of several early medieval works are available: L. Sherley-Price, trans., *Bede: A History of the English Church and Peoples** (1962); M. Alexander, trans., *The Earliest English Poems** (1972); D. L. Sayers, trans., *The Song of Roland**; and D. Wright, trans., *Beowulf** (1957).

PROBLEMS FOR FURTHER INVESTIGATION

How did Merovingian and Carolingian government work? How did the concept of kingship evolve? Was Christianity as important as claimed? These and other questions are answered in P. Wormald et al., *Ideal and Reality in Frankish and Anglo-Saxon Society* (1984). What were the contributions of women in medieval society? Begin your inquiry with D. Baker, ed., *Medieval Women** (1981).

What were the motives of the pope and Charlemagne at the time of the coronation on Christmas Day in the year 800? Of what significance is the fact that the church gave the title to the king? These and other questions are considered in a collection of interpretations entitled *The Coronation of Charlemagne** (1959), edited by R. E. Sullivan. How much did the Islamic movement shape the course of European history? The classic statement on this is Henri Pirenne, *Mohammed and Charlemagne** (1958).

*Available in paperback.

CHAPTER 9

REVIVAL, RECOVERY, AND REFORM

CHAPTER OBJECTIVES

After reading and studying this chapter you should be able to answer the following questions:

Q-1. How did the revival of Europe come about?
Q-2. What was the social and political impact of the recovery of Europe?
Q-3. How did the reform of the Christian church affect relations between church and civil authorities?
Q-4. What were the crusades and how did they manifest the influence of the church and the ideals of society?

CHAPTER SYNOPSIS

When Charlemagne died in 814, Europe was thrown into a century and a half of disorder. Then, around the year 1000, Europe began to recover from this long, bitter winter of violence. This chapter deals with two of the most important signs of that European springtime: political recovery and the spiritual and political revival of the church. These two revivals were of great importance for the evolution of individual freedom and for the political and intellectual growth of Europe.

One of the earliest signs of revival was the success feudalism achieved—as in Normandy--in bringing peace and unity to Europe in the tenth and eleventh centuries. The reduced level of warfare in this period, together with favorable changes in climate, resulted in both population explosion and agricultural improvement, and explains why the German nobility was able to dominate German politics. Further, another forceful testimony to the dynamism of the age was the Crusades. Growing out of the influence of the papacy and religion in medieval society, and the efforts toward the *reconquista* in Spain, the Crusades provided an outlet for the spiritual and political energy of Europe.

The religious revival also began, with a monastic reform at the abbey of Cluny in the eleventh century, and spread across Europe. When monastic life was subsequently threatened by materialism and lay interference, there were fresh demands for reform by the Cistercians at the abbey of Citeaux. At the same time, and partly as a result of the Cistercian reforms, the papacy set out to purify itself and to redefine its relationship with the emperors, kings, and other lay political authorities of Europe. This led to the investiture controversy, which reached its height in the conflict between Pope Gregory VII and the German emperor Henry IV. The struggle between the popes and the emperors turned out to be one of the most important and long-lasting political conflicts in European history.

STUDY OUTLINE

I. Political revival in western Europe in the tenth and eleventh centuries
    A. The decline of invasions and civil disorder
        1. The Northmen were Christianized and brought into the kingdom of France
        2. The Norman dukes Rollo and William made Normandy a strong territory
        3. The Vikings slowly became assimilated into European society
        4. Beginning with Hugh Capet in 987 the Capetian kings made the French crown hereditary and strengthened their territory—the Ile-de-France
        5. West Saxon victory in 878 led to English unity based on the *fyrd* and royal law
        6. The Danish king Canute made England part of a large Scandinavian empire
        7. The German king Otto halted the Magyars and revived the Holy Roman Empire in central Europe (Germany and Italy)
            a. Otto brought peace and stability to Germany and Italy
            b. The base of his power was his alliance with the church, which he used to weaken the feudal lords
            c. His coronation in 962 advanced German interests
        8. The Italian cities broke Muslim control of Mediterranean trade
    B. Increasing population and a milder climate
        1. The decline in war and disease meant a rise in population
        2. The warmer climate meant better agricultural production
    C. The peace movements of the church
        1. Church laws—called the Peace of God—protected certain people and places from war and violence

2. The Truce of God restricted the times for fighting to three or fewer days of the week

II. Revival and reform in the Christian church in the eleventh century
   A. The monastic revival
      1. Monastic activity had declined as the Carolingian Empire disintegrated
      2. The abbey of Cluny led the way in a tenth-century monastic revival
         a. Cluny stood for reform of abuses such as *simony*, for high religious standards, and for sound economic management
         b. The Cluniac reform spread throughout Europe
      3. The monastic reform led by abby of Gorze stood for literary culture, simple life style, and lay authority
      4. By the eleventh century, wealth and lay interference caused corruption
      5. The Cistercians (beginning in 1098) isolated themselves from laymen and elaborate ritual
         a. Their reform movement was widespread
         b. It centered on farming and a simple communal life
   B. The reform of the papacy
      1. The tenth-century papacy was corrupt and materialistic and provided little leadership to the people of Europe
      2. Leo IX made the first sweeping reforms
      3. Later reforms included decreeing that the college of cardinals would henceforth elect the pope

III. The Gregorian revolution in church reform
   A. Pope Gregory VII's ideas for reform of the church
      1. Gregory believed that the pope could hold kings accountable
      2. He wanted the church to be free from lay control
   B. The controversy over lay investiture
      1. The church outlawed the widespread practice of lay investiture but Germany presented certain problems
      2. Emperor Henry IV of the Holy Roman Empire protested Pope Gregory's stand on investiture
      3. Their conflict was resolved by Henry's submission to the pope at Canossa in 1075
      4. But the problem was not yet settled; a compromise was not reached until 1122
         a. The emperor surrendered the right to invest bishops
         b. But lay rulers retained a veto over ecclesiastical choices
      5. In the long run, the investiture crisis perpetuated the political division of Germany, and it encouraged the rise of noble dynasties
   C. The papacy in the High Middle Ages

1. Pope Urban II laid the foundation for the papal monarchy
2. The papal curia, which henceforth formulated church law for all of Europe, was established and became important

IV. The Crusades of the eleventh and twelfth centuries
   A. The Crusades reflect papal influence in the society and the fact that the military class had assumed an ecclesiastical function
   B. The Crusades, or holy wars, were seen as a reflection of the religious zeal and secular vitality of the High Middle Ages
      1. They grew out of the Christian-Muslim conflict in Spain and the Christian reconquista
      2. The Eastern emperor appealed to the West for help against the Muslim Turks
      3. Many people responded to Pope Urban II's plea for a crusade to take Jerusalem from the Turks
   C. The results of the Crusades
      1. The First Crusade (1096) resulted in new feudal states—"Crusader kingdoms"—at Jerusalem, Edessa, Tripoli, and Antioch
      2. The Fourth Crusade, which resulted in Christians fighting Christians, was a disaster
      3. The Crusades brought few cultural changes
         a. Crusades were also used to purge Europe out of its domestic enemies, such as the heretical Albigensians
         b. The Crusades encouraged greed and intolerence
         c. Deep bitterness between Christian and Muslim society was established, but the Christian West benefited from commercial contact with the Middle East

REVIEW QUESTIONS

Q-1. Describe the political revival that took place in the ninth and tenth centuries. Who were the chief participants in this revival and what did they accomplish?

Q-2. What role did the church play in the recovery of Europe from a period of war and invasion?

Q-3. Soon after about 1000 the population of Europe began to increase. Why?

Q-4. What were the goals of the Cluniac reformers? Why were they interested in isolation from lay society?

Q-5. Describe the condition of the clergy and church leadership prior to Leo IX's reform movement. What were its major abuses?

Q-6. Was it inevitable that Pope Gregory would come into conflict with the monarchs of Europe? Explain.

Q-7. What was the investiture controversy? Where did ultimate power in medieval society rest?

Q-8. Describe the conflict between Pope Gregory VII and Henry IV. Who had the best weapons and what was the outcome?

Q-9. In the long run who were the winners in the investiture controversy? How did this controversy affect the political development of Germany?

Q-10. What were the reasons for the Crusades?

Q-11. Were the Crusades a "steam valve" for late medieval society?

Q-12. What changes did the Crusades bring to Western European society? Did the benefits outweigh the disadvantages?

STUDY-REVIEW EXERCISES

Define the following key concepts and terms.

capitalism

the fyrd

simony

lay investiture

curia

investiture

Peace of God

guild

laymen

Identify each of the following and give its significance.

treaty of Saint Claire-sur-Epte

investiture controversy

Cluniac reforms

Gorze reforms

Cistercians

Canossa

college of cardinals

the Worms conference of 1122

Explain why the following people were important.

Canute, king of England

Henri Pirenne, historian

Rollo, duke of Normandy

Henry IV, Holy Roman Emperor

Otto, king of Germany

Pope Leo IX

Pope Gregory VII

Test your understanding of the chapter by answering the following questions.

1. The Crusades resulted in an *increase/decrease* in greed and social-religious intolerence, while it *improved/deteriorated* relations between Christians and Muslim societies.

2. It appears that between the ninth and eleventh centuries the European climate became significantly *warmer/cooler*.

3. The church law called the _____ proclaimed that certain people and places were to be protected from war.

4. The *increase/decrease* of warfare in the eleventh century led to an *increase/decrease* in the population of Europe.
5. The important monastic revival began in the tenth century at the abbey of

_____ in Burgundy.
6. According to the Worms (1122) settlement, bishops were henceforth to be chosen

by the _____, but veto power was to be held by the

_____.
7. The important German monastic reform movement was centered at the abbey

of _____.

MULTIPLE-CHOICE QUESTIONS

1. The curia was
   a. the headquarters for the Italian bishops.
   b. the papal financial office.
   c. the location of the imperial court.
   d. the papal bureaucracy and court of law.

2. Emperor Henry IV challenged the pope, Gregory VII, because
   a. the pope wanted ownership of Germany.
   b. the pope was a peasant.
   c. the pope restricted lay investiture.
   d. Henry wanted control over all of Italy.

3. The battle of Edington in 878 marked
   a. West Saxon political revival and unity.
   b. the rise of Normandy.
   c. Danish control of northern Europe.
   d. the fall of Anglo-Saxon law and culture in England.

4. The Anglo-Saxon *fyrd* was
   a. free foot soldiers.
   b. a system of castles.
   c. a civil law code.
   d. ecclesiastical office.

5. The real winner in the eleventh-century investiture controversy was
   a. the nobility.
   b. the papacy.
   c. the emperor.
   d. the college of cardinals.

6. The Truce of God
   a. disallowed any fighting on church land.
   b. ended the Magyar invasions.
   c. disallowed fighting on certain days.
   d. was enforced by all the monastic orders in Europe.

7. The curia was
   a. the headquarters for the Italian bishops.
   b. the papal financial office.
   c. the location of the imperial court.
   d. the papal bureaucracy and court of law.

8. In 962 which German king was crowned Holy Roman Emperor, thereby reviving imperial authority in central Europe?
   a. William
   b. Otto
   c. Gregory
   d. Charles V

9. It was at which Burgundian abbey that the famous tenth-century monastic reform and religious revival had its origins?
   a. Cluny
   b. Canossa
   c. Flanders
   d. Worms

10. The system of papal election was changed in the eleventh century in order that henceforth the pope was elected by whom?
    a. Emperor
    b. College of cardinals
    c. Townspeople
    d. Roman citizens

11. The duchy of Normandy became the strongest territory under William I because he practiced all *except* one of the following:

a. He controlled the currency.
b. He forbade the construction of private castles.
c. He ruthlessly punished vassals who defaulted on military obligations.
d. He allowed the church autonomy.

12. The power of the German emperor Otto I rested on
    a. an alliance with William of Normandy.
    b. heavy taxation of the merchants of his territories.
    c. papal approval.
    d. the support of ecclesiastical officials in Germany.

13. The peace movements of the Christian church worked
    a. to establish Sunday as a day of rest.
    b. to improve relations with the Muslims.
    c. to end the chronic violence and destruction.
    d. to secure a treaty with William of Normandy.

14. In the tenth and eleventh centuries, Nicolaites were
    a. reformed monks.
    b. married priests.
    c. priests who bought and sold church offices.
    d. none of the above

15. Crusades originated as reaction to
    a. Christian-Muslim conflict in Spain.
    b. the decline of Christian influence in Turkey.
    c. the decline of Christian influence in Italy.
    d. new economic opportunities in southern Italy.

16. The goal of the Gregorian Reform movement was
    a. the end of Philip I's adulterous marriage.
    b. the abolition of simony.
    c. the moral reform of the clergy and the centralization of the Catholic
        church under papal authority.
    d. the excommunication of William of Normandy.

17. The German emperor Henry IV opposed Gregory VII because
    a. the pope was too inflexible.
    b. Gregory VII was a peasant.
    c. the pope wanted Henry's strict obedience.
    d. Henry relied on the services of churchmen whom the pope wanted to make
        responsible solely to papal authority.

18. The pontificate of Innocent III represents the high point of medieval papal authority because
    a. Innocent launched the crusades.
    b. he composed important legal treatises.
    c. he exerted power all over Europe.
    d. he secured the end of clerical marriage.

19. The papal or Roman curia in the High Middle Ages was important as
    a. a symbol of papal power and authority.
    b. the first strong monarchial bureaucracy.
    c. a final court of appeals for Christians all over Europe.
    d. all of the above

20. The Crusade that resulted in Christian fighting Christian was the
    a. Fourth Crusade.
    b. Second Crusade.
    c. Eastern Crusade.
    d. First Crusade.

UNDERSTANDING HISTORY THROUGH READING AND THE ARTS

What was life like for the serfs of the early Middle Ages? This is one subject dealt with in the fascinating book *Medieval People** (1963) by E. Power. G. Barraclough's *Medieval Papacy** (1968) is an interesting study for anyone interested in the power of the papacy and the Cluniac movement.

What were the ideas and stories that inspired the imagination and dreams of medieval people? Who were their heroes? The myths of any period are important because they make up the backbone of the culture. Seven myths and hero stories of the Middle Ages are retold in N. L. Goodrich, *The Medieval Myths** (1961).

PROBLEMS FOR FURTHER INVESTIGATION

What was the relationship between politics and religion in medieval society? Politics and royal justice? Begin your investigation with the standard work on medieval political ideals, J. Morrall, *Political Thought in Medieval Times* (1962). The success, glory, idealism, and political aspects of the religious Crusades have fascinated historians for generations. Students interested in further research in this area should begin with *The Crusades** (1939) by J. A. Brundage.

*Available in paperback.

CHAPTER 10

LIFE IN CHRISTIAN EUROPE IN THE
HIGH MIDDLE AGES

CHAPTER OBJECTIVES

After reading and studying this chapter you should be able to answer the following questions:

Q-1. How did the peasants, nobles, and monks of the Middle Ages live and what were their interests?
Q-2. How much social mobility existed in the Middle Ages?

CHAPTER SYNOPSIS

This chapter surveys life in medieval society. It focuses on the three major classes within medieval society: the peasants, who worked; the nobles, who fought; and the monks, who prayed. Despite the rise of towns and the beginning of a merchant class, most of the people were peasants or serfs, who lived and labored on the land. Men and women toiled on the land of the manors to scratch out a meager existence for themselves and to support their noble lords in noble fashion. The agricultural productivity of the average manor was low because there was a lack of fertilizer and it was necessary to leave as much as half of the land fallow each year. Between the ninth and thirteenth centuries, however, it appears that agricultural productivity doubled—a remarkable achievement. Yet the diet of the peasantry was very limited and seldom adequate. A major problem of the Middle Ages was that the birthrate tended always to outpace the food supply.

The manor was the basic unit of medieval rural life, and Christianity was the center of the day-to-day world on the manor. The church provided an explanation for the meaning of life, and it also supplied the community with much of its entertainment and political leadership. Women held a pivotal position in the family and village economy.

The aristocratic nobility was a class with special power and legal status. It had its own lifestyle and goals. The size of noble families, aristocratic patterns of child-rearing, marriage, and sex, and women's role were determined by the fact that males were the holders of property.

The monasteries of Europe had a great civilizing influence. They contributed to both literacy and agricultural improvement in the Middle Ages, and they were important in providing careers for the children of the aristocracy. Monastic life varied from order to order and from district to district, but daily life in all monasteries centered around the liturgy.

STUDY OUTLINE

I. Life in Christian Europe: those who work
    A. The status of the peasantry varied widely all across Europe
    B. Slavery, serfdom, and upward mobility
        1. Slavery was not common in Europe
        2. Serfs had no freedom, but they could not be bought and sold
        3. All serfs were obligated to perform certain duties and pay levys
        4. Only freemen could move and live as they wished
        5. Serfs could obtain freedom in several ways: from their lord, by purchase by a third party, or by being in a town guild for a year and a day
        6. Settlement on new land meant social mobility and freedom
    C. The manor as the basic unit of medieval rural life
        1. The manor—the estate of the lord—was a farming community of varying size
        2. Both the peasant's and the lord's land were divided into strips
        3. Each manor usually had meadows and forests
    D. Agricultural methods
        1. Usually half the land was left fallow (the open-field system)
        2. Animal manure was the major form of fertilizer
        3. The increase in iron production after 1100 meant better tools
        4. The development of the horse collar led to the use of horses in agriculture and thus a great increase in productivity
        5. Yields were low, but they improved from the ninth to the thirteenth centuries
    E. Life on the manor
        1. Medieval village life was provincial but secure
        2. Family life was important, and women played a central economic role

       3. Diet was limited to grains and beer with possibly a great increase in meat consumption by the mid-thirteenth century

       4. Children contributed to the family economy

  F. Popular religion

       1. The Christian religion infused and regulated daily life

       2. Religious ritual and practice synthesized many elements—Jewish, pagan, Roman, and Catholic

       3. The church was the center of village social and political life

       4. The peasants believed strongly in a personal God, and pilgrimages were very popular

       5. In the eleventh century a great emphasis on the devotion to Mary evolved

       6. Religion offered the peasants hope and adventure in a world of gloom

II. Life in Christian Europe: those who fight

  A. The legal and social status of the nobility varied from region to region

  B. The aristocratic nobility

       1. The nobility was an elite, self-conscious social class

       2. Nobles held political power and had a special legal status

       3. Nobles were professional fighters; all nobles were knights but some (like the German ministrials) never attained noble status

  C. Infancy and childhood in aristocratic families

       1. Ignorant medical care contributed to the high infant mortality rate

       2. It is unclear whether infanticide increased during this period

       3. Wet-nursing and swaddling were common practices

       4. Aristocrats had large families but *primogeniture* led to favoring of first born son

       5. Aristocratic boys received a military education—which culminated in "knighthood" in France and England

  D. Youth in aristocratic families

       1. Because "adulthood" could come only with property ownership, it was often difficult to obtain

       2. Knighted men whose fathers were alive had to find activities to occupy themselves

       3. Aristocratic women married early, but many did not marry at all

       4. Generational disputes were common in aristocratic families

       5. Sexual tensions arose from aristocratic marriage practices, which brought together young wives, older husbands, and young, unmarried men

  E. Power and responsibility in the aristocracy

       1. Adulthood meant property and authority

       2. Aristocrats saw lavish living as a sign of status and power, but it often meant debt

       3. Military and economic needs meant frequent travel

       4. Aristocratic women often had considerable power

III. Life in Christian Europe: those who pray
   A. Prayer was a vital social service performed by monks; they also performed other important cultural and economic services
   B. Recruitment
      1. Many who became monks did so because of their parents' decision
      2. Monasteries provided careers for aristocratic children
      3. In the later Middle Ages the monasteries recruited from the middle class
   C. Prayer and other work
      1. Daily life centered around the liturgy
      2. The monasteries—often supported by manorial lords—engaged in farming, stock breeding, iron production, and so on
      3. Various responsibilities were divided among the monks
      4. The monasteries contributed to learning and agricultural progress
   D. Economic difficulties
      1. Monasteries depended on lay endowments
      2. By the late Middle Ages many monasteries, such as Cluny, did not have enough income to support their lavish lifestyle
   E. The effect of the monasteries
      1. They exercised a strong Christian influence on Europe
      2. They were also a civilizing force
      3. The fate of the great abbey of Cluny is an example of the financial crisis of the twelfth century

REVIEW QUESTIONS

Q-1. What were the ways in which a serf (villein) could obtain his or her freedom?

Q-2. Describe a medieval manor. How did it work and what agricultural methods governed its existence? Was it "efficient"?

Q-3. What was the role of women in medieval society? What evidence exists to suggest that women might have held considerable power within the family unit?

Q-4. How important was religion in medieval manor life?

Q-5. What do you believe to have been the world-view of the average medieval peasant? How would peasant men and women have thought about themselves and their environment?

Q-6. What was the function of the nobility? What were its characteristics as a class?

Q-7. How did medieval people treat their children? What were some of the common child-care practices?

Q-8. Aristocratic men married late and aristocratic women married early. Why?

Q-9. Aristocratic society was marked by sexual tension and generational conflict. Why?

Q-10. Discuss the responsibilities and lifestyles of adult aristocratic men and women.

Q-11. What was the social background of most medieval monks? How did this tend to change in the later Middle Ages?

Q-12. What were the major functions of the medieval monasteries? Were they solely spiritual institutions?

Q-13. Why was the monastic movement important to the aristocratic families of Europe?

Q-14. Describe the economic dilemma that many monasteries faced in the late Middle Ages.

STUDY-REVIEW EXERCISES

Identify each of the following and give its significance.

ministerials

Abbey of Cluny

Cistercian Order

Orderic Vitalis

The Leech Book of Bald

chevaliers

wet nurse

knighthood

Salve Regina

Define the following key concepts and terms.

villeins

serf

nobility

almoner

choir monks

lay brothers

open-field system

manor (demesne)

swaddling

Explain each of the following important aspects of medieval life.

monastic recruitment

aristocratic "adulthood"

medieval agricultural system

aristocratic marriage patterns

medieval peasants' diet

Test your understanding of the chapter by answering the following questions.

1. The common practice in medieval society of binding up an infant, often strap-

    ping it to a board, is known as _____ .
2. The evidence about infanticide makes it *certain/uncertain* that it increased in the
    Middle Ages.
3. The use of horses rather than oxen in farming meant *greater/less* productivity.
4. In medieval society, women *did/did not* play an important economic role in the
    medieval manor and the family.

5. The word _____ derives from a Latin term
    meaning "dwelling," "residence," or "homestead."
6. In medieval society women were *frequently/never* raised to the nobility.
7. By the late Middle Ages it was the *groom/bride* who provided the marriage dowry.

8. Most noble men married relatively *early/late* in life.
9. Formal military training for the medieval aristocratic boy was concluded with

    the ceremony of _____ .
10. Slavery *was/was not* common in medieval European society.

11. Some scholars believe that the use of the _____ in
    agriculture was one of the decisive ways in which Europe advanced over the rest
    of the world.

MULTIPLE-CHOICE QUESTIONS

1. Which of the following statements about the medieval village church is *false*?
   a. It was often a business center.
   b. It was often a center for medieval drama.
   c. It was the chief educational center.
   d. It was often open only to aristocratic participation.

2. In the twelfth century many of the older monastic houses found themselves in
   economic difficulties because
   a. they could no longer recruit monks.
   b. peasants refused to pay their levies.
   c. building and living expenses increased faster than revenue.

3. Which of the following statements about medieval nobility is *false*?
   a. All nobles were knights.
   b. Their function was primarily military and political.
   c. Father-son ties tended to be strong and loving.
   d. A castle was an aristocratic status symbol.

4. Generally, the monasteries recruited their members from
   a. the middle class.
   b. the aristocracy.
   c. the peasantry.
   d. village church schools.

5. For noble men, "adulthood" came with
   a. knighthood.
   b. the age of eighteen.
   c. the acquisition of property.
   d. the demonstration of military prowess.

6. The difference between a free person and a serf was that the
   a. free person was tied to the land and the serf was not.
   b. serf had no obligations to the lord, while the free person had many.
   c. serf paid rent to his lord, while the free person paid nothing at all.
   d. serf was bound to the land by the obligations he owed his lord, while the free person usually just paid rent.

7. Medieval farmers
   a. generally farmed the land in strips scattered throughout the manor.
   b. were too ignorant to use any kind of fertilizer.
   c. never used iron for tools.
   d. were unable to show any improvement in nearly a thousand years.

8. Medieval peasants
   a. traveled widely and visited many foreign countries.
   b. had a sense of community and pride of place.
   c. hardly ever drank alcoholic beverages.
   d. refused to let women work in the fields.

9. Peasants usually did *not* consume
   a. vegetables, particularly cabbage.
   b. large quantities of meat.
   c. bread.
   d. beer.

10. Characteristics of medieval infancy and childhood included
    a. a high rate of mortality.
    b. wet nurses for babies of the nobility.
    c. swaddling.
    d. all of the above.

11. Noblewomen
    a. were confined strictly to domestic duties.
    b. were always relegated to the life of a nunnery.
    c. primarily managed the household and often the estate in the absence of their husbands.
    d. generally married men younger than themselves.

12. Monastic life in general was
    a. a combination of attention to liturgy and manual work.
    b. devoted exclusively to prayer.
    c. so different from place to place that it is impossible to generalize about it.
    d. centered exclusively on manufacturing and farming.

13. Serfs could acquire their freedom by
    a. immigrating to new frontier territories.
    b. purchasing it.
    c. fleeing from the manor and living in town for a year and a day.
    d. any of the above

14. *Chevaliers* were
    a. wealthy monks.
    b. members of a religious order that stressed agricultural reform.
    c. horsemen, or knights.
    d. court painters and architects.

15. A medieval manor was
    a. an estate of at least ten villages.
    b. a plantation.
    c. the estate of a lord and his dependent tenants.
    d. an estate of at least three villages.

16. To provide food for all the people on the manor, the land had to yield at least
    a. six times the amount seeded.
    b. ten times the seed.
    c. three times the seed.
    d. five times the seed.

17. A person became a noble by
    a. thrift, hard work, and sobriety.
    b. clever business acumen.
    c. birth or remarkable service to king or lord.
    d. buying a patent of nobility.

18. Most of the education of medieval aristocrats was in
    a. the Bible.
    b. the Latin classics.
    c. canon law.
    d. the arts of war and chivalry.

19. The basic responsibility of aristocratic women in the Middle Ages was
    a. holding the manorial courts when their husbands were away on crusade.
    b. bearing and raising children.
    c. managing the household.
    d. all of the above.

20. Until the fourteenth century, most monks were drawn from the
    a. business classes.
    b. peasantry.
    c. petty bourgeoisie.
    d. nobility.

21. Management of the monastic estate was the basic responsibility of the
    a. abbot.
    b. novices.
    c. cellarer.
    d. almoner.

UNDERSTANDING HISTORY THROUGH READING AND THE ARTS

Did the peasants really starve? What are some of the modern world's mistaken beliefs about sex, marriage, and family in medieval times? These and other questions are considered in a ground-breaking social history, *The World We Have Lost** (1965) by P. Laslett.

From the profoundly moral to the bawdy, the tales of an odd assortment of pilgrims in Geoffrey Chaucer's *The Canterbury Tales** reflect the manners and morals of medieval England.

"Carmina Burana" by C. Orff is a series of songs based on poems written in the thirteenth century by wandering students and disillusioned monks who celebrated their carousing and lovemaking in verse. The poems, written in medieval Latin, German, and French, were discovered in 1830 in the archives of the Benedictine monastery at Bevern near Munich. Orff put these intensely physical, scenic, and entertaining poems to vibrant music in 1937.

PROBLEMS FOR FURTHER INVESTIGATION

Did aristocratic women have any power in the churches or households of this military society? Were children maltreated in the medieval family? Historians are just beginning to investigate how childhood and the status of women in society have changed over the course of history. A good starting point for research on childhood is L. de Mause, ed., *The History of Childhood** (1974) and the journal *The History of Childhood Quarterly*. For medieval women see E. Power, *Medieval Women,** M. M. Postan, ed. (1976). Most of the work on medieval women is on women in the world of religion. The best of these works is J. Nichols and L. Shank, *Medieval Religious Women*,

*Available in paperback.

Vol. 1: "Distant Echoes" (1984). A good place to begin a study on women as mystics and the masculine-feminism issues in religion is C. Bynum, *Jesus as a Mother: Studies in the Spirituality of the High Middle Ages* (1982).

Did the emergence of urban life result in a clash between Christianity and urban values? Did urbanization force Christianity to reevaluate its traditional antimaterialistic position? A good place to begin your investigation is with an excellent synthesis of the new urban life and Christianity: L. Little, *Religion, Poverty, and the Profit Economy in Medieval Europe* (1978).

CHAPTER 11

THE CREATIVITY AND VITALITY OF
THE HIGH MIDDLE AGES

CHAPTER OBJECTIVES

After reading and studying this chapter you should be able to answer the following questions:

Q-1. How did medieval towns originate and how do they reflect radical change including heresy?

Q-2. How did medieval rulers in England, France, and Germany solve their problems of government and lay the foundations of the modern state?

Q-3. How did universities develop and what needs of medieval society did they serve?

Q-4. What does the Gothic cathedral reveal about the ideals, attitudes, and interests of medieval people?

CHAPTER SYNOPSIS

The High Middle Ages—roughly, the twelfth and thirteenth centuries—was an era of remarkable achievement in law, the arts, philosophy, and education. Of central importance, the modern idea of the sovereign nation-state took root in this period. By means of war, taxation, and control over justice the kings of England and France were able to strengthen royal authority and establish a system of communication with all of their people.

The Normans were important in bringing a centralized feudal system to England by using the sheriff, the writ, and other devices to replace baronial rule with royal power. Out of this process emerged the concept of common law and, with the Magna Carta, the idea of supremacy of the law. The process, however, was not altogether smooth, as the conflict between Henry II and Becket illustrates. The evolution of the territorial state in France was not quite as rapid as in England. France was less of a geographical unit than England, and the creation of strong royal authority involved more armed conflict between king and barons. And in Germany, royal power failed to develop at all, despite a good start by Emperor Frederick Barbarossa. Part of the reason was the historic connection between Germany and Italy. The church-state struggle was also a major reason why royal authority in Germany was destined to remain weak.

The rise of the universities accompanied the emergence of the strong secular states because the new states needed educated administrators to staff their bureaucracies. The new universities became centers for the study of law and medicine. They were loosely organized institutions, where curriculum and faculty status were often dictated by rioting students.

Improvement in agriculture, coupled with a reopening of the Mediterranean to Christian traders, fostered a great, but gradual, rise of towns and commerce. Flanders and Italy led the way in this urban revival. The growth of towns was one of the most important developments in Western history. Towns meant a new culture and social order, increased economic opportunities, and the beginnings of modern capitalism.

Connected to this process of urbanization, the author claims, religious heresy grew up as the traditional Christian religion was unable to meet the needs of urban dwellers. The result of the heretical crisis was the evolution of several new religious orders of Friars, which counteracted the heretical movement by putting emphasis on a nonmaterialistic clergy that could preach to the needs of the people and at the same time manage the Inquisition process of reconversion.

Few periods in history can make claim to artistic achievement as can the High Middle Ages. The Gothic cathedrals, shimmering in stone and glass, stand not only as spiritual and artistic testimony to the age but also as a reflection of the economic power and civic pride of the great cities. By 1300, the energy of the High Middle Ages had been spent.

STUDY OUTLINE

I. The medieval origins of the modern state
    A. Royal desire to extend authority and increase public order
        1. The modern state uses law, bureaucracy, and money to provide its citizens with order and protection
    B. Unification and communication in England
        1. England was unified earlier than other countries
        2. William the Conqueror used local people to enforce royal law
        3. Sheriffs, the writ, the Norman inquest, and *Domesday Book* were used to centralize royal power

    4. The English "Angevin empire" began with William and Matilda's son, Henry II

C. Unification and communication in France
    1. The cult of *Saint Denis* generated national devotion and loyalty to the French king
    2. Philip II began the process of unifying France
    3. By the end of the thirteenth century, the king of France was stronger than his nobles
    4. Philip Augustus devised a system of royal agents called baillis and seneschals to help enforce royal law
    5. Unlike England, where administration was based on unpaid local officials, royal administration in France rested on a professional class

D. Unification and communication in Germany
    1. Germany was split into many states
    2. The German emperors were weak and lacked a strong royal domain to serve as a source of revenue and a power base
    3. Frederick Barbarossa tried to unify Germany by creating royal officials to enforce his will
    4. But he became involved in Italian affairs, which were costly and caused disorder at home

E. The financial problems of medieval kings
    1. Henry I of England established a state finance bureau called the Exchequer to keep track of income
    2. French kings relied on royal taxes, mostly from the church, the tallage, and the conversion of feudal dues to cash payments
    3. Medieval society believed that royal taxation should be imposed only at times of emergency
    4. The Sicilian state is a good example of an efficient financial bureaucracy
        a. Roger de Hauteville introduced feudalism to the island
        b. Frederick II Hohenstaufen centralized royal power in Sicily
        c. He received the permission of his people to tax them regularly

F. Law and justice in medieval Europe
    1. A system of royal justice, founded by Louis IX, unified France
    2. Beginning with Henry II the English kings developed and extended the common law, which was accepted by the whole country
    3. Henry II established a jury system and improved legal procedure
    4. The trial by jury replaced the trial by ordeal
    5. Becket and Henry II quarreled over legal jurisdiction
        a. Becket claimed that crimes by clerics should be tried in church courts
        b. He was assassinated by the king's friends
    6. King John's conflict with church and barons led to the Magna Carta (1215), which claims that everyone, including the king, must obey the law

7. The English common law system was strikingly different from the system of continental (Roman) law
8. The various factors led to prejudice against homosexuals so that by 1300 homosexuality had been declared illegal

II. The rise and development of towns
  A. The rise of towns in the tenth and eleventh centuries
    1. Some historians believe that towns began as fortifications, while the historian Henri Pirenne claimed that towns resulted from trade
    2. Others believe that towns sprang up around religious centers
    3. All towns had a few common characteristics: a town wall, a central market, a legal system, and a monetary system
    4. The bourgeoisie, or townspeople, became a new class in medieval society
    5. Many towns benefited from having a literate and industrious Jewish population
  B. Town liberties
    1. Townspeople worked hard to acquire social, political, and legal freedoms
    2. Merchant and craft guilds evolved, and their members bargained for town liberty from local lords or the king
    3. Women played an important role in the household, the guilds, and the town economy
    4. Townspeople's great wealth bought them liberty
  C. Town life
    1. Medieval towns served as places of trade and protection
    2. Towns grew without planning or regulation
    3. The church was important in town life
    4. William of Newburgh's description of London shows that towns were centers for economic advancement, social mobility, and entertainment
  D. The revival of long-distance trade in the eleventh century
    1. Italian and Flemish cities dominated the trade market
      a. Venice led the West in trade and controlled the oriental market
      b. Flanders controlled the cloth trade
      c. Bruges, Ghent, and Ypres became cloth manufacturers
    2. England was the major supplier of wool for Flanders
      a. Wool was the cornerstone of the English economy
      b. Eventually cloth manufacture was taken up in English towns
  E. The commercial revolution of the eleventh through thirteenth centuries
    1. The growth of medieval commerce meant the rise of capitalist ideas and practices
    2. The Hanseatic League developed new trade routes and established new "factories" and business techniques
    3. The commercial revolution meant a higher standard of living and new opportunities

4. Kings allied with the middle classes to defeat feudal lords and build modern states, while many serfs used the commercial revolution to improve their social position

III. Medieval universities
  A. Origins
    1. Prior to the twelfth century, only monasteries and cathedral schools existed
    2. Universities grew up along with interest in law and medicine
    3. The first universities were at Bologna and Salerno in Italy
    4. The learning community at Paris was made a *universitas*—an educational guild—in 1200
  B. Instruction and curriculum
    1. The scholastic method of teaching was used
      a. In this method of reasoning and writing, questions were raised and authorities cited on both sides of the question
      b. It applied Aristotelian axioms to science and theology
      c. The scholastics sought to organize all knowledge into *summa*, or reference books
      d. Aquinas used reason to obtain knowledge of everything, including the existence of God
    2. The lecture and the gloss, or interpretation of a reading, were the main learning methods
    3. Oral examinations came at the end of a period of study
  C. Student life
    1. Most students came from the middle classes
    2. Students held considerable power, partly through their guilds
    3. Riot and rebellion were common among students
IV. Gothic art
  A. Medieval church building was innovative and reflected the wealth, pride, and religious faith of the townspeople
  B. From Romanesque gloom to "uninterrupted light"
    1. Eleventh-century peace encouraged church building
    2. The Gothic style was created by the abbot of St.-Denis
    3. The Gothic style has several distinct features: the pointed arch, the ribbed vault, flying buttresses, and interior brightness
  C. The creative outburst of cathedral building
    1. Bishops, nobility, and the commercial classes supported cathedral building
    2. Cathedrals became symbols of civic pride
    3. Cathedrals served many purposes
      a. They were used on feast days
      b. Local guilds met in them

      c. Political meetings were held in them

    4. Architecture became a means of religious instruction

    5. Tapestry making and drama were first used to convey religious themes to ordinary people

V. Heresy and the Friars

  A. Heresy flourished most in the most economically advanced and urbanized areas

    1. Neither traditional Christian theology nor the isolated monastic orders addressed the problems of mercantile society

    2. Townspeople desired a pious clergy who would meet their needs

  B. Heresy, originally meaning "individual choosing," was seen as a threat to social cohesion and religious unity

    1. The Gregorian injunction against clerical marriage made many priests vulnerable to Donatist and other claims of immorality

    2. Various heretics, such as Arnold of Brescia, Peter Waldo, the Albigensians, and others denounced wealth, the sacraments, and material things

    3. The Albigensian heresy grew strong in southern France and was the subject of a political-religious crusade against it

  C. As a response to heretical cults, two new religious orders (the Friars) were founded

    1. The Spaniard Saint Dominic's mission to win back the Albigensians led to the founding of a new religious order of Preaching Friars (the Dominicans)

    2. Francis of Assisi founded an order (the Franciscans) based on preaching and obsolute poverty of the clergy

    3. These new orders of Friars were urban, based on the idea of poverty, and their members were drawn from the burgher class

  D. The Friars met the spiritual and intellectual needs of urban peoples

    1. The Friars stressed education and intellectual pursuit

    2. Their emphasis on an educated and nonmaterialistic clergy won them the respect of the bourgeoisie

    3. The Friars successfully administered the Inquisition process so that heresy was virtually extinguished

REVIEW QUESTIONS

Q-1. Define the "modern state." What are its characteristics and goals?

Q-2. Describe the unification and centralization of royal power in England. Who were the participants and what methods did they use?

Q-3. What problems did the French kings face in unifying France under royal authority? What techniques did they use?

Q-4. Why was unification in Germany so much more difficult than in England and France? What were the factors that weakened and divided Germany?

Q-5. Evaluate the work of Frederick Barbarossa. In what did he succeed, and why, in the end, did he fail?

Q-6. Why was Frederick II Hohenstaufen called "The Transformer of the World"? What was so modern about him? What effect did he have on Germany?

Q-7. Describe the evolution of common law and royal justice in England. Who were the important participants and what were their methods and accomplishments?

Q-8. What were the principal reasons for the rise of urban society in the eleventh century?

Q-9. Evaluate the various theories advanced to explain the rise of towns in late medieval society. Which do you believe to be the most plausible?

Q-10. How did the new townspeople manage to gain political status and liberty for their towns?

Q-11. Why did Venice and the Flemish towns come to lead in the long-distance trade?

Q-12. What impact did the rise of towns and the so-called commercial revolution have on the way people lived?

Q-13. Describe the purpose and the origins of the medieval universities.

Q-14. Who were the medieval scholastics? What were their basic beliefs about knowledge and education and what were their methods of acquiring knowledge?

Q-15. Describe the Gothic style. What were its chief features?

Q-16. The cathedrals became symbols of civic pride. Explain.

Q-17. The author claims that in the High Middle Ages architecture became the servant of theology. What does he mean? Give examples.

Q-18. What were the reasons for the rise of heretical cults? Why and how were they extinguished?

STUDY-REVIEW EXERCISES

Define the following key concepts and terms.

Gothic

scholasticism

universitas

common law

Roman law

the modern state

Hanseatic League

Explain each of the following terms and explain how it contributed to the evolution of the modern state.

writ

sheriff

baillis and seneschals

Exchequer

jury

tallage

Identify each of the following and give his significance.

the cult of Saint Denis

heresy

Frederick II Hohenstaufen

Philip II of France

Saint Thomas Aquinas

Suger, abbot of St.-Denis

Henry II of England

Peter Abélard

Louis IX of France

Saint Dominic

Saint Francis of Assisi

Explain what the following events were and why they are important in understanding the High Middle Ages.

Domesday survey

the crusade against the Albigensians

reconquista

Frederick Barbarossa's Italian wars

William of Normandy's conquest of England

the conflict between Pope Boniface VIII and King Philip the Fair of France

the church building activity of the twelfth and thirteenth centuries

Test your understanding of the chapter by answering the following questions.

1. This letter declared that everyone must submit to the papacy.

    _____

2. The English royal bureau of finance. _____

3. The emperor of Germany who tried to unify Germany. _____

4. William the Conqueror's survey of English wealth. _____

5. The European country best known for its common law. _____
6. The area that underwent development by Frederick II Hohenstaufen.

    _____

7. This document implied that in English society the law is above the king.

    _____

8. The French cathedral school famous for its curriculum and students.

    _____

9. The architectural style that reflects Roman and early Christian models.

    _____

10. Medieval reference books. _____

11. A league of German cities with its center at Lubeck. _____

12. A Paris teacher, author of *Sic et Non*. _____
13. The bishop who was murdered as a result of a church-state struggle.

    _____
    _____

14. A kind of French supreme court. _____

MULTIPLE-CHOICE QUESTIONS

1. Historians maintain that medieval towns probably developed from
    a. old Roman army camps.
    b. fortifications.
    c. ecclesiastical centers.
    d. all of the above

2. By origin and definition, a burgher or bourgeois was
    a. a person involved in trade or commerce.
    b. a person who lived within town walls.
    c. a resident of Hamburg, Germany.
    d. a person who lived on hamburgers.

3. The modern scholar who identified the growth of medieval towns with the development of trade was
    a. Josiah Cox Russell.
    b. Eileen Power.
    c. Henri Pirenne.
    d. Marc Bloch.

4. *Town Liberty* meant
   a. citizenship.
   b. the right to buy and sell in the town.
   c. personal freedom.
   d. all of the above

5. Artisians and craftspeople in medieval towns formed
   a. courts to try corrupt businessmen.
   b. craft guilds.
   c. merchant guilds.
   d. the AFL-CIO.

6. The French government, as conceived by Philip Augustus, was characterized by
   a. centralization at the local level and diversity at the top.
   b. diversity at the local level and centralization at the top.
   c. complete local government.
   d. a system identical to England's.

7. Frederick Barbarossa's success in restoring order to the Holy Roman Empire was spoiled by his involvement in
   a. France.
   b. Germany.
   c. England.
   d. Italy.

8. The principle implied in Magna Carta was
   a. democracy.
   b. that all people, even the king, are subject to the law.
   c. that the king is above the law.
   d. that the people rule the monarch.

9. Which of the following is *not* a characteristic of a Gothic cathedral?
   a. pointed arches
   b. ribbed vaults
   c. thick walls
   d. flying buttresses

10. The surge of cathedral building in the twelfth and thirteenth centuries was closely associated with
    a. the increase of university-trained architects.
    b. financial hard times, which caused people to turn to faith.
    c. the low cost of building materials.
    d. the growth of towns and the increase of commercial wealth.

11. The university in the Europe of the High Middle Ages
    a. was borrowed from the Muslims.
    b. was a unique contribution of western Europe.
    c. was copied from the Greek model.
    d. was copied from the Roman model.

12. The duties of sheriffs in Norman England included
    a. maintaining law and order.
    b. collecting taxes when instructed by the king.
    c. raising infantry at the king's request.
    d. all of the above

13. Heresy flourished
    a. in the most economically advanced and urbanized areas.
    b. in backward rural areas.
    c. only in southern France.
    d. in urban areas suffering from plague and economic depression.

14. The two European states that first developed efficient state bureaucracies were
    a. England and Sicily.
    b. England and France.
    c. England and Italy.
    d. Sicily and France.

15. Which of the following financial problems eventually forced England's King John to sign the Magna Carta?
    a. the debts incurred from Richard the Lionhearted's crusading zeal
    b. the ransom paid for Richard the Lionhearted
    c. the war debt caused by John in his attempt to regain Normandy from France
    d. all of the above

16. The first European universities were located in
    a. England.
    b. France.
    c. Italy.
    d. Germany.

17. Prior to the systematization of law in the thirteenth century, homosexuality was
    a. socially accepted.
    b. outlawed.
    c. uncommon.
    d. unknown.

18. The majority of university students in the Middle Ages came from the
    a. peasantry.
    b. middle class.
    c. aristocracy.
    d. none of the above

19. Of the following, which university was founded as a result of student dissatisfaction at another university?
    a. Cambridge
    b. Bologna
    c. Oxford
    d. Paris

20. Common law differed from the system of Roman law in that
    a. common law was applied only to the peasant class.
    b. common law was more permanent and static.
    c. it relied on precedents.
    d. it relied heavily on torture.

GEOGRAPHY

1. Using the map in the text on page 357 and outline map on page 152, trace the routes of the four crusades. Then, using the space below, explain the outcome of each crusade.

2. How do the crusades reflect the tension among the three cultural areas of the European-Mediterranean world: Western Europe, Byzantium, and the Muslim empire?

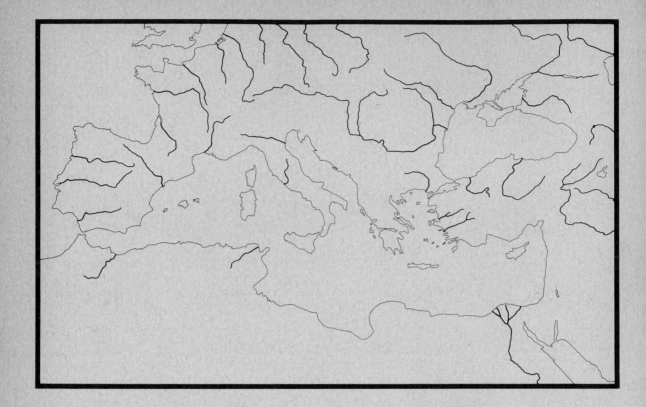

3. Describe the geographic and political relationship between England and the Norman state of France. What impact did the Normans have on England?

UNDERSTANDING HISTORY THROUGH READING AND THE ARTS

The conflict between King Henry II and Archbishop Becket has produced some interesting literature, such as Jean Anouilh, *Becket; or the Honor of God*, L. Hill, trans. (1960) and T. S. Eliot, *Murder in the Cathedral* (1935). One of the most fascinating women of the Middle Ages was Eleanor of Aquitaine, wife to the king of France and the king of England and mother to two kings of England. She is the subject of a spellbinding biography, *Eleanor of Aquitaine and the Four Kings** (1950) by A. Kelly.

Those interested in medieval cathedral building will want to see J. Harvey, *The Medieval Architect* (1972). And, by the same author is one of the most readable surveys of Gothic architecture, *The Master Builders* (1971). See also Chapters 3 and 4 of N. Pevsner, *An Outline of European Architecture** (7th ed., 1963).

PROBLEMS FOR FURTHER INVESTIGATION

What caused the rise of "individualism" in European life? What impact did the cult of individualism have on European society? The best book on this subject is M. Colin, *The Discovery of the Individual, 1050-1200** (1973). See also R. Hanning, *The Individual in Twelfth Century Romance* (1977).

New interpretations and ideas for research on the rise of the modern state are found in a collection of essays edited by H. Lubasz, *The Development of the Modern State** (1964). The success, glory, idealism, and political aspects of the religious crusades have fascinated historians for generations. Students interested in further research in this area should begin with *The Crusades** (1939) by J. A. Brundage, a book in the Heath series on historical problems. Many possible research and term-paper topics are suggested in T. M. Jones, ed., *The Becket Controversy* (1970).

*Available in paperback.

CHAPTER 12

THE CRISIS OF THE
LATER MIDDLE AGES

CHAPTER OBJECTIVES

After reading and studying this chapter you should be able to answer the following questions:

Q-1. What were the causes and the effects of the fourteenth-century disasters?
Q-2. Was war a catalyst for change?
Q-3. What provoked the division in the church in the fourteenth century?

CHAPTER SYNOPSIS

The fourteenth century was a time of disease, war, crime, and violence. The art and literature of the period are full of the portrayal of death, just as the historical accounts are full of tales of conflict and violence. There were several major causes for this century of human suffering. Natural disasters—including changes in climate and horrible new diseases—attacked Europe. A long series of wars between France and England not only brought death and economic ruin but increased personal violence and crime as well. In addition, a serious shortage of labor, created by the bubonic plague, resulted in intense social conflict among landlords. Economic crisis during the century also resulted in a bitter struggle between urban workers and their guild masters.

Amid such violence the church lost power and prestige, partly because of the religious disillusionment that accompanied the plague. In short, the institutional church failed to fill the spiritual vacuum left by the series of disasters. A more immediate reason for the decline of the church's influence and prestige was the Babylonian captivity and the Great Schism. The call for reform, often in the form of the conciliar movement, by people such as Marsiglio of Padua and John Wyclif, was a signal of things to come in the sixteenth-century Reformation.

But the century of disaster was also a century of change, some of it for the good of ordinary people. It is in this light that the chapter examines some important changes in marriage practices, family relations, and the life of the people. The decline in population meant that those who survived had better food and higher wages. Peasants in western Europe used the labor-shortage problem to demand higher wages and freedom from serfdom. These demands often resulted in conflict with their lords. The disillusionment with the organized church also led to greater lay independence and, ultimately, ideas of social and political equality. The wars actually fostered the development of constitutionalism in England. All in all, it was a period of disaster but of disaster that brought with it important changes.

STUDY OUTLINE

I. Death and disease in the fourteenth century
   A. Disaster in the fourteenth century
      1. Climate changes and inflation caused economic decline
      2. Diseases killed many people and animals
      3. The population was undernourished, and population growth came to a halt
      4. Weak governments were unable to deal with these problems
   B. The Black Death
      1. Genoese ships brought the plague—the Black Death—to Europe in 1347
      2. This bubonic bacillus lived in fleas that infested black rats
      3. Unsanitary and overcrowded cities were ideal breeding grounds for the black rats
      4. Most people had no rational explanation for the disease, and out of ignorance and fear many blamed it on Jews
      5. The disease, which killed millions, recurred often and as late as 1700
   C. The social and psychological consequences of the Black Death
      1. The plague hit the poor harder than the rich, but all classes suffered
      2. The decline in population meant labor shortages, thus wages went up and social mobility increased
      3. The psychological consequences of the plague were enormous: depression, gross sensuality, flagellantism, and obsession with death
II. The Hundred Years' War (1337-1453)
   A. The causes of the war
      1. Edward III of England, the grandson of the French king Philip the Fair, claimed the French crown
         a. French barons used Edward's claim as a way to check their king

      2. Flemish wool merchants supported the English claim to the crown

      3. Both the French and the English saw military adventure as an excuse to avoid domestic problems

      4. The French barons passed the crown to Philip Valois and not Edward III

  B. The popular response to the war

      1. Royal propaganda for war and plunder was strong on both sides

      2. The war meant opportunity for economic or social mobility for poor knights, criminals, and great nobles

  C. The Indian summer of medieval chivalry during the Hundred Years' War

      1. Chivalry was a code of conduct for the knightly class

         a. Knights were supposed to be brave, loyal, courteous, and generous

         b. Chivalry and feudal society glorified war

      2. Chivalry enjoyed its final days of glory during the war

  D. The course of the war to 1419

      1. The battles took place in France and the Low Countries

      2. At the battle of Crécy (1346), the English disregarded the chivalric code and used new military tactics: the longbow and cannon

  E. Joan of Arc and France's victory

      1. Joan of Arc's campaigns meant a turning point and victory for France

      2. Joan was turned over to the English and burned as a heretic

  F. Costs and consequences

      1. The war meant economic and population decline for France and England

      2. War financing caused a slump in the English wool trade

      3. In England, returning soldiers caused social problems

      4. The war encouraged the growth of parliamentary government, particularly in England

         a. The "Commons" acquired the right to pass on taxation and developed its own organization

         b. In France, neither king nor the Provincial assemblies wanted a national assembly

      5. The war generated feelings of nationalism in England and France

III. Vernacular literature

  A. The emergence of national consciousness is seen in the rise of literature written in national languages—the vernacular

  B. Three literary masterpieces manifest this new national pride

      1. Dante's *Divine Comedy*, a symbolic pilgrimage to the City of God, embodies the psychological tensions of the age and contains bitter criticism of some church authorities

      2. Chaucer, in his *Canterbury Tales*, uses a religious setting to depict the materialistic and worldly interests of a variety of English people in the fourteenth century

       3. Villon used the language of the lower classes to talk about the reality, beauty, and hardships of life here on earth

IV. The decline of the church's prestige

    A. The Babylonian Captivity (1309-1377)

       1. The pope had lived at Avignon since the reign of King Philip the Fair of France and thus was subject to French control

       2. This Babylonian Captivity damaged papal power and prestige

       3. Pope Gregory XI brought the papacy back to Rome in 1377, but then a split occurred when the newly elected Urban VI alienated the church hierarchy in his zeal to reform the church

       4. A new pope, Clement VII, was elected, and the two popes both claimed to be legitimate (the Great Schism)

    B. The Great Schism lasted until 1417

       1. England and Germany recognized Pope Urban VI

       2. France and others recognized Pope Clement VII

    C. The conciliar movement was based on the idea of reform through a council of church leaders

       1. Marsiglio of Padua claimed that authority within the church should rest with a church council and not the pope

       2. The English teacher John Wyclif attacked papal authority and called for even more radical reform of the church

       3. Wyclif's ideas were spread to Bohemia by John Hus and then to the University of Paris

       4. Finally, the council at Constance (1414-1418) ended the schism with the election of Pope Martin V

V. The life of the people in the fourteenth and fifteenth centuries

    A. Fur-collar crime

       1. In England, nobles returning from war had little to do and were in need of income; thus they resorted to crime at home

       2. Kidnaping, extortion, and terrorism by the upper classes were widespread

       3. Central governments were not able to stop abuses

       4. As a result, "outlaws" such as Robin Hood sought to protect the people

    B. Peasants' revolts

       1. Peasants revolted in France in 1358 and in England in 1381

       2. One cause was the lords' attempt to freeze wages

       3. In general, the revolts were due to rising expectations

       4. The 1381 revolt in England began as a protest against taxes

       5. As in England, workers in Italy, Germany, and Spain revolted

    C. Marriage and the family

       1. Economic factors, rather than romantic love, usually governed the decision to marry

2. Marriage usually came at 16 to 18 years for women and later for men; divorce did not exist
3. Many people, however, did not observe church regulations and married without a church ceremony

D. Life in the parish
   1. The land and the religion were the centers of life
   2. Mobility within guilds declined in the fourteenth century, and strikes and riots within guilds became frequent
   3. Cruel sports, such as bullbaiting, and drunkenness reflect the violence and frustrations of the age
   4. Lay people increasingly participated in church management

E. Catalysts for change
   1. The crises and wars of the fourteenth and fifteenth centuries altered traditional ways of life
   2. Rising social consciousness, changes in government, and advances in technology were some of the changes brought by the events of the times

REVIEW QUESTIONS

Q-1. What were the causes of the population decline that began in the early fourteenth century?

Q-2. What was the source of the bubonic plague and why did it spread so rapidly in Europe?

Q-3. What impact did the plague have on wages and the demand for labor? Can you guess what happened to land values?

Q-4. Describe the psychological effects of the plague. How did people explain this disaster?

Q-5. What were the immediate and other causes of the Hundred Years' War?

Q-6. Why did the people support their kings in war?

Q-7. In your opinion, did feudalism tend to encourage or prevent war? Explain.

Q-8. What were the results of the Hundred Years' War? Who were the winners and losers within both countries?

Q-9. Why did a national representative assembly emerge in England but not in France?

Q-10. Drawing on the writings of Dante, Chaucer, and Villon, describe vernacular literature in terms of its form and subject matter. What makes it "modern"?

Q-11. The Babylonian Captivity greatly weakened the power and prestige of the church. Explain.

Q-12. In 1409 there were three popes. Why? Who were they and how and why did this situation occur?

Q-13. What was the conciliar movement and who were its advocates? Was this a revolutionary idea?

Q-14. Why was Wyclif a threat to the institutional church? Even many powerful and rich lords feared the Lollards. Why?

Q-15. What was fur-collar crime and why did it become a central feature of European life in the fourteenth and fifteenth centuries?

Q-16. Did peasant conditions improve or deteriorate in the fourteenth and fifteenth centuries? Explain.

Q-17. What were the reasons for the French *Jacquerie* of 1358 and the English Peasants' Revolt of 1381?

Q-18. Describe how guilds worked, and explain why a great amount of conflict and frustration was evident among guild members in the fourteenth century.

STUDY-REVIEW EXERCISES

Define each of the following key concepts and terms.

fur-collar crime

English Statute of Labourers

conciliar movement

Pasteurella pestis

vernacular

craft guild

Identify each of the following and give its significance.

Robin Hood

Marsiglio of Padua

Battle of Crécy (1346)

Martin V

Joan of Arc

Babylonian Captivity

Margaret Paston

Lollards

House of Commons

Edward III

John Hus

John Wyclif

Jacquerie

<u>Explain</u> *the importance of each of the following concepts in late medieval life and describe what changes it was subject to in this period.*

pluralism

marriage and womanhood

feudal chivalry

individual Christian faith

leisure time

nationalism

<u>Provide</u> *approximate dates for the following important events.*

1. The first instance of the bubonic plague in Europe

2. The Babylonian Captivity

3. The Hundred Years' War

4. The Council of Constance

5. The battle of Crécy

6. The French Jacquerie revolt

7. Dante's *Divine Comedy* (1321)

Test your understanding of the chapter by answering the following questions.

1. In reaction to the calls for reform in the fourteenth century, the church *did/ did not* enter into a period of reform and rejuvenation.
2. Prior to the plague in 1348, Europe experienced a period of unusually *good/bad* harvests.

3. The Hundred Years' War was between the kings of _____

    and _____ .

4. The followers of the English theologian Wyclif were called _____ .
5. Up to the nineteenth century, *economic/romantic* factors usually determined whom and when a person married.
6. For the most part, job mobility within the late medieval guilds tended to *increase/ decrease.*

MULTIPLE-CHOICE QUESTIONS

1. The conciliar movement was
    a. an effort to give the pope the power to use councils to wipe out heresy.
    b. the effort by the French lords to establish a parliament.
    c. a new monastic order vowing poverty.
    d. an attempt to place ultimate church authority in a general council.

2. The plague was probably brought into Europe by
    a. Chinese soldiers.
    b. Spanish warriors returning from South America.
    c. English soldiers pushing into France.
    d. Genoese ships from the Crimea.

3. In general, farm laborers who survived the bubonic plague faced
   a. higher wages.
   b. food shortages.
   c. the need to migrate.
   d. excommunication from the church.

4. Generally, the major new source of criminals after the Hundred Years' War was
   a. the urban mobs.
   b. the rural peasants.
   c. the nobility.
   d. the bourgeoisie.

5. Which of the following statements about the fourteenth century is *false*?
   a. The population declined.
   b. The standard of living fell drastically.
   c. The power of the church declined.
   d. War between England and France was frequent.

6. Most people in the fourteenth century believed that the plague (Black Death) was caused by
   a. bad air.
   b. poor sanitation and housing.
   c. a bacillus living in fleas.
   d. black rats.

7. Generally, the plague disaster of the fourteenth century resulted in all but one of the following for European society.
   a. higher wages for most workers
   b. a severe decline in the number of German clergymen
   c. a decline in flagellantism
   d. an obsession with death

8. Which of the following was *not* a participant in the Hundred Years' War?
   a. Edward III of England
   b. King Philip the Fair
   c. Joan of Arc
   d. the Dauphin Charles of France

9. One reason for peasant-landlord conflict in the fourteenth century was
   a. peasants' opposition to declining wages and inflation.
   b. landlords' attempts to legislate wages.
   c. land scarcity.
   d. peasants' refusal to be drafted for war service.

10. The author of *Defensor Pacis* and proponent of the idea that authority in the Christian church rested in a general council rather than in the papacy was
    a. Cardinal Robert of Geneva.
    b. Pope Urban V.
    c. John Wyclif.
    d. Marsiglio of Padua.

11. The Hundred Years' War had all but one of the following effects on English society.
    a. It encouraged representative government.
    b. It depressed the English wool trade.
    c. It increased the amount of arable land in England.
    d. It created a severe manpower shortage.

12. The followers of the English theologian-reformer Wyclif were called
    a. Protestants.
    b. Outlaws.
    c. Lollards.

13. Which of the following was not a social consequence of the agricultural catastrophes of the fourteenth century?
    a. people married earlier
    b. unemployment
    c. increase in crime
    d. increased serfdom

14. After 1347, the Black Death generally moved
    a. from north to south.
    b. from west to east.
    c. from south to north.
    d. from east to west.

15. Initially the Hundred Years' War was fought over
    a. Aquitaine.
    b. King Edward III's claim to the French crown.
    c. the control of the Flemish wool trade.
    d. religion.

16. English military innovation(s) during the Hundred Years' War included
    a. the crossbow.
    b. the cannon and the longbow.
    c. cavalry.
    d. the pike.

17. Each of the following statements represents marriage during the Middle Ages
    except
    a. some marriages were made privately.
    b. most marriages were arranged.
    c. divorce did not exist except in rare cases.
    d. divorce was common.

18. Who of the following was not a writer of vernacular literature?
    a. Dante
    b. Villon
    c. Clement VII
    d. Chaucer

19. All but one of the following was true of Joan of Arc.
    a. She dressed like a man.
    b. The English king was her greatest supporter.
    c. She was accused of being a heretic and was burned.
    d. She was from a peasant family.

20. For the French, the turning point of the Hundred Years' War was
    a. the relief of Paris.
    b. the defeat of the English fleet in the English Channel.
    c. the relief of Orleans.
    d. the battle of Poitiers.

GEOGRAPHY

A. Using Map 12.2 in the text
   1. Locate the extent of the English possessions in France. What were the origins
      of English claims to French land?

   2. Why was it unlikely that England could have held these territories permanent-
      ly?

B. Using Map 12.3 in the text
    1. Locate the main centers of popular revolt in France and England.
    2. Why were so many of the English revolts in the highly populated and advanced areas of the country?

UNDERSTANDING HISTORY THROUGH READING AND THE ARTS

One of the results of the Black Death was a revival of Christian mysticism—a search for meaning in life through a personal relationship with God. One of the most popular books of this movement was *The Imitation of Christ** by Thomas à Kempis.

An excellent introduction to the music of this period is a recording, *Instruments of the Middle Ages and Renaissance*, with an accompanying illustrated book by David Munro (Angel recording number SB2-3810 [1976]), and for the French chansons and the English Madrigals listen to the recording titled *The King's Singers Sing of Courtly Pleasures*, which includes text and translations (Angel recording number s-37025 [1974]).

Students interested in the history of disease in general or in the plague in particular should check the chapter bibliography. Three interesting accounts of the subject are G. C. Coulton, *The Black Death* (1929); P. Zeigler, *The Black Death* (1960); and W. McNeill, *Plagues and Peoples* (1976). E. Perroy, *The Hundred Years' War** (1951), is a good start for anyone interested in that subject. Boccaccio's *Decameron* is a series of bawdy tales told by a group of Florentine men and women who fled to the countryside to escape the plague.

PROBLEMS FOR FURTHER INVESTIGATION

What was the cause of the conflict between Philip the Fair of France and the pope? Was the French king out to destroy the power of the papacy? These and other questions are debated by a number of historians in C. T. Wood, ed., *Philip the Fair and Boniface VIII** (1967).

*Available in paperback.

CHAPTER 13

EUROPEAN SOCIETY IN THE AGE OF THE RENAISSANCE

CHAPTER OBJECTIVES

After reading and studying this chapter you should be able to answer the following questions:

Q-1. What does the term "Renaissance" mean?
Q-2. How did the Renaissance influence politics, government, and social organization?
Q-3. Did the Renaissance cause shifts in religious attitudes?
Q-4. What developments occurred in the evolution of the nation-state?
Q-5. What were the intellectual and artistic hallmarks of the Renaissance?

CHAPTER SYNOPSIS

While the fourteenth century is often described in terms of death and violence, the following two centuries are usually regarded as composing an era of intellectual and artistic brilliance unsurpassed in European history. This period, which is called the Renaissance, is difficult to define. Yet it is clear that some thinking people in this era saw themselves living in an age more akin to that of the bright and creative ancient world than that of the recent dark and gloomy Middle Ages. Although many of the supposedly "new" Renaissance ideas are actually found in the Middle Ages, scholars generally agree that the Renaissance was characterized by a number of distinctive ideas about life and humanity—individualism, secularism, humanism, materialism, and hedonism.

The Renaissance began in Florence, Italy, in the fourteenth century. It subsequently spread to the rest of Italy—particularly Rome—and then to northern Europe, where it developed somewhat differently. The best-known manifestations of the bold new Renaissance spirit can be seen in the painting, sculpture, and architecture of the period. But new attitudes were also found in education, politics, and philosophy and in Northern Europe in ideas of social reform. Although the Renaissance brought some benefits to the masses of people, such as the printing press, it was basically an elitist movement. One negative feature of the age was a deterioration in the power and position of women in society.

The political side of the Renaissance expressed itself in an approach to power and the state that historians often call the theory and practice of "new monarchies." The best known and most popular theoretician of this school was the Florentine Niccolo Machiavelli. Its most able practitioners are the fifteenth- and sixteenth-century monarchs of France, England, and Spain. In Italy, the city-state system led to wealthy and independent cities that were marvelously creative but also vulnerable to invasion and control from the outside by powerful Spanish and French kings.

STUDY OUTLINE

I. The origins and hallmarks of the Renaissance
   A. The evolution of the Italian Renaissance
      1. The "Renaissance" was a period of cultural achievement in two phases—from 1050 to 1300 and from 1300 to about 1600
      2. The wealth of the northern Italian cities was a cause of the Renaissance; it was an artistic and intellectual movement sustained by urban wealth
      3. Florence, the first city of the Renaissance, was a banking and manufacturing center
   B. Communes and republics
      1. Northern Italian "communes" were cities wherein the feudal nobility and the commercial aristocracy merged and ruled
         a. The *popolo*, or middle class was excluded from power
         b. Popolo-led republican governments failed—which led to the rule of despots or oligarchies
         c. In the fifteenth century, the princely courts of the rulers were centers of wealth and art
      2. Italy had no political unity; it was divided into city-states such as Milan, Venice, and Florence, a papal area, and a kingdom of Naples in the south
      3. The political and economic competition among the city-states was damaging
      4. After 1494 a divided Italy became a European battleground
II. Intellectual hallmarks of the Renaissance
   A. Many, like the poet and humanist Petrarch, saw the fourteenth century as a new age and a revival of ancient Roman culture
   B. Individualism

       1. Medieval people usually saw themselves as members of a group
       2. Renaissance people believed in individual will and genius

  C. The revival of antiquity
       1. Italians copied the ancient Roman lifestyle
       2. The study of the classics led to humanism, or an emphasis on human beings
          a. Humanists sought to understand human nature through a study of pagan antiquity *and* Christian thought
          b. The humanist writer Pico della Mirandola believed that there were no limits to what human beings could accomplish
       3. Ancient Latin style was considered superior to medieval Latin

  D. Secular spirit
       1. *Secularism* means a concern with materialism rather than religion
       2. Unlike medieval people, Renaissance people were concerned about money and the accumulation of wealth
       3. They were also interested in pleasure and the enjoyment of life on earth
       4. The church did little to combat secularism; in fact, many popes were Renaissance patrons and participants

  E. Art, the artist, and power in the fourteenth century
       1. The *quattrocento* and the *cinquecento* saw great artistic activity as the center of activity shifted from Florence to Rome
       2. Art served a social function during the Renaissance
          a. It was patronized by corporate groups such as guilds and religious bodies, and by rich individuals
          b. It was a means of glorifying politicians and rich families
       3. The purpose and style of art changed in the fifteenth century
          a. It became more secular
          b. Painting and sculpture became more naturalistic and realistic
          c. The human body was glorified in art—for example, by Michelangelo
          d. A new "international-style" emphasized color, decoration, and curvilinear rhythms
       4. The status and personality of the artist were affected by the Renaissance
          a. The status of the artist improved during the Renaissance; most work was done by commission from a prince
          b. The creative genius of the artist was recognized
          c. The Renaissance was largely an elitist movement that cared little for ordinary people

III. Social change during the Renaissance
  A. Education and political thought
       1. Vergerio's humanism represents the Renaissance concern for education
       2. The Renaissance man was well rounded

      3. Castiglione's *The Courtier* describes the model Renaissance gentleman as a man of many talents, including intellectual and artistic skills

      4. Machiavelli's *The Prince* describes how to acquire political power

          a. Machiavelli believed that the politician may use any means to gain power

          b. He viewed the state not as a utopia but as an amoral force

B. The printed word

      1. The invention of movable type by Gutenberg, Fust, and Schöffer—all at Mainz, Germany—revolutionized life

      2. Printing brought about new possibilities for propaganda, encouraged wider "common identity," and improved literacy

      3. It meant the spread of ideas—ideas that were often critical of the existing order

C. Women in Renaissance society

      1. The status of upper-class women declined during the Renaissance

      2. Nevertheless, the Renaissance meant improved educational opportunities for women

      3. Women's position declined with regard to sex and love

      4. The rape of women by upper-class men was frequent and not considered serious

      5. Infanticide and abandonment of children was frequent and eventually led to the establishment of foundling hospitals

D. Blacks in Renaissance society

      1. Beginning in the fifteenth century, black slaves were brought into Europe in large numbers

      2. Black slaves filled a variety of positions, from laborers to dancers and musicians

      3. The Europeans perceived blacks from both positive and negative religious perspectives

IV. The Renaissance in the north of Europe

A. The Renaissance in the north began about 1475

      1. It was more Christian than the Renaissance in Italy, and it stressed social reform based on Christian ideals

      2. Christian humanists sought to create a more perfect world

          a. Humanists like Lefèvre and Colet believed in the use of the Bible by common people

          b. Thomas More, the author of *Utopia*, believed that society, not people, needed improving

          c. The Dutch monk Erasmus best represents Christian humanism in his emphasis on education and inner Christianity

      3. French humanist writers were more secular

          a. Rabelais satirized social institutions and behavior while he promoted individual instinct and enjoyment of life

      4. Northern art and architecture were more religious than in Italy and less influenced by classical themes and motifs

        a. van Eyck painted realist works based on human themes

        b. Bosch used religion and folk legends as themes

V. Politics and the state in the Renaissance (ca. 1450-1521)

  A. The "new" monarchs

    1. The fifteenth century saw the rise of many powerful and ruthless rulers interested in the centralization of power and the elimination of disorder and violence

    2. Many of them seemed to be acting according to Machiavelli's principles

    3. The ideas of the new monarchs were not entirely original—some of them had their roots in the Middle Ages

  B. France after the Hundred Years' War

    1. Charles VII ushered in an age of recovery and ended civil war

      a. He expelled the English

      b. He made the church subject to the state

    2. Louis XI expanded the French state and laid the foundations of later French absolutism

  C. England

    1. Feudal lords controlled England in the fifteenth century

    2. Edward IV and his followers began to restore royal power

    3. The English Parliament had become a power center for the aristocracy but was manipulated by Henry VII into becoming a tool of the king

      a. Henry VII used the royal council and the Court of Star Chamber to check aristocratic power

      b. He rebuilt the monarchy and restored the economy

  D. Spain

    1. The marriage of Ferdinand and Isabella united Spain into a loose confederation

    2. They used the *hermandades*, or local police forces, to administer royal justice

    3. The royal council checked aristocratic power

    4. The church was used to strengthen royal authority

    5. Ferdinand and Isabella completed the *reconquista*—the expulsion or conversion of Arabs and Jews

    6. Anti-Semitic riots, called *conversos*, were frequent

REVIEW QUESTIONS

Q-1. Describe the evolution of government and social class relations in the Italian cities from the time of the emergence of the urban nobility to the rise of the *signori*.

Q-2. Medieval people saw themselves as a part of a corporate society. Explain. How did the men and women of the Renaissance differ?

Q-3. Define the Renaissance by discussing the interests and characteristics of Renaissance people.

Q-4. How do Valla and Boccaccio illustrate and represent what Renaissance people were like?

Q-5. Do you believe that it is possible, through education, to perfect mankind? What did the Renaissance thinkers believe the keys to this process to be?

Q-6. According to Vergerio, what is the purpose of education? Was he a humanist?

Q-7. How does Castiglione's *The Courtier* define the "perfect Renaissance man"? How does this book represent the philosophy of humanism?

Q-8. In what ways does Machiavelli represent a Renaissance thinker? What were his suggestions for and philosophy of the acquisition and meaning of political power?

Q-9. Explain why the invention of movable type revolutionized European life.

Q-10. What were the similarities and differences between the Renaissance in northern Europe and that of Italy?

Q-11. Discuss Christian humanism by describing the works and ideas of Thomas More and Desiderius Erasmus.

Q-12. Describe the makeup of the Italian city-state political system. How well did it work?

Q-13. "After 1494, Italy became a battleground for the European superpowers." Explain.

Q-14. What were the obstacles to royal authority faced by the kings of France in the fifteenth century? How did Charles VII and his successors strengthen the French monarchy?

Q-15. What devices did Henry VII of England use to check the power of the aristocracy and strengthen the monarchy?

Q-16. The reign of Ferdinand and Isabella is one of the most important in Spanish history. Why? What were their achievements in the areas of national power and national expansion?

Q-17. Why were blacks valued in Renaissance society? What roles did they play in the economic and social life of the times?

STUDY-REVIEW EXERCISES

Define the following key concepts and terms.

oligarchies

signori

communes

popolo

reconquista

Renaissance

humanism

secularism

individualism

materialism

hermandades

Machiavellian

Explain the importance of each of the following.

English Royal Council and Court of Star Chamber

conquest of Granada

Habsburg-Valois wars

Brunelleschi's Foundling Hospital in Florence

Identify each of the following people and give his significance.

Pico della Mirandola

Desiderius Erasmus

Jan Van Eyck

Thomas More

Donatello

Baldassare Castiglione

Niccolo Machiavelli

Johan Gutenberg

Lefèvre d'Etaples

Saint John Chrysostom

Lorenzo Valla

Savonarola

Jerome Bosch

François Rabelais

Explain why each of the following is often considered to be a "new monarch."

Louis XI of France

Henry VII of England

Ferdinand and Isabella of Spain

Charles VII of France

Cesare Borgia

Test your understanding of the chapter by answering the following questions.

1. He was the author of a best-selling political critique called *The Prince*.

   _____

2. Renaissance humanists tended to be *more/less* concerned about religion than about people.

3. In the fifteenth century, infanticide *increased/decreased*.
4. He was an important English humorist and the author of *Utopia*.

---

5. Generally, the legal status of upper-class women *improved/declined* during the Renaissance.
6. It *is/is not* clear that the economic growth and the material wealth of the Italian cities were direct causes of the Renaissance.

MULTIPLE-CHOICE QUESTIONS

1. Which of the following statements about the earliest printed books is *false*?
   a. They dealt mainly with economic and business subjects.
   b. They encouraged literacy.
   c. Movable type was first developed in Mainz, Germany.
   d. They had an effect on the process of learning.

2. The Renaissance began in
   a. the Low Countries.
   b. Rome.
   c. France.
   d. Florence

3. The patrons of the Renaissance were mostly
   a. churchmen.
   b. the popes.
   c. the common people.
   d. merchants and bankers.

4. The frail and ugly king who began French economic and political recovery in the early fifteenth century was
   a. Henry Tudor.
   b. Charles VII.
   c. Philip the Fair.
   d. Louis XI.

5. It appears that in Renaissance society blacks were
   a. valued as soldiers.
   b. valued as servants and entertainers.
   c. considered undesirable and were not allowed in society.

6. A major difference between Northern and Italian humanism is that Northern humanism stressed
   a. economic gain and materialism.
   b. social reform.
   c. pagan virtues.

7. Local groups in Spain that were given royal authority to administer justice were the
   a. *conversos*.
   b. liberals.
   c. *hermandades*.
   d. royal tribunals.

8. The court of Star Chamber in England was
   a. a common law court.
   b. under the control of the barons in the House of Lords.
   c. done away with by the powerful Tudors.
   d. used to check aristocratic power.

9. The superiority of the French monarch over the church was the object of the
   a. Pragmatic Sanction of Bourges.
   b. Habsburg-Valois wars.
   c. Declaration of Calais.
   d. Hundred Years' War.

10. Most of the northern Renaissance thinkers agreed that
    a. democracy, not monarchy, was the only workable political system.
    b. humanity is basically sinful.
    c. Christianity is unacceptable.
    d. society is perfectable.

11. The late fifteenth-century ruler of England who ended the civil war and strengthened the crown was
    a. John I.
    b. William III.
    c. Henry II.
    d. Henry VII.

12. Which of the following statements about Florence at the time of the Renaissance is *false*?
    a. Its major industry was wool production.
    b. It lost probably half its population to the Black Death.

c. It was a major banking center.

d. It was an important Mediterranean port city.

13. The High Renaissance masterpiece, the dome of St. Peter's in Rome, is considered to be the greatest work of
a. Brunelleschi.
b. Donatello.
c. Michelangelo.
d. Ghiberti.

14. The term *Renaissance* means
a. a rise in the average standard of living among the masses.
b. a resurgence of art and culture out of a concern for individualism and study of the ancients.
c. an increase in the population after the ravaging effects of the "Four Horsemen of the Apocalypse."
d. the recovery of the church from economic and moral decline.

15. The financial and military strength of the towns of northern Italy was directly related to
a. their wealth, which enabled them to hire mercenary soldiers to protect their commercial interests.
b. their contractual and marital alliances with the rural nobility.
c. protections provided them by the Holy Roman Emperor.
d. their alliance with the papacy.

16. The northern Renaissance differed from the Italian Renaissance in that the former was characterized by
a. interest in biblical scholarship.
b. an emphasis on the use of reason.
c. the combination of the best aspects of antiquity and Christianity.
d. all of the above

17. Erasmus advocated
a. paganism.
b. Christian education for moral and intellectual improvement.
c. monastic life of contemplation and divorce from the material world.
d. obedience to church doctrine and ritual.

18. The Renaissance artist of talent and ability often lived a life
a. of economic desperation.
b. of economic security through patronage.

    c. of luxury, but without social status.
    d. like that of the masses.

19. The most influential book on Renaissance court life and behavior was
    a. Castiglione's *The Courtier*.
    b. Machiavelli's *The Prince*.
    c. Augustine's *The City of God*.
    d. Boccaccio's *Decameron*.

20. Machiavelli's *The Prince* is considered by scholars to be
    a. an accurate description of politics in Renaissance Italy.
    b. a satire on sixteenth-century politics.
    c. a call for Italian nationalism.
    d. all of the above

21. The Wars of the Roses were
    a. civil wars between the English ducal houses of York and Lancaster.
    b. between England and France.
    c. civil wars between the English king, Henry VI, and the aristocracy.
    d. minor disputes among English gentry.

22. Just before the advent of Ferdinand and Isabella, the Iberian peninsula could
    best be described as
    a. a homogeneous region sharing a common language and cultural tradition.
    b. a heterogeneous region consisting of several ethnic groups with a diversity
        of linguistic and cultural characteristics.
    c. a culturally poor and backward region.
    d. a region dominated equally by Arabs and Jews in both numbers and politi-
        cal powers.

UNDERSTANDING HISTORY THROUGH READING AND THE ARTS

The music of the Renaissance is introduced in the recordings *From the Renaissance*
(STL-150) and *From the Renaissance-Concert* (STL-160) in the Time-Life series *The
Story of Great Music* (1967), which includes a book with a good introduction to the
period and its musical styles, art, and history. Another good introduction to Renaissance music is H. Brown, *Music in the Renaissance** (1976).
    One of the best ways to understand the Renaissance is to read the works of its
participants. Three works dealt with in this chapter are Niccolo Machiavelli, *The

*Available in paperback.

*Prince** (a number of paperback translations are available); Baldassare Castiglione, *The Courtier**, Charles Singleton, trans. (1959); and Thomas More, *Utopia**.

Urban and rural life, court life, war, and witchcraft are among the many aspects of Renaissance life covered in E. R. Chamberlin, *Everyday Life in Renaissance Times** (1967).

Color, genius, romance, intrigue, brilliance, energy—the Renaissance had all of these. The best portrait of the age is J. H. Plumb, *The Renaissance* (1961), which includes biographies of Michelangelo, Petrarch, Da Vinci, and others and includes hundreds of color plates and a comprehensive history of Renaissance art. One of the best sources on Renaissance music is G. Reese, *Music in the Renaissance* (1954). Among the most admired poetry of this period is that of Petrarch, the poet laureate of the Renaissance and often called the first modern man. The vanity and secularism of Renaissance life is reflected in the fascinating *Autobiography* of Benvenuto Cellini, one of the best known Renaissance craftsmen.

PROBLEMS FOR FURTHER INVESTIGATION

Students interested in women in the Renaissance should begin with M. Rose et al., *Women in the Middle Ages and the Renaissance: Literary and Historical Perspectives* (1986).

The Swiss historian Jacob Burckhardt called the Renaissance the "mother" of our modern world. Was the Renaissance as important as Burckhardt and others have claimed? Did it dramatically change the way people acted and the direction history was to take? These and other questions are considered in several historical debates on the Renaissance: D. Hay, ed., *The Renaissance Debate** (1965); B. Tierney, et al., *Renaissance Man—Medieval or Modern?** (1967); and K. H. Dannenfeldt, ed., *The Renaissance—Medieval or Modern?** (1959). What impact did Renaissance thinking have on the arts? Fine illustrations and a discussion of new directions in the arts are woven into a number of interesting essays on the age in D. Hay, *The Renaissance* (1967).

*Available in paperback.

READING WITH UNDERSTANDING
EXERCISE 3

LEARNING HOW TO IDENTIFY MAIN POINTS THAT ARE EFFECTS, RESULTS, CONSEQUENCES

In the introduction to this *Study Guide* and in Reading with Understanding Exercises 1 and 2 we noted that learning to underline properly plays an important part in college work. Underlining (or highlighting with a felt-tipped pen) provides a permanent record of what you study and learn. It helps you review, synthesize, and do your best on exams.

We suggested three simple guidelines for effective underlining or highlighting:*

1. Be selective; do not underline or highlight too much.
2. Underline or highlight the main points.
3. Consider numbering the main points.

These guidelines will help you in courses in many different subjects.

Cause and Effect in History

The study of history also requires learning to recognize special kinds of main points. These points are *explanatory* in nature. *They answer why and how questions*, thereby helping you to interpret and make sense of the historical record.

Two particularly important types of why and how questions focus on *cause* and *effect* in history. You are already familiar with questions of this nature, questions that provide much of history's fascination and excitement. "Why did the Roman Empire

---

*The guidelines for underlining are from *RSVP: The Houghton Mifflin Reading, Study, & Vocabulary Program*, second edition, by James F. Shepherd (Houghton Mifflin, 1984). We urge students to consult this very valuable book for additional help in improving their reading and study skills.

decline and fall?" That is, what *causes* explain the decline and fall of the Roman Empire? "What were the *effects* of the Black Death?" You should pay particular attention to questions of cause and effect. They give history meaning. They help you increase your ability to think and reason in historical terms.

Two other insights will help you greatly in identifying main points involving cause and effect. First, historians use a number of different words and verbal constructions to express these concepts. Thus "causes" often become "reasons" or "factors," or things that "account for," "contribute to," or "play a role in" a given development. "Effects" often become "results" or "consequences," or are "the product of an impact." In most cases students can consider such expressions as substitutes for cause and effect, although they should be aware that historians are not of one mind on these matters.

Second, cause and effect are constantly interrelated in the historical process. Yesterday's results become today's causes, which will in turn help bring tomorrow's results. To take examples you have studied, the *causes* of the fall of the Roman Empire (such as increasing economic difficulties) brought *results* (such as the self-sufficient agrarian economy) which contributed to—helped *cause*—the rise of Benedictine monasticism. In short, *a historical development can usually be viewed as a cause or an effect, depending on what question is being answered.*

Exercise A

Read the following passage once as a whole. Read it a second time to underline or highlight it in terms of main points identified as effects or results. Consider numbering the effects in the margin. Then do Exercise B at the end of the passage.

The effects of the invention of movable-type printing were not felt overnight. Nevertheless, within a half-century of the publication of Gutenberg's Bible of 1456, movable type brought about radical changes. The costs of reproducing books were drastically reduced. It took less time and money to print a book by machine than to make copies by hand. The press also reduced the chances of error. If the type had been accurately set, all the copies would be correct no matter how many were reproduced. The greater the number of pages a scribe copied, the greater the chances for human error.

Between the sixteenth and eighteenth centuries, printing brought about profound changes in European society and culture. Printing transformed both the private and the public lives of Europeans. Governments that "had employed the cumbersome methods of manuscripts to communicate with their subjects switched quickly to print to announce declarations of war, publish battle accounts, promulgate treaties or argue disputed points in pamphlet form. Theirs was an effort 'to win the psychological war.'" Printing made propaganda possible, emphasizing differences between various groups, such as crown and nobility, church and state. These differences laid the basis for the formation of distinct political parties.

Printed materials reached an invisible public, allowing silent individuals to join causes and groups of individuals widely separated by geography to form a common identity; this new group consciousness could compete with older, localized loyalties. Book shops, coffee shops, and public reading rooms gradually appeared and, together with print shops, provided sanctuaries and meeting places for intellectuals and wandering scholars. Historians have yet to assess the degree to which such places contributed to the rise of intellectuals as a distinct social class.

Printing also stimulated the literacy of lay people and eventually came to have a deep effect on their private lives. Although most of the earliest books and pamphlets dealt with religious subjects, students, housewives, businessmen, and upper- and middle-class people sought books on all subjects. Printers responded with moralizing, medical, practical, and travel manuals. Pornography as well as piety assumed new forms. Broadsides and flysheets allowed great public festivals, religious ceremonies, and political events to be experienced vicariously by the stay-at-home. Since books and printed materials were read aloud to the illiterate, print bridged the gap between written and oral cultures.

Exercise B

Study the last paragraph again. Can you see how it is a good example of the historical interaction of cause and effect? Do you see how a given development is an effect or a cause *depending on what historical question is being asked?* Be prepared for such "reversals" in the text, in lecture and class discussion, and on exams.

Hint: In the last paragraph, what is an *effect* of the invention of the printing press? (Ideas could be spread more rapidly.) What "stimulated"—helped *cause*—the spread of literacy? (The invention of the printing press. The author develops this point further in Chapter 14.)

CHAPTER 14

REFORM AND RENEWAL IN THE
CHRISTIAN CHURCH

CHAPTER OBJECTIVES

After reading and studying this chapter you should be able to answer the following questions:

Q-1. What religious developments paved the way for Protestant thought?
Q-2. What role did social and political factors play in the several reformations?
Q-3. What were the consequences of religious division?
Q-4. Why did Luther's ideas trigger political, social, and economic reactions and how did the Catholic Church respond?

CHAPTER SYNOPSIS

A great religious upheaval called the Protestant Reformation ended the centuries-long religious unity of Europe and resulted in a number of important political changes. In the sixteenth century, cries for reform were nothing new, but this time they resulted in revolution. There were a number of signs of disorder within the church, pointing to the need for moral and administrative reform. For example, it was the granting of indulgences (remissions from the penalties for sin) that propelled the German professor Martin Luther into the movement for doctrinal change in the church. Luther had come to the conclusion that salvation could not come by good works or indulgences, but only through faith. This was to be one of the fundamental tenets of Protestantism and one of the ideas that pushed Luther and the German nobility to revolt against not only Rome but Rome's secular ally, the Holy Roman Emperor.

It is important to recognize that Luther's challenge to the authority of the church and to Catholic unity in Europe invited and supported an attack on the emperor by the German nobility. The pope and the emperor, as separate powers and allies, represented religious and political unity and conformity in Germany. Thus, the victory of Luther and the nobility was a victory for decentralized authority; it meant the collapse of Germany as a unified power in Europe. This is one reason Catholic France usually supported the German Protestants in their quarrel with Rome.

Outside of Germany the Protestant reformer Calvin had a greater impact on Europe than Luther. Calvin's harsh and dogmatic religion spread from Geneva into northern Europe, England, and Scotland. It was England, in fact, that eventually became the political center of Protestantism. Initiated by Henry VIII, the English Protestant Reformation was at first motivated by the personal and political interests of the king himself. The type of Protestantism eventually adopted by the Church of England was much more moderate—and closer to Catholicism—than that of Scotland.

With the Council of Trent of 1545-1563, the Catholic church, finding the Habsburgs unable to destroy the heretical Protestantism, launched a massive and somewhat successful Counterreformation to convince dissidents to return to the church.

All in all, Protestantism developed and spread for economic and political reasons as well as religious ones. In the end Protestantism meant greater spritual freedom for some individuals, but spiritual disunity and disorganization for Europe as a whole. In England, Scotland, the Scandinavian states, and elsewhere, it contributed to the power of the nation and thus meant a further political division of Europe, while in Germany it slowed down the movement toward nationhood.

STUDY OUTLINE

I. The condition of the church (ca. 1400-1517)
   A. The declining prestige of the church
      1. The Babylonian captivity and the Great Schism damaged the church's prestige
      2. Humanists such as Erasmus and Machiavelli satirized and denounced moral corruption within the church
      3. The exact amount of corruption is difficult to ascertain, however, because many local priests brought spiritual help to the poor
   B. Signs of disorder in the early sixteenth century
      1. Critics wanted moral and administrative reform in three areas
         a. Clerical immorality created a scandal among the faithful
         b. The lack of education of the clergy was condemned by Christian humanists
         c. The absenteeism, pluralism (holding of several *benefices*, or offices), and wealth of the greater clergy bore little resemblance to Christian gospel

      2. The prelates and popes of the period lived like secular princes; they did not set a good example

  C. Signs of vitality in the late fifteenth and early sixteenth centuries

      1. Sixteenth-century Europe remained deeply religious

      2. New organizations were formed to educate and minister to the poor

      3. Thomas à Kempis and the Brethern of the Common Life urged ordinary people to achieve spiritual perfection by means of the simple life

      4. The Italian Oratorians devoted themselves to ministering to society

      5. Pope Julius II summoned an ecumenical council on reform in the church called the Lateran Council (1512-1527)

II. Martin Luther and the birth of Protestantism

  A. Luther's early years

      1. Luther was a middle-class German trained as a monk and a professor of religion

      2. Luther's search for identity and salvation led him to the religious life

      3. He concluded that faith was central to Christianity and the only means to salvation

  B. Luther's Ninety-five Theses (October 1517)

      1. Luther's opposition to the sale of indulgences (remissions of penalities for sin) prompted his fight with Rome

      2. His Ninety-five Theses, or propositions on indulgences, raised many theological issues and initiated a long period of debate in Europe

      3. Luther was excommunicated by the pope and declared an outlaw by Charles V at Worms in 1521

  C. Protestant thought (1520-1530)

      1. Protestant thought was set forth in the Confession of Augsburg, in which Luther modified four basic theological issues

          a. He believed that salvation derived through faith alone

          b. He stated that religious authority rests with the Bible, not the pope

          c. He believed that the church consists of the entire community of Christian believers

          d. And he believed that all work is sacred and everyone should serve God in his or her individual vocation

      2. Protestantism, therefore, was a reformulation of Christian beliefs and practices

III. The social impact of Luther's beliefs

  A. By 1521 Luther's religious ideas had a vast following among all social classes and eventually led to social revolt

      1. Luther's ideas were popular because of popular resentment of clerical wealth

      2. Prosperous burghers encouraged preaching of sermons while peasants found in Luther a reason to demand land

   3. In the end Luther did not support them; he believed in obedience to
      civil authority
   4. Widespread peasant revolts were brutally crushed but some land was re-
      turned to common use
   5. Luther's greatest weapon was his mastery of the language, and his words
      were spread by the advent of printing
      a. Zwingli and Calvin were greatly influenced by his writings
      b. The publication of Luther's translation of the New Testament in
         1523 democratized religion
   B. Luther held enlightened views on sex and marriage—although he claimed
      that women should be no more than efficient wives
IV. Germany and the Protestant Reformation
   A. The Holy Roman Empire in the fourteenth and fifteenth centuries
      1. By the Golden Bull of 1356 each of the seven electors had virtual sover-
         eignty
      2. Localism and chronic disorder allowed the nobility to strengthen their
         territories
   B. The rise of the Habsburg dynasty
      1. The Habsburgs gave unity to much of Europe, especially with the mar-
         riage of Maximilian I of Austria and Mary of Burgundy in 1477
      2. Charles V, their grandson, dominated Europe and was committed to the
         idea of its religious and political unity
   C. The political impact of Luther's beliefs
      1. The Protestant Reformation stirred nationalistic feelings in Germany
         against the wealthy Italian papacy
      2. Luther's appeal to patriotism earned him the support of the princes,
         who used religion as a means of gaining more political independence
      3. Thus, Luther's teachings prevailed, despite his condemnation by the
         pope and the Holy Roman Emperor
      4. Charles V did not understand or take any interest in the Luther
         issue
         a. The Turkish threat blocked Charles V's position in Germany
         b. He was also involved in numerous wars against France, which kept
            Germany a divided and weakened royal power
      5. By the Peace of Augsburg of 1555, Charles recognized Lutheranism as a
         legal religion with the Peace of Augsburg
 V. The growth of the Protestant Reformation
   A. Calvinism
      1. Calvin believed that God selects certain people to do His work and that
         he was selected to reform the city of Geneva
      2. Under Calvin, Geneva became a theocracy, in which the state was sub-
         ordinate to the church

3. Calvin's central idea was his belief in the omnipotence of God and the insignificance of humanity and *predestination*
   a. People lacked free will
   b. God decided ahead of time who would be saved (predestination)
4. Austere living and intolerance characterized Calvin's Geneva
5. The city was the model for international Protestantism, and Calvinism became the most dynamic and influential form of Protestantism

B. The Anabaptists
   1. This Protestant sect believed in adult baptism, revelation, and the separation of church and state
   2. Their beliefs and practices were humane but too radical for the times, and they were bitterly persecuted

C. The English Reformation
   1. As early as the fourteenth century the English Lollards stressed the idea of a direct relationship between the individual and God
   2. Wolsey's career represents corruption in the English church
   3. Henry VIII desired a divorce from his queen, Catherine, daughter of Ferninand and Isabella of Spain
   4. Pope Clement VII (because he did not wish to admit papal error) and Charles V blocked the divorce
   5. The pro-Protestant Archbishop Cranmer engineered the divorce
   6. The result was the nationalization of the English church and a break with Rome as Henry used Parliament to legalize the Reformation
      a. Henry needed money so he dissolved the monasteries and confiscated their lands, but this did not lead to more equal land distribution
      b. Some traditional Catholic practices, such as confession and the doctrine of transubstantiation, were maintained, however
      c. Nationalization of the church led to new form of government
   7. Under Edward VI, Henry's heir, England shifted closer to Protestantism
   8. Mary Tudor attempted to bring Catholicism back to England
   9. Under Elizabeth I a religious settlement—mainly Protestant—was made

D. The establishment of the Church of Scotland
   1. Scotland was an extreme case of church abuse
   2. John Knox brought Calvinism to Scotland from Geneva
   3. The Presbyterian Church became the national church of Scotland

E. Protestantism in Ireland
   1. The English ruling class in Ireland adopted the new faith
   2. The Irish defiantly remained Catholic

F. Lutheranism in Scandinavia
   1. In Sweden, Norway, and Denmark the monarchy led the religious reformation

      2. The result was Lutheran state churches

VI.   The Catholic and counter reformations

    A. New religious orders

       1. The Ursuline order, dedicated to combating heresy through education, spread to France and America

       2. The Jesuits were interested in fighting heresy, reforming the church, and converting pagans

    B. The slowness of institutional reform

       1. Too often the popes were preoccupied with politics or sensual pleasures

       2. Popes feared conciliarism because it would limit their authority, so they resisted calls for a council

    C. The Council of Trent

       1. Pope Paul III called the Council of Trent (1545-1563)

          a. An attempt to reconcile with the Protestants was made, but it failed

          b. International politics hindered the theological debates and attempts at reconciliation

       2. The principle of papal authority was maintained

       3. Considerable reform was undertaken, and the spiritual renewal of the church was begun

          a. Tridentine decrees forbade the sale of indulgences and outlawed pluralism and simony

          b. Attempts were made to curb clerical immorality and to encourage education

    D. The Sacred Congregation of the Holy Office

       1. The Roman Inquisition—founded in 1542 by Pope Paul III—was an arm of the Counterreformation empowered to combat heresy

       2. Under the direction of religious fanatics, it had the power to arrest, imprison, and execute

       3. Its influence was confined to Italy

VII.   The significance of the Reformation

    A. The paradoxical nature of the Reformation

       1. The unity of Europe was destroyed but religious beliefs remained strong

       2. Individualism in religion won out but confusion existed

       3. The sixteenth century and the Reformation are a dividing line between the medieval and the modern world

REVIEW QUESTIONS

Q-1. Describe the condition of the church in 1517. Were the village clergy useless and corrupt?

Q-2. What were some of the signs of disorder within the early sixteenth-century church? What impact did church wealth have on the condition of the church?

Q-3. What were some of the signs of religious vitality in fifteenth- and early sixteenth-century society?

Q-4. Describe the circumstances that prompted Luther to post his Ninety-five Theses.

Q-5. Describe the practice of indulgence selling. What authority did Luther question and on what argument did he base his position?

Q-6. What were Luther's answers, as delineated in the Confession of Augsburg, to the four basic theological issues?

Q-7. What effect did Luther's concept of state authority over church authority have on German society and German history?

Q-8. Calvin's Geneva was called "the city that was a church." Explain. What is a theocracy?

Q-9. In what ways were the Anabaptists radical for their time? Why did many of their beliefs cause them to be bitterly persecuted?

Q-10. Explain the causes and results of the English Reformation.

Q-11. What was the Elizabethan Settlement?

Q-12. Compare and contrast the religious settlements made in Scotland and Ireland. Why was Protestantism in one way a source of national strength and in the other a source of national weakness?

Q-13. What were the repercussions of the marriage of Maximilian and Mary? What impact did this marriage have on France?

Q-14. Charles V has been considered a medieval emperor. In what respects is this true? What were the origins of his empire?

Q-15. Why was the condemnation of Luther in 1521 at Worms not enforced by the German nobility? What was the result?

Q-16. What were the goals and methods of the Ursuline order and the Society of Jesus?

Q-17. Why was reform within the Catholic church often unwelcome and slow in coming?

Q-18. What were the achievements of the Council of Trent? What circumstances surrounding the calling of the council to make its task difficult and its goal of reconciliation with Protestantism unattainable?

Q-19. What was the Roman Inquisition? How extensive was its power?

Q-20. Discuss the overall impact of the Reformation on European society. Do you see it as a blessing or a disaster for the people of Europe?

STUDY-REVIEW EXERCISES

Identify each of the following and give its significance.

Brethern of the Common Life

John Knox

Pope Paul III

Archbishop Cranmer

John Tetzel

Martin Luther

Angela Merici

Henry VIII

Charles V

Mary Tudor

Pope Alexander VI

Council of Trent

Counterreformation

Elizabethan Settlement

Act of Restraint of Appeals

pluralism

benefices

Peace of Augsburg

Ninety-five Theses

preacherships

Explain the subject matter and historical significance of the following books. How does each relate to the question of religion in society?

Erasmus, *The Praise of Folly*

Chaucer, *Canterbury Tales*

Thomas à Kempis, *The Imitation of Christ*

Luther, *Appeal to the Christian Nobility of the German Nation*

Calvin, *The Institutes of the Christian Religion*

Define the basic beliefs of the following Christian religions and churches.

Roman Catholicism

Lutheranism

Calvinism

Anabaptism

Church of England

Presbyterian Church of Scotland

Test your understanding of the chapter by answering the following questions.

1. The Council of Trent *did/did not* reaffirm the seven sacraments, the validity of tradition, and transubstantiation.

2. The English Supremacy Act of 1534 declared the _____ to be the Supreme Head of the Church of England.
3. For the most part, the English Reformation under Henry VIII dealt with *political/ theological* issues.
4. He wrote: "How comes it that we Germans must put up with such robbery and such extortion of our property at the hands of the pope?"

5. This pope's name became a synonym for moral corruption.

_____

6. Mary Tudor, the English queen and daughter of Henry VIII, *was/was not* interested in the restoration of Catholicism in England.
7. In general, Protestantism tended to *strengthen/weaken* Germany as a political unit.
8. During the reign of Elizabeth, the English church moved in a moderately *Protestant/Catholic* direction.

MULTIPLE-CHOICE QUESTIONS

1. Under the Presbyterian form of church government, the church is governed by
   a. bishops.
   b. the king of Scotland.
   c. ministers.
   d. the people.

2. Which one of the following was not of the Anabaptist tradition?
   a. Congregationalists
   b. Puritans
   c. Quakers
   d. Jesuits

3. According to Luther, salvation comes through
   a. good works.
   b. faith.
   c. indulgences.
   d. a saintly life.

4. The cornerstone of Calvin's theology was his belief in
   a. predestination.
   b. indulgences.
   c. the basic goodness of man.
   d. religious tolerance and freedom.

5. John Knox and the Reformation movement in Scotland were most influenced by which of the following theological positions?
   a. Catholicism
   b. Calvinism
   c. Lutheranism
   d. the Church of England

6. Which of the following is *not* identified with corrupt practices in the early sixteenth-century church?
   a. pluralism
   b. the Brethren of the Common Life
   c. Pope Alexander VI
   d. absenteeism

7. Which of the following clearly did *not* support Luther?
   a. the German peasants
   b. the German nobility
   c. Charles V
   d. Ulrich Zwingli

8. Overall, Henry VIII's religious reformation in England occurred
   a. strictly for economic reasons.
   b. for religious reasons.
   c. mostly for political reasons.
   d. mostly for diplomatic reasons.

9. The Reformation in Germany resulted in
   a. a politically weaker Germany.
   b. a politically stronger Germany.
   c. no political changes of importance.
   d. a victory for imperial centralization.

10. The great Christian humanists of the fifteenth and sixteenth centuries believed that reform could be achieved through
    a. the use of violent revolution.
    b. education and social change.
    c. mass support of the church hierarchy.
    d. none of the above

11. Luther tacked his Ninety-five Theses to the door in Wittenberg as a response to
    a. the sale of indulgences and papal wealth.
    b. a revelation he experienced instructing him to start a new church.
    c. the illiteracy of the clergy.
    d. the oppressive rule of Frederick of Saxony.

12. The peasants who revolted in 1524 wanted
    a. the abolition of serfdom.
    b. the reform of the clergy.
    c. an end to taxes and tithes.
    d. all of the above

13. Luther's success was a result of
    a. a strong command of language.
    b. the development of the printing press.
    c. his appeal to the nobility and the middle classes.
    d. all of the above

14. The Holy Roman Emperor who tried to suppress the Lutheran revolt was
    a. Charles II.
    b. Henry VIII.
    c. Alexander V.
    d. none of the above

15. By 1555 the Protestant Reformation had spread to all but
    a. England.
    b. Scandinavia.
    c. Spain.
    d. Scotland.

16. The chief center of the Protestant Reformers in the sixteenth century was
    a. Paris.
    b. Geneva.
    c. Zurich.
    d. Cologne.

17. The Anabaptists appealed to
    a. the nobility.
    b. the poor, uneducated, and unemployed.
    c. the intellectuals.
    d. the merchant classes.

18. Henry VIII dissolved the monasteries largely because
    a. they were corrupt and mismanaged.
    b. they were symbolic of papal authority.
    c. he needed the wealth they would bring.
    d. they were a burden on the state.

19. The Scandinavian countries were most influenced by the religious beliefs of
    a. Martin Luther.
    b. John Knox.
    c. Roger Brown.
    d. the Jesuits.

20. A vow of the Jesuit order making it uniquely different from others was
    a. poverty.
    b. chastity.
    c. obedience to the pope.
    d. pacifism.

UNDERSTANDING HISTORY THROUGH READING AND THE ARTS

Few men in history have been the subject of more biographies than Martin Luther, the German reformer. One of the most important is a psychological study by E. Erikson entitled *Young Man Luther: A Study in Psychoanalysis and History** (1962). Other books about Luther include R. Bainton, *Here I Stand** (1950); E. Schwiebert, *Luther and His Times* (1952); G. Forel, *Faith Active in Love* (1954); and J. Atkinson, *Martin Luther and the Birth of Protestantism** (1968).

King Henry VIII of England is the subject of a number of interesting biographies. Three of the best are L. B. Smith, *Henry VIII* (1971); A. F. Pollard, *Henry VIII** (1905); and J. Scarisbrick, *Henry VIII* (1968). Henry's marital problems, as seen from his wife's side, are the subject of the fascinating and exciting *Catherine of Aragon** (1941) by G. Mattingly.

PROBLEMS FOR FURTHER INVESTIGATION

Students interested in further study of the religious revolution of the sixteenth century will find some of the problems of interpretation and investigation relative to that subject set out in L. W. Spitz, ed., *The Reformation** (1972) and K. Sessions, ed., *Reformation and Authority: The Meaning of the Peasant's Revolt** (1968). The relationship between the Protestant religion and economic growth has long interested historians. This historical problem is defined in R. Green, ed., *Protestantism, Capitalism, and Social Science* (1973). Students interested in the Counterreformation should begin with E. M. Burns, *The Counter Reformation** (1964), and those interested in the political implications of Calvinism should see R. Kingdon, *Calvin and Calvinism: Sources of Democracy** (1970).

*Available in paperback.

CHAPTER 15

THE AGE OF EUROPEAN EXPANSION
AND RELIGIOUS WARS

CHAPTER OBJECTIVES

After reading and studying this chapter you should be able to answer the following questions:

Q-1. Why and how did Europeans gain control over distant continents?
Q-2. What effect did overseas expansion have on Europe and conquered societies?
Q-3. What were the causes of religious wars in France, the Netherlands, and Germany?
Q-4. How did the religious wars affect the status of women?
Q-5. How and why did African slave labor become the dominant form of labor organization in the New World?
Q-6. What religious and intellectual developments led to the growth of skepticism?
Q-7. What literary masterpieces did this period produce?

CHAPTER SYNOPSIS

In this chapter we see how the trends in the High Middle Ages toward centralized nations ruled by powerful kings and toward European territorial expansion were revitalized. The growth of royal power and the consolidation of the state in Spain, France, and England accompanied and supported world exploration and a long period of European war.

The Portuguese were the first to push out into the Atlantic, but it was Spain, following close behind, that built a New World empire that provided the economic basis for a period of Spanish supremacy in European affairs. In the short run, Spanish gold and silver from the New World made the Spanish Netherlands the financial and manufacturing center of Europe, and Spain became Europe's greatest military power.

In the long run, however, overseas expansion ruined the Spanish economy, created massive European inflation, and brought the end of Spain's empire in Europe.

The attempts by Catholic monarchs to re-establish European religious unity and by both Catholic and Protestant monarchs to establish strong centralized states led to many wars among the European states. Spain's attempt to keep religious and political unity within her empire led to a long war in the Netherlands—a war that pulled England over to the side of the Protestant Dutch. There was bitter civil war in France, which finally came to an end with the reign of Henry of Navarre and the Edict of Nantes in 1598. The Thirty Years' War in Germany from 1618 to 1648 left that area a political and economic shambles.

The sixteenth century also saw a vast increase in witch-hunting and the emergence of modern racism, sexism, and skepticism. Generally, the power and status of women in this period did not change. Protestantism meant a more positive attitude toward marriage, but the revival of the idea that women were the source of evil and the end of the religious orders for women caused them to become increasingly powerless in society. North American slavery and racism had their origins in the labor problems in America and in Christian and Muslim racial attitudes. Skepticism was an intellectual reaction to the fanaticism of both Protestants and Catholics and a sign of things to come, while the Renaissance tradition was carried on by Shakespeare's work in early sixteenth-century England.

STUDY OUTLINE

I.   Discovery, reconnaissance, and expansion (1450-1650)
  A. Overseas exploration and conquest
    1. The spread of the Ottoman Turks frightened the Europeans and overshadowed their international exploits at first
    2. Political centralization in Spain, France, and England prepared the way for expansion
    3. The Portuguese, under the leadership of Prince Henry the Navigator, pushed south from North Africa
      a. Da Gama, Diaz, and Cabral set routes to India
      b. The Portuguese gained control of the Indian trade by overpowering Muslim forts in India
    4. Spain began to play a leading role in exploration and exploitation
      a. Columbus sailed under the Spanish flag and discovered the Caribbean
      b. Spanish exploitation in the Caribbean led to the destruction of the Indian population
      c. Magellan sailed southwest across the Atlantic for Charles V of Spain, and his expedition circumnavigated the earth

       d. Pizarro crushed the Inca empire in Peru and opened the Potosi mines to Spanish use

       e. New Spain brought great wealth to Spain

   5. The Low Countries, particularly the cities of Antwerp and Amsterdam, became the center of European trade

       a. The Dutch East India Company became the major organ of Dutch imperialism

       b. The Dutch West India Company gained control of much of the African and American trade

   6. France and England made sporadic efforts at exploration and settlement

B. The explorers' motives

   1. The desire to Christianize the Muslims and pagan peoples played a central role in European expansion

   2. Limited economic and political opportunity for upper class men in Spain led to emigration

   3. Government encouragement was also important

   4. Renaissance curiosity caused people to seek out new worlds

   5. The economic motive—the quest for material profit—was the basic reason for European exploration and expansion

C. Technological stimuli to exploration

   1. The development of the cannon aided European expansion

   2. New sailing and navigational developments—such as the caravel ship and the compass—also aided the expansion

D. The economic effects of Spain's discoveries in the New World

   1. Enormous amounts of American gold and silver poured into Spain

   2. It is probable that population growth and not empire building caused inflation in Spain

   3. Spanish gold caused European inflation, which hurt the poor the most

E. Colonial administration

   1. The Spanish monarch divided his new world into four viceroyalties, each with a viceroy and *audiencia*

   2. Spanish economic policy toward its colonies was that of mercantilism

   3. Portuguese administration and economic policy was similar

II. Politics, religion, and war

A. The Spanish-French wars ended in 1559 with a Spanish victory, thus leading to a variety of wars centering on religious and national issues

   1. These wars used bigger armies, with gun powder, and with a need for better financial administration

   2. Governments had to use various propaganda devices, including the printing press, to arouse public opinion

   3. The Peace of Westphalia (1648) ended religious wars but also ended the idea of a unified Christian society

B. The origins of difficulties in France (1515-1559)
1. By 1500, France was recovering from plague and disorder, and the nobility began to lose power
2. The French kings, such as Francis I and Henry II, continued the policies of centralization but spent more money than they raised
3. The wars between France and Emperor Charles V—the Habsburg-Valois wars—were costly
4. To raise money, Francis signed the Concordat of Bologna (1516), in which he recognized the supremacy of the papacy in return for the right to appoint French bishops
    a. This settlement established Catholicism as the national religion
    b. It also perpetuated corruption within the French church
    c. The corruption made Calvinism attractive to Christians eager for reform: some clergy and members of the middle and artisan classes
C. Religious riots and civil war in France (1559-1589)
1. The French nobility, many of them Calvinist, attempted to regain power
2. Frequent religious riots symbolized the struggle for power
3. The Saint Bartholomew's Day massacre of Calvinists led to the War of the Three Henrys, a conflict for secular power
4. King Henry IV's Edict of Nantes (1598) saved France from further civil war by allowing Protestants to worship
D. The Netherlands under Charles V
1. The Low Countries were part of the Habsburg empire and enjoyed relative autonomy
2. Charles V divided his empire between his brother Ferdinand and his son, King Philip of Spain
E. The revolt of the Netherlands (1556-1587)
1. Regent Margaret attempted to destroy Protestantism by establishing the Inquisition in the Netherlands
2. Popular support for Protestantism led to the destruction of many Catholic churches
3. The Duke of Alva and his Spanish troops were sent by Philip II to crush the disturbances in the Low Countries
4. Alva's brutal actions only inflamed the religious war, which raged from 1568 to 1578
5. The Low Countries were finally split into the Spanish Netherlands in the south and the independent United Provinces of the Netherlands in the north
    a. The north was Protestant and ruled by the commercial aristocracy
    b. The south was Catholic and ruled by the landed nobility
6. Elizabeth I of England supported the northern, or Protestant, cause as a safeguard against Spain's attacking England

        a.   This was for economic reasons

        b.   She had her rival Mary Queen of Scots beheaded

F. Philip II and the Spanish Armada

    1. Philip II planned war on England for several reasons

        a.   He wanted to keep England in the Catholic fold

        b.   He believed he would never conquer the Dutch unless he defeated England first

    2. The failure of the Spanish invasion of England—the armada of 1598—did not mean the end of the war, but it did prevent Philip from forcibly unifying western Europe

    3. In 1609, Philip III agreed to a truce, recognizing the independence of the United Provinces

G. The Thirty Years' War (1618-1648)

    1. Protestant Bohemian revolt over religious freedom led to war in Germany

    2. The Bohemian phase was characterized by civil war in Bohemia for religious liberty and political independence from the Habsburgs; the Catholics won

    3. The Danish phase led to further Catholic victory

    4. The Swedish phase ended the Habsburg plan to unite Germany

    5. The French phase ended with a destroyed Germany and an independent Netherlands

H. Germany after the Thirty Years' War

    1. The war was economically disastrous for Germany

    2. The war led to agricultural depression in Germany, which in turn encouraged a return to serfdom for many peasants

III. Changing attitudes

A. The status of women

    1. Literature on women and marriage called for a subservient wife with the household as her first priority and a protective, firm-ruling, and loyal husband

        a.   Catholic marriages could not be dissolved while Protestants held that divorce and remarriage were possible

        b.   Women did not lose their identity or meaningful work, but their subordinate status did not change—although a few women (like Bess of Hardwick) gained wealth and power

    2. Sexual indulgence was popular and widespread

        a.   Prostitution was common—as brothels were licensed—but Protestant Moralists fought it

    3. Protestant reformers believed that convents were antifeminist and that women should be free to marry and enjoy sex

     a. However, it was understood even by Protestants that religious orders for women provided upper class women with an outlet for their talents

B. The great European witch-hunt
1. Growth in religion and advent of religious struggle led to a rise in the belief in the evil power of witches
2. The thousands of people executed as witches represent society's drift toward social and intellectual conformity
3. Reasons varied but all in all witch hunting reflects widespread misogyny

C. European slavery and the origins of American racism
1. Black slavery originated with the end of white slavery (1453) and the widespread need for labor, particularly in the new sugar-producing settlements
2. Africans were brought to America to replace the Indians
3. A few, like Las Casas, called for the end of slavery
4. North American racist ideas originated in Christian and Muslim ideas

D. The origins of modern skepticism
1. Skeptics doubt whether definitive knowledge is ever attainable
2. Montaigne is the best representative of early modern skepticism
     a. He was a humanist graced with open-mindedness and tolerance
     b. He believed that the beginning of wisdom lies in the confession of ignorance
3. Montaigne's skepticism represents a sharp break with the past; it is a forerunner of modern attitudes

IV. Elizabethan and Jacobean literature
A. The golden age of English literature: the late sixteenth and early seventeenth centuries
1. Shakespeare reflects the Renaissance in that his great plays express national consciousness and human problems
2. The Authorized Bible of King James I is a masterpiece of English vernacular writing

REVIEW QUESTIONS

Q-1. Describe the Portuguese explorations. Who were the participants and what were their motives?

Q-2. Describe the American-Spanish-Dutch economic arrangement. How did it work? Who were the winners and who were the losers?

Q-3. The sixteenth century was a century of money inflation. Why?

Q-4. What role did technology play in European expansion?

Q-5. Overall, what do you believe to be the major reasons for European expansion in the fifteenth and sixteenth centuries?

Q-6. What impact did Protestantism have on the economic and political development of France? Why is the Edict of Nantes an important event in French history?

Q-7. What were the causes and consequences of the French civil war of 1559-1589? Was it chiefly a religious or a political event?

Q-8. Discuss the origins and the outcome of the war between the Netherlands and Spain in the late sixteenth and early seventeenth centuries.

Q-9. What were the circumstances surrounding Elizabeth's decision to aid the United Netherlands in their war against Spain? What was the Spanish reaction?

Q-10. Why did Catholic France side with the Protestants in the Thirty Years' War?

Q-11. What were the political, religious, and economic consequences of the Thirty Years' War in Europe?

Q-12. Describe the social status of women between 1560 and 1648.

Q-13. What were the origins of North American racism?

Q-14. What is skepticism? Why did faith and religious certainty begin to come to an end in the first part of the seventeenth century?

Q-15. What were the major literary masterpieces of this age? In what ways can the English playwright Shakespeare be regarded as a true Renaissance man?

Q-16. What do the witch hunts tell us about social attitudes toward women?

STUDY-REVIEW EXERCISES

Identify each of the following.

politiques

Elizabeth I of England

Huguenots

Philip II of Spain

Prince Henry the Navigator

Michel de Montaigne

Christopher Columbus

Bartholomew Diaz

Hernando Cortez

Elizabeth Hardwick

Council of Blood

Habsburg-Valois wars

quinto

audiencia

corregedores

Thirty Years' War

defeat of the Spanish Armada

Concordat of Bologna

Peace of Westphalia

Saint Bartholomew's Day massacre

War of the Three Henrys

Edict of Nantes

Define the following key concepts and terms.

mercantilism

inflation

sexism

racism

skepticism

misogyny

Test your understanding of the chapter by answering the following questions.

1. The war that brought destruction and ensured division in Germany.

    _____

2. The Spanish explorer who conquered the Aztecs. _____
3. The Spanish priest and defender of the American Indians.

    _____

4. The law of 1598 that granted religious freedom to French Protestants.

    _____

5. Spain's golden century. _____
6. The king of Sweden who intervened in the Thirty Years' War.

    _____

7. After 1551, the seven northern provinces of the Netherlands were called

    _____ .

8. The city that became the financial capital of Europe by 1600.

    _____

9. The monarch of Britain at the time of the Spanish Armada.

    _____

10. The idea that nothing is completely knowable.

    _____

11. The emperor who divided the Habsburg empire into two parts.

    _____

12. The 1516 compromise between church and state in France.

    _____

13. The first European country to establish sea routes to the east.

    _____

MULTIPLE-CHOICE QUESTIONS

1. Which of the following was *not* a motive for Portuguese exploration in the late fifteenth and sixteenth centuries?
   a. the search for gold
   b. Christianizing the Muslims
   c. the discovery of sea routes to India
   d. the conquest of Constantinople

2. Beginning in 1581, the northern Netherlands revolted against their political overlord,
   a. France.
   b. Spain.
   c. Elizabeth I of England.
   d. Florence.

3. North American racist attitudes toward African blacks originated in
   a. South America.
   b. Spain.
   c. France.
   d. England.

4. In the Thirty Years' War, France supported
   a. the German Catholics.
   b. the Holy Roman Emperor.
   c. Spain.
   d. the German Protestants.

5. Which of the following statements about the Spanish Armada of 1588 is *false*?
   a. It was the beginning of a long war with England.
   b. It failed in its objective.
   c. It prevented Philip II from reimposing unity on western Europe by force.
   d. It made possible Spanish conquest of the Netherlands.

6. The nation that considered itself the international defender of Catholicism was
   a. France.
   b. Spain.
   c. Italy.
   d. England.

7. Columbus, like many of his fellow explorers, was principally motivated by
   a. a desire to discover India.
   b. a desire to Christianize the Americans.
   c. the desire of Spain to control the New World.
   d. the Spanish need to control the Mediterranean.

8. The earliest known explorers of North America were
   a. the Spanish.
   b. the Vikings.
   c. the Italians.
   d. the English.

9. Select the one which was *not* a feature of Spanish colonial administration:
   a. The New World was divided into four vice-royalties.
   b. Each territory had an *audiencia*, or judicial council.
   c. Each territory had royal officials, or intendants, responsible to the crown.
   d. The crown had only indirect and limited control over colonies.

10. In order to gain control of the spice trade of the Indian Ocean, the Portuguese were thrown into direct competition with
    a. Spain.
    b. England.
    c. the Muslims.
    d. France.

11. The main contribution of Cortez and Pizzaro to Spain was
    a. the tapping of the rich silver resources of Mexico and Peru.
    b. the Christianizing of the New World peoples.
    c. the further exploration of the Pacific Ocean.
    d. the discovery of South Africa.

12. The flow of huge amounts of gold and silver from the New World caused
    a. serious inflation in Spain and in the rest of Europe.
    b. the Spanish economy to become dependent on New World gold and silver.
    c. the suffering of the poor because of the dramatic rise in food prices.
    d. all of the above

13. Of the following, which was not a technological improvement that facilitated the "Age of Expansion"?

a. the galley
b. the magnetic compass
c. the cannon
d. the caravel

14. France was saved from religious anarchy when religious principles were set aside for political necessity by the new king,
    a. Henry III.
    b. Francis I.
    c. Henry IV of Navarre.
    d. Charles IX.

15. Calvinism was appealing to the middle classes for each of the following reasons *except*
    a. its heavy moral emphasis.
    b. its stress on leisure and ostentatious living.
    c. its intellectual emphasis.
    d. its approval of any job well done, hard work, and success.

16. The vast palace of the Spanish monarchs, built under the direction of Philip II, was called
    a. Versailles.
    b. the Escorial.
    c. Tournai.
    d. Hampton Court.

17. The Treaty of Westphalia, which ended the Thirty Years' War (1618-1648),
    a. further strengthened the Holy Roman Empire.
    b. completely undermined the Holy Roman Empire as a viable state.
    c. maintained that only Catholicism and Lutheranism were legitimate religions.
    d. refused to recognize the independence of the United Provinces of the Nether-lands.

18. Of the following, the best representative of early modern skepticism is
    a. Las Casas.
    b. James I.
    c. Calvin.
    d. Montaigne.

19. The Spanish missionary Las Casas convinced Charles V to import Africans to Brazil because

    a. church law did not strictly forbid the use of black slavery.
    b. blacks were better able to withstand the rigors of hard work in a hot climate.
    c. the native Indians were not durable enough under such harsh conditions.
    d. all of the above

20. The Portuguese explorer who first reached India was
    a. Bartholomew Diaz.
    b. Prince Henry the Navigator.
    c. Vasco da Gama.
    d. Hernando Cortez.

21. The origin of racial attitudes found in North America was
    a. England.
    b. Spain.
    c. Catholic teaching.
    d. the Dutch.

22. The appearance of gunpowder in Europe
    a. put a common soldier on equal footing with a gentleman soldier.
    b. changed the popular belief that warfare bettered the individual.
    c. created the need for governments to use propaganda to convince their people to support war.
    d. all of the above

GEOGRAPHY

A. Using Map 15.1 in the text as a guide:
    1. Show on the outline map the exploration routes of da Gama, Columbus, and Magellan.
    2. Mark the location of the Aztec and Inca empires and locate and label the following places.

Cueta	Cape of Good Hope	Amsterdam	Guinea Coast of Africa
Calicut	Cape Horn	London	Lisbon
Goa	Antwerp	Mexico City	Moluccas

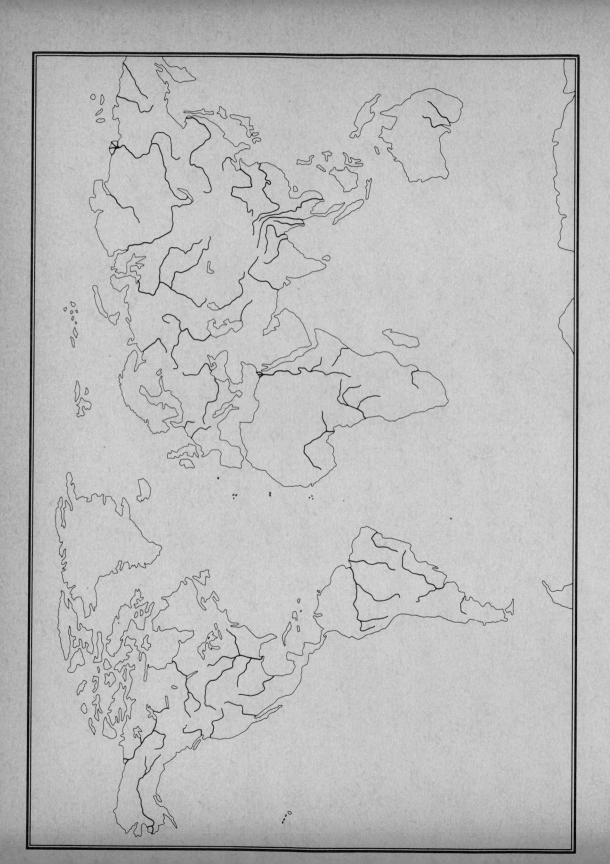

3. Why did the Spanish and Portuguese gain an early lead in European expansion? What were the goals of the early explorers, such as Columbus?

4. Explain, in geographic and economic terms, the reasons for the growth of the Flemish (Netherland) towns such as Antwerp and Amsterdam.

5. Explain the important economic relationship that developed among Spain, the Americas, and the Netherlands.

B. Using Map 15.4 in the text as a reference, list below the areas that were the main sources of African slaves and the main areas of slave importation into the New World. Do the latter areas illustrate the economic origins of the slave trade?

UNDERSTANDING HISTORY THROUGH READING AND THE ARTS

Those interested in skepticism and the life of its finest representative will want to read M. Lowenthal, ed., *Autobiography of Michel de Montaigne* * (1935). There were a number of extremely important and powerful women of the sixteenth century whose biographies make for fascinating reading: R. Roeder, *Catherine de Medici and the Lost Revolution* * (1937); J. E. Neal, *Queen Elizabeth I* * (1934, 1966); and A. Fraser, *Mary Queen of Scots* * (1969). An interesting seventeenth-century woman is Gustavus Adolphus's daughter, whose life is told in G. Masson, *Queen Christina* (1968); N. Harvey, *The Rose and the Thorn* (1977) is an account of the lives and times of Mary and Margaret Tudor.

*Available in paperback.

PROBLEMS FOR FURTHER INVESTIGATION

Those interested in doing work in the area of European expansion should begin with D. L. Jensen, ed., *The Expansion of Europe: Motives, Methods, and Meaning* (1967). A discussion of some of the problems faced in studying the religious conflict in France is found in J. H. M. Salmon, *The French Wars of Religion** (1967), and anyone interested in research on the Thirty Years' War should begin with S. H. Steinberg, *The Thirty Years' War and the Conflict for European Hegemony, 1600-1660** (1966) and T. K. Rabb, *The Thirty Years' War** (1964). Those interested in understanding how the vast Spanish Empire worked will want to see C. H. Haring, *The Spanish Empire in America** (1947, 1963). This book includes an excellent bibliography on the subject.

*Available in paperback.

CHAPTER 16

ABSOLUTISM AND CONSTITUTIONALISM IN WESTERN EUROPE (CA 1589-1715)

CHAPTER OBJECTIVES

After reading and studying this chapter you should be able to answer the following questions:

Q-1. How did absolute monarchy and constitutionalism differ from the feudal and dynastic monarchies of earlier centuries?

Q-2. Which countries best represent absolutism and constitutionalism?

CHAPTER SYNOPSIS

This chapter examines how the political system of absolutism succeeded gloriously in France and failed dismally in England in the seventeenth century. Few kings have been as successful in establishing complete monarchial sovereignty as the great Sun King of France, Louis XIV. Louis gave Europe a masterful lesson on how to reduce the power of the class that historically had been a constant competitor of the monarchy, the nobility. He was a superb actor and propagandist, who built on the earlier achievements of Henry IV and Richelieu and used his magnificent palace of Versailles to imprison the French nobility in a beautiful golden cage. He succeeded in expanding France at the expense of the Habsburgs, and his patronage of the arts helped form the great age of French classicism. However, the economic progress he first made was later checked by his policy of revoking religious toleration.

While the France of Louis was the classic model of modern absolutism, Spain was the classic case of imperial decline. By 1600 Spain was in trouble, and by 1700 it was no longer a major European power. Not only did the silver and labor of America run out, but this great American wealth ruined the Spanish economic and social structure.

War with the Dutch, the English, and the French also helped turn Spain into a backwater of Europe.

England and the United Provinces of the Netherlands provide a picture of constitutionalism triumphing over absolutism. For England, the seventeenth century was a long period of political conflict, complete with a bitter civil war and a radical experiment with republicanism. The causes of this era of conflict were varied, but it is clear that by 1689 the English army and Parliament had destroyed the Stuart quest for divine-right absolutism. The period that followed witnessed some important changes in the way the state is managed.

The Netherlands was important not only because it became the financial and commercial center of Europe, but also because it provided the period's third model of political development—a loosely federated, middle-class constitutional state.

STUDY OUTLINE

I. Absolutism
   A. Absolutism defined
      1. Under absolutism, sovereignty resided in kings—not the nobility or the parliament—who considered themselves responsible to God alone
      2. Absolute kings created new state bureaucracies and armies, and they regulated all the institutions
      3. However, the ambitions of absolute monarchs were limited and not the same as those of leaders of modern totalitarian states
   B. Henry IV and the foundations of French absolutism
      1. Henry IV achieved peace and curtailed the power of the nobility
      2. His minister, Sully, brought about financial stability and economic growth
   C. The cornerstone of French absolutism: Louis XIII and Richelieu
      1. Cardinal Richelieu, the ruler of France under King Louis XIII, broke the power of the French nobility
      2. He also brought about administrative reform that helped centralize the state's power
      3. However, his financial actions were unsound and created problems for the future
      4. Richelieu regarded the Protestant Huguenots as a source of aristocratic power
      5. Under Richelieu, France sought to break the Habsburg power
      6. Mazarin's policies gave rise to the *Fronde*
II. The absolutism of Louis XIV
   A. Louis the "Sun King" was selfish, an insatiable eater, a great actor, and fearful of the nobility

   B. He made the court at Versailles a fixed institution and used it as a means of preserving royal power and as the center of French absolutism
      1. The court at Versailles was a device to ruin the power of the aristocracy
      2. The architecture and art of Versailles was a means of carrying out state policy
      3. The French language and culture became the international style
   C. Economic management under Louis XIV: Colbert and mercantilism
      1. Mercantilism is a collection of governmental policies for the regulation of the economy by the state
      2. Louis XIV's finance minister, Colbert, tried to achieve a favorable balance of trade and make France self-sufficient so the flow of gold to other countries would be halted
         a. Colbert encouraged French industry, enacted high tariffs, and created a strong merchant marine
         b. He hoped to make Canada part of a French empire
         c. Though France's industries grew, its agricultural economy declined
   D. The revocation of the Edict of Nantes
      1. In 1685, Louis revoked the Edict of Nantes, which had given religious freedom to French Protestants
      2. This revocation caused many Protestants to flee the country; but it had little effect on the economy and it caused fear and hatred abroad
III. French classicism in art and literature
   A. French classicism imitated and resembled the arts of the ancients and the Renaissance
   B. Poussin best illustrates classical idealism in painting, while Le Nain is an important realistic painter
   C. Louis XIV was a patron to the music composers Lully, Couperin, and Charpentier
   D. The comedies of Molière and the tragedies of Racine best illustrate the classicism in French theater
IV. Louis XIV's wars
   A. The French army under Louis XIV was modern because it employed mercenaries rather than nobles
   B. Louis XIV's foreign policy was expansionist
   C. The height of French expansion was reached in 1678 with victory over Spain and the Holy Roman Empire
   D. Louis then fought the new Dutch king of England, William III and the League of Augsburg
   E. The War of the Spanish Succession (1701-1713) involved the issue of the succession to the Spanish throne: Louis claimed Spain but was opposed by the Dutch, English, Austrians, and Prussians

1. The war was also an attempt to check French economic growth in the world
2. The war was concluded by the Peace of Utrecht in 1713, which forbade the union of France and Spain
3. The war left France on the brink of bankruptcy with widespread misery

V. The decline of absolutist Spain in the seventeenth century
   A. Factors contributing to Spain's decline:
      1. Fiscal disorder, political incompetence, population decline, intellectual isolation, and psychological malaise contributed to the decline
      2. The defeat of the "Invincible Armada" in 1588 was a crushing blow to Spain's morale
      3. Spain's economy began to decline by 1600
         a. Royal expenditure increased, but income from the Americas decreased
         b. Business and agriculture suffered
      4. Spanish kings lacked force of character and could not deal with all these problems
      5. Spain could not escape from her past: military glory, Roman Catholicism, and easy money from America

VI. Constitutionalism in England and the Netherlands
   A. Constitutionalism defined
      1. Under constitutionalism, the state must be governed according to law, not royal decree
         a. It implies a balance between the power of the government and the rights of the subjects
         b. A nation's constitution may be written or unwritten, but the government must respect it
      2. Constitutional government is not the same as full democracy because not all of the people have the right to participate
   B. The decline of royal absolutism in England (1603-1649)
      1. The Stuart kings of England lacked the political wisdom of Elizabeth I
      2. James I was devoted to the ideal of rule by divine right
      3. His absolutism ran counter to English belief
      4. James I faced a new, educated merchant-gentry class that opposed absolutism
      5. This new class controlled the House of Commons, which the Stuarts attempted to control
   C. The Protestant or "capitalist ethic" and the problem of religion in England
      1. Many English people were attracted by the values of hard work, thrift, and self-denial implied by Calvinism; these people were called Puritans
      2. The Puritans, who were dissatisfied with the Church of England, saw James I as an enemy

     3. Charles I and his archbishop, Laud, appeared to be pro-Catholic

D. The English Civil War (1642-1649)

     1. Charles I had ruled without Parliament for eleven years

     2. A revolt in Scotland over the religious issue forced him to call a new Parliament into session to finance an army

        a. The Commons passed an act compelling the king to summon Parliament every three years

        b. It also impeached Archbishop Laud

        c. Religious differences in Ireland led to a revolt there, but Parliament would not trust Charles with an army

     3. Charles initiated military action against Parliament

        a. The Civil War revolved around the issue of whether sovereignty should reside in the king or in Parliament

        b. The problem was not resolved, but Charles was beheaded in 1649

E. Puritanical absolutism in England: Cromwell and the Protectorate

     1. Kingship was abolished in 1649 and a commonwealth proclaimed

     2. In actuality, the army—led by Cromwell—controlled the government

     3. Cromwell's Protectorate became a military dictatorship—absolutist and puritanical

        a. Cromwell allowed religious toleration for all Christians, except Roman Catholics, and savagely crushed the revolt in Ireland

        b. He censored the press and closed the theaters

        c. He regulated the economy according to mercantilist principles

F. The restoration of the English monarchy (1660-1688)

     1. The restoration of the Stuart kings failed to solve the problems of religion and authority in society

     2. Charles II's Cabal was the forerunner of the cabinet system, and it helped create good relations with the Parliament

     3. Charles's pro-French policies led to a Catholic scare

     4. James II violated the Test Act, which prevented Catholics from holding government posts

     5. Fear of Catholicism led to the expulsion of James II and the Glorious Revolution

     6. The Bill of Rights of 1689 stated that sovereignty henceforth resided with Parliament

        a. Locke argued that all people have natural rights—including that of rebellion

        b. Locke's ideas served as the foundation of English and American liberalism

     7. The cabinet system, which developed in the eighteenth century, reflects the victory of aristocratic government over absolutism

G. The Dutch republic in the seventeenth century
1. The Dutch republic emerged from the sixteenth-century struggle against Spain
2. Power in the republic resided in the local Estates
    a. The republic was a confederation: a weak union of strong provinces
    b. The republic was based on middle-class ideas and values
3. Religious toleration fostered economic growth
4. The province of Holland became the commercial and financial center of Europe

REVIEW QUESTIONS

Q-1. In what way does the French minister Richelieu symbolize absolutism? What were his achievements?

Q-2. It has been said that the palace of Versailles was a device to ruin the nobility of France. Explain. Was Versailles a palace or a prison?

Q-3. Define mercantilism. What were the mercantilist policies of the French minister Colbert?

Q-4. The revocation of the Edict of Nantes has been considered a great error on the part of Louis XIV. Why?

Q-5. What were the reasons for the fall of the Spanish Empire?

Q-6. Discuss the foreign policy goals of Louis XIV. Was he successful?

Q-7. Define absolutism. How does it differ from totalitarianism?

Q-8. What was the impact of Louis XIV's wars on the French economy and French society?

Q-9. What were the causes of the War of the Spanish Succession? What impact did William III of England have on European events after about 1689?

Q-10. What was constitutionalism? How does it differ from democratic form of government?

Q-11. Discuss John Locke's political theory. Why is it said that Locke was the spokesman for the liberal English Revolution of 1689 and for representative government?

Q-12. What were the attitudes and policies of James I that made him so unpopular with his subjects?

Q-13. Who were the Puritans? Why did they come into conflict with James I?

Q-14. What were the immediate and the long-range causes of the English Civil War of 1642-1649? What were the results?

Q-15. Why did James II flee from England in 1688? What happened to the kingship at this point?

Q-16. Were the events of 1688-89 a victory for English democracy? Explain.

Q-17. Compare and contrast constitutionalism and absolutism. Where does sovereign power reside in each system?

Q-18. What accounts for the phenomenal economic success and political stability of the Dutch republic?

STUDY-REVIEW EXERCISES

Define the following key concepts and terms.

mercantilism

absolutism

totalitarianism

republicanism

constitutionalism

cabinet government

French classicism

sovereign power

quixotic

commonwealth

Identify each of the following and give its significance.

Molière

Poussin

Versailles

Dutch Estates General

intendants

Peace of Utrecht

Cabal of Charles II

Instrument of Government

Puritans

Oliver Cromwell

Cardinal Richelieu

Louis XIV of France

James II of England

English Bill of Rights

John Churchill

Philip II of Spain

Thomas Hobbes

Richelieu's *Dictionary*

Explain what each of these men believed about the placement of authority within society.

James I of England

Thomas Hobbes

Louis XIV of France

John Locke

Sully

Explain what the following events were and why they were important.

revocation of the Edict of Nantes

Scottish revolt of 1640

War of the Spanish Succession

Glorious Revolution

English Civil War of 1642-1646

Treaty of the Pyrenees

Test your understanding of the chapter by answering the following questions.

1. The highest executive office of the Dutch republic. _____

2. Louis XIV's able minister of finance was _____ .
3. During the age of economic growth in Spain, a vast number of Spaniards *entered/left* religious orders.
4. For Louis XIV of France the War of the Spanish Succession was a *success/disaster*.
5. The Englishman who inflicted defeat on Louis XIV at Blenheim was

   _____ .

6. The archbishop whose goal was to enforce Anglican unity in England and Scot-

   land was _____ .

MULTIPLE-CHOICE QUESTIONS

1. Mercantilism
   a. was a military system.
   b. insisted on a favorable balance of trade.
   c. was adopted in England but not in France.
   d. claimed that state power was based on land armies.

2. French Protestants tended to be
   a. poor peasants.
   b. the power behind the throne of Louis XIV.
   c. a financial burden for France.
   d. clever business people.

3. The War of the Spanish Succession began when Charles II of Spain left his territories to
   a. the French heir.
   b. the Spanish heir.
   c. Eugene of Savoy.
   d. the archduke of Austria.

4. This city was the commercial and financial capital of Europe in the seventeenth century.
   a. London
   b. Hamburg
   c. Paris
   d. Amsterdam

5. Of the following, the country most centered on middle-class interests was
   a. England.
   b. Spain.
   c. France.
   d. the Netherlands.

6. Which of the following Englishmen was a Catholic?
   a. James II
   b. Oliver Cromwell
   c. Archbishop Laud
   d. William III

7. Which of the following is *not* a characteristics of an absolute state?
   a. sovereignty embodied in the person of the ruler
   b. bureaucracies solely accountable to the king
   c. a strong voice expressed by the nobility
   d. permanent standing armies

8. Cardinal Richelieu's most notable accomplishment was
   a. the creation of a strong financial system for France.
   b. the creation of a highly effective administration system.
   c. winning the total support of the Huguenots.
   d. allying the Catholic church with the government.

9. The statement "There are no privileges and immunities which can stand against a divinely appointed king" forms the basis of the
   a. Stuart notion of absolutism.
   b. Stuart notion of constitutionalism.
   c. English Parliament's notion of democracy.
   d. English Parliament's notion of constitutionalism.

10. The English Long Parliament
    a. enacted legislation supporting absolutism.
    b. supported the Catholic tendencies of Charles I.
    c. supported Charles I as a military leader.
    d. enacted legislation against absolutism.

11. Cromwell's government is best described as a
    a. constitutional state.
    b. democratic state.
    c. military dictatorship.
    d. monarchy.

12. Absolute monarchs secured mastery over the nobility by
    a. the creation of a standing army.
    b. the creation of a state bureaucracy.
    c. the use of war.
    d. all of the above

13. Cardinal Richelieu consolidated the power of the French monarchy by each of the following *except* for
    a. destroying the castles of the nobility.
    b. ruthlessly treating conspirators who threatened the monarchy.
    c. keeping nobles from gaining high government offices.
    d. eliminating the "intendant" system of local government.

14. One way in which Louis XIV controlled the French nobility was by
    a. maintaining standing armies in the countryside to crush noble uprisings.
    b. requiring the presence of the major noble families at Versailles for at least part of the year.
    c. periodically visiting the nobility in order to check on their activities.
    d. none of the above

15. Features of the French army under Louis XIV included the following *except* for

   a. standarized uniforms and weapons.
   b. living off the countryside.
   c. the ambulance corps caring for the troops.
   d. a system of recruitment, training, and promotion.

16. The Peace of Utrecht in 1713
   a. enlarged the British Empire significantly.
   b. reflected the balance-of-power principle.
   c. ended Spain's role as a major power in Europe.
   d. all of the above

17. The downfall of Spain in the seventeenth century from being a major European power can be blamed on
   a. a weak monarchy.
   b. a decline in industry and trade.
   c. a contraction of slave labor.
   d. all of the above

18. When Archbishop Laud tried to make the Presbyterian Scots accept the Anglican Book of Common Prayer, the Scots
   a. revolted.
   b. reluctantly accepted the archbishop's directive.
   c. ignored the directive.
   d. none of the above

19. Acting as spokesman for the landowning class and proponent of the idea that the purpose of government is to protect life, liberty, and property was
   a. Thomas Hobbes.
   b. William of Orange.
   c. John Locke.
   d. Edmund Burke.

20. After the United Provinces of the Netherlands won independence from Spain, their structure of government was
   a. a strong monarchy.
   b. a centralized parliamentary system.
   c. a weak union of strong provinces.
   d. a democracy.

21. The Dutch economy was based on
   a. fishing and the merchant marine.
   b. silver mining in Peru.
   c. export of textiles.
   d. all of the above

GEOGRAPHY

1. Using Map 16.1 in the text as a guide, on the outline map shade in the territory added to France as a result of the wars and foreign policy of King Louis XIV.
2. Explain how each of the territories was acquired and from whom.

3. Louis XIV declared in 1700 that "the Pyrenees no longer exist." What did he mean?

4. What changes in the balance of power came about as a result of the Treaty of Utrecht in 1713?

UNDERSTANDING HISTORY THROUGH READING AND THE ARTS

Louis XIV and the magnificence of his court at Versailles are re-created with color and spirit in W. H. Lewis, *The Splendid Century* * (1953), and a vivid picture of life of the English upper classes—how they ran their estates, entertained, and when possible ran the country—is found in Mark Girouard, *Life in the English Country House: A Social and Architectural History* (1979).

The seventeenth century was a period of architectural splendor in France and in England. Some of the great achievements of this period are discussed in Chapter 7 of N. Pevsner, *An Outline of European Architecture* (7th ed., 1963). The splendor of Versailles and French and British baroque painting and architecture are the subjects of Chapter 7, "The Baroque in France and England," in H. W. Janson, *History of Art* (1962).

Much good reading is found in the literature of the seventeenth century. The great comic writer of the age was Molière, whose *Tartuffe* is still a source of entertainment. LaFontaine's *Fables* are a lively reworking of tales from antiquity and Cervantes's *Don Quixote* continues to inspire its readers. The greatest writer to emerge from the Puritan age in England was John Milton, whose *Paradise Lost* is a classic.

*Available in paperback.

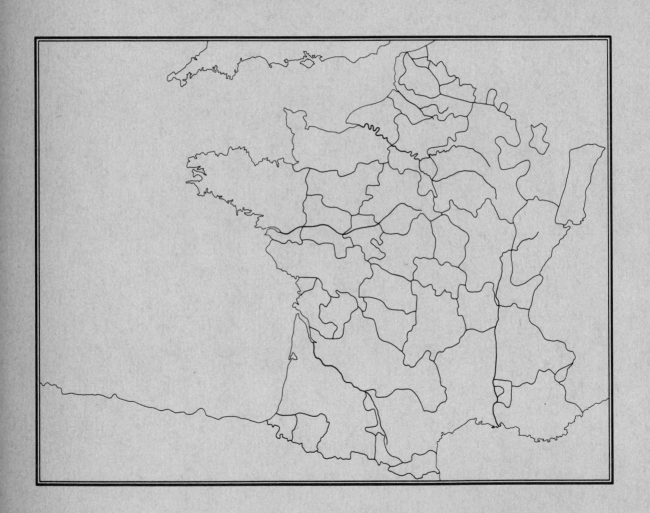

PROBLEMS FOR FURTHER INVESTIGATION

James Stuart was a successful king in Scotland but a failure in England. Why? See D. Willson, *King James VI and I* * (1956). Was the Glorious Revolution of 1688-89 in England a victory for modern political democracy or a palace revolution by a group of aristocrats? This and other problems surrounding this political event are discussed in G. M. Straka, ed., *The Revolution of 1688 and the Birth of the English Political Nation* * (rev. ed., 1973). Some of the problems in interpretation of the crucial period 1642 to 1649 in Britain are considered in P. A. M. Taylor, ed., *The Origins of the English Civil War* * (1960), L. Stone, ed., *Social Change and Revolution in England, 1540-1640* * (1965)—and B. Manning deals with popular participation in the wars and revolution in *The English People and the English Revolution* (1976).

Students interested in research on absolutism and Louis XIV in France will want to consider H. G. Judge, ed., *Louis XIV* (1965); William F. Church, ed., *The Greatness of Louis XIV: Myth or Reality?* * (rev. ed., 1972); and R. F. Kierstead, ed., *State and Society in Seventeenth-Century France* * (1975). The best biography of Louis XIV is *Louis XIV* (1968) by J. Wolf.

*Available in paperback.

arising from external conflicts and a multicultural state by building a strong, central-ized military state. Prussian absolutism—intended to check the power of the nobility—was achieved by the Hohenzollern monarchs, while Russian absolutism was largely the outgrowth of the Mongol conquest and internal power struggles.

Some of the absolute monarchs were enlightened reformers, but their good in-tentions were often thwarted by internal problems. But if reform from above was not overly effective, the absolute monarchs' use of architecture and urban planning—much of which was in the so-called baroque form—to enhance their images was a noteworthy success. They created buildings and cities that reflected their growing power, and they hired baroque painters and musicians such as Rubens and Bach to glorify them and to fill their palaces with paintings and music.

STUDY OUTLINE

I. Lords and peasants in eastern Europe
   A. The medieval background (1400-1650)
      1. Personal and economic freedom for peasants increased between 1050 and 1300
      2. Thus, living conditions improved and serfdom was reduced
      3. After 1300, powerful lords in eastern Europe reinstituted serfdom to combat their economic problems
      4. Laws restricted freedom, and labor obligations were increased in eastern Europe
   B. The consolidation of serfdom
      1. The re-establishment of hereditary serfdom took place in Poland, Prussia, and Russia between 1500 and 1650
      2. This was a result of the growth of estate agriculture
         a. Lords seized peasant land for their own estates
         b. They then demanded unpaid serf labor on those estates
   C. Political reasons for changes in serfdom in eastern Europe
      1. Serfdom increased because of political, not economic, reasons
      2. Weak monarchs could not resist the demands of the powerful noble land-lords
      3. The absence of the Western concept of sovereignty meant that the king did not think in terms of protecting the people of the nation
      4. Overall, the peasants of the East were weaker than those of the West, and the urban middle class was undermined by the landlords
II. The rise of Austria and Prussia (1650-1750)
   A. Austria and the Ottoman Turks
      1. After the end of the Thirty Years' War in 1648, the Austrian Habsburgs, having failed to destroy Protestantism, turned inward and eastward to unify their holdings

2. Austria became absorbed in a war against the Turks for the conquest of Hungary and Transylvania
3. Under Suleiman the Magnificent the Turks built the most powerful empire in the world, which included part of central Europe
   a. The Turkish sultan was the absolute head of the state
   b. There was little private property, and a bureaucracy staffed by slaves
4. The Turkish attack on Austria in 1683 was turned back, and the Habsburgs conquered all of Hungary and Transylvania
5. The Habsburg possessions consisted of Austria, Bohemia, and Hungary, which were joined in a fragile union
   a. The Pragmatic Sanction (1713) stated that the possessions should never be divided
   b. The Hungarian nobility resisted accepting Habsburg rule

B. Prussia in the seventeenth century
1. The Hohenzollern family ruled the electorate of Brandenburg but had little real power
2. The Thirty Years' War weakened the representative assemblies of the realm and allowed the Hohenzollerns to consolidate their absolutist rule
3. Frederick William (the Great Elector) used military force and taxation to unify his holdings into a strong state

C. The consolidation of Prussian absolutism
1. Frederick William I encouraged Prussian militarism and created the best army in Europe plus an efficient bureaucracy
2. The nobility—the Junker class—became the military elite

III. The development of Russia
A. The Vikings and the Kievan principality
1. Eastern Slavs moved into Russia between the fifth and ninth centuries
2. Slavic-Viking settlements grew up in the ninth century
3. The Vikings unified the eastern Slavs politically and religiously, creating a ruling dynasty and accepting Eastern Orthodox Christianity for themselves and the Slavs
4. A strong aristocracy (the boyars) and a free peasantry made it difficult to strengthen the state

B. The Mongol yoke and the rise of Moscow
1. The Mongols conquered the Kievan state in the thirteenth century and unified it under their rule
2. The Mongols used Russian aristocrats as their servants
   a. The princes of Moscow served the Mongols well and became the hereditary great princes
   b. Ivan I served the Mongols while using his wealth and power to strengthen the principality of Moscow

      c. Ivan III stopped acknowledging the Mongol Khan and assumed the headship of Orthodox Christianity

C. Tsar and people to 1689
1. By 1505, the prince of Moscow—the tsar—had emerged as the divine-right ruler of all the lands of the eastern Slavs
2. The tsars and the boyars struggled over who would rule the state, and the tsars won
3. Ivan the Terrible was an autocratic tsar who expanded Muscovy and further reduced the power of the boyars
    a. He murdered leading boyars and confiscated their estates
    b. Many peasants fled his rule to the newly conquered territories, forming groups called Cossacks
    c. Businessmen and artisans were bound to their towns and jobs
4. The Time of Troubles (1598-1613) was a period characterized by internal struggles and invasions
    a. There was no heir
    b. Cossack bands slaughtered many nobles and officials
    c. Swedish and Polish armies invaded
5. Michael Romanov was elected tsar by the nobles (1613), and he re-established tsarist autocracy
6. The Romanovs brought about the total enserfment of the people
7. A split in the church over religious reforms led to mass protests by the peasants, and the church became dependent on the state for its authority

D. The reforms of Peter the Great
1. Peter wished to create a strong army for protection and expansion
    a. He forced the nobility to serve in the army or in the civil service
    b. He created schools to train technicians for his army
2. Army and government became more efficient and powerful as an interlocking military-civilian bureaucracy was created and staffed by talented people
3. Russian peasant life under Peter became more harsh
4. Modest territorial expansion took place under Peter, and Russia became a European Great Power
5. Peter borrowed many western ideas

IV. Absolutism and the Baroque
A. Baroque art and music
1. Baroque art fulfilled the needs of the Catholic Church and the absolute rulers
2. In painting, the baroque is best seen in the work of Rubens; in music, it reached its height with Bach
B. Palaces and power

    1. Architecture played an important role in politics because it was used by kings to enhance their image and awe their subjects

    2. The royal palace was the favorite architectural expression of absolutist power

    3. The dominant artistic style of the age of absolutism was baroque—a dramatic and emotional style

C. Royal cities and urban planning

    1. The new St. Petersburg is an excellent example of the tie among architecture, politics, and urban development

       a. Peter the Great wanted to create a modern, baroque city from which to rule Russia

       b. The city became a showplace for the tsar paid for by the Russian nobility and built by the peasants

D. The growth of St. Petersburg

    1. During the eighteenth century, St. Petersburg became one of the world's largest and most influential cities

    2. The new city was modern or "baroque" in its layout and design

    3. All social groups, including the peasants, paid heavily in the construction of the city

    4. Tsarina Elizabeth and architect Rastrelli crowned the city with great palaces

REVIEW QUESTIONS

Q-1. What were the reasons for the re-emergence of serfdom in eastern Europe in the early modern period (1400-1650)? Build a case for either an economic or a political explanation.

Q-2. In western Europe the conflict between the king and his vassals resulted in gains for the common man. Why did this not happen in eastern Europe?

Q-3. Why would the reign of the Great Elector be regarded as "the most crucial constitutional struggle in Prussian history for hundreds of years"? What did he do to increase royal authority? Who were the losers?

Q-4. Prussia has traditionally been considered one of the most militaristic states in Europe. How do you explain this development? Who or what was responsible?

Q-5. How did war (the Thirty Years' War) and invasion (by the Ottoman Turks) help the Habsburgs consolidate power?

Q-6. What was the Pragmatic Sanction and why were the Hungarian and Bohemian princes opposed to it?

Q-7. What role, if any, did war play in the evolution of absolutism in eastern Europe?

Q-8. Use the following to illustrate the relationship between baroque architecture and European absolutism: St. Petersburg, Karlesruhe, Upper and Lower Belvedere, Schönbrunn. Was it simply that "every fool likes his own hat"? Explain.

Q-9. It has been said that the common man benefited from the magnificant medieval cathedrals as much as the princes. Can the same be said about the common man and the building projects of the absolute kings and princes? Explain.

Q-10. Discuss the influence of the Vikings and the Mongols on Russian history.

Q-11. Why do you think the history of Russia is more a history of servitude than of freedom? How do you account for the enormous amount of violence in Russian history?

Q-12. Why was territorial expansion "the soul of tsardom"?

Q-13. Trace the fortunes and political power of the boyar class in Russia from the time of the Kievan state to the death of Peter the Great.

Q-14. Peter the Great of Russia and Frederick William I of Prussia are often viewed as heroes and "reformers" in the histories of their own countries. How valid is this assessment in terms of the peasants of the early eighteenth century?

STUDY-REVIEW EXERCISES

Identify the following people and explain their importance.

Bartolomeo Rastrelli

Suleiman the Magnificent

Frederick the Great

Charles VI of Austria

Jenghiz Khan

Ivan the Terrible

J. S. Bach

Peter the Great

Frederick William the Great Elector

Ivan III

Peter Paul Rubens

<u>*Define*</u> *the following key concepts and terms.*

absolutism

baroque

Prussian Junkers

Hohenzollern

kholops

Romanov

boyar

autocracy

Vikings

Hapsburg

Mongol Yoke

Pragmatic Sanction

<u>*Explain*</u> *and describe baroque architecture by referring to the pictures in the textbook.*

<u>*Explain*</u> *what the following events were, who participated in them, and why they were important.*

Building of the Winter Palace of St. Petersburg

Siege of Vienna, 1683

War of the Austrian Succession

Time of Troubles

Battle of Poltava

Test your understanding of the chapter by answering the following questions.

1. He was the founder of the new Russian city on the coast of the Baltic Sea.

    _____

2. He is the unsurpassed master of baroque music. _____
3. After 1500, serfdom in eastern Europe *increased/decreased*.
4. The Ottoman Turkish leader who captured Vienna in 1529 was

    _____ .

5. In the struggle between the Hungarian aristocrats and the Austrian Habsburgs, the Hungarian aristocrats *maintained/lost* their traditional privileges.
6. This Prussian monarch doubled the size of Prussia in 1740 by taking Silesia from

    Austria. _____
7. Number the following events in correct chronological order.

    _____ The election of the first Romanov tsar

    _____ The establishment of the Kievan state

    _____ The Time of Troubles

    _____ Invasion by the Mongols

    _____ The building of St. Petersburg

    _____ The battle of Poltava

8. The monarchs of eastern Europe in the sixteenth and seventeenth centuries were generally *stronger/weaker* than the kings of western Europe.

MULTIPLE-CHOICE QUESTIONS

1. The unifiers and first rulers of the Russians were the
    a. Mongols.
    b. Turks.
    c. Romanovs.
    d. Vikings.

2. By the seventeenth century, in Russia commercial activity, manufacturing, and mining were owned or controlled by the
    a. rising urban capitalists.
    b. Cossacks.
    c. Tsar.

3. The monarchs of eastern Europe used their increased power after 1600 to do all of the following *except*
    a. impose taxes without consent.
    b. maintain standing armies.
    c. control the treatment of serfs by their lords.
    d. conduct foreign affairs independently.

4. The principality called the "sandbox of the Holy Roman Empire" was
    a. Brandenburg-Prussia.
    b. Hungary.
    c. Sweden.
    d. Austria.

5. Ivan the Terrible
    a. failed to conquer Kazan.
    b. was afraid to call himself tsar.
    c. monopolized a great deal of mining and business activity.
    d. abolished the system of compulsory service for noble landlords.

6. Peter the Great's reforms included all but which one of the following?
    a. Compulsory education away from home for the higher classes
    b. A lessening of the burdens of serfdom for Russian peasants
    c. A fourteen-rank merit-system bureaucracy
    d. A strengthening of the Russian army

7. The dominant artistic style of the seventeenth and early eighteenth centuries was

a. Gothic.
b. Romantic.
c. impressionistic.
d. baroque.

8. The noble landowners of Prussia were known as
    a. Boyars.
    b. Junkers.
    c. Vikings.
    d. Electors.

9. Apparently the most important reason for the return to serfdom in eastern Europe from about 1500 to 1650 was
    a. political.
    b. economic.
    c. military.
    d. religious.

10. The eastern European nobility gained power from struggling monarchs during the late Middle Ages because of
    a. the many wars that occurred during the period.
    b. disputed royal successions.
    c. the absence of a well-developed concept of sovereignty.
    d. all of the above

11. After the disastrous defeat of the Czech nobility by the Habsburgs at the battle of White Mountain in 1618, the
    a. old Czech nobility in great numbers accepted Catholicism.
    b. majority of Czech noble land was given to soldiers who had fought for the Habsburgs.
    c. conditions of the enserfed peasantry improved.
    d. Czech nobility continued their struggle effectively for many years.

12. After the Thirty Years' War and the creation of a large standing army, Austria turned its attention to control of
    a. northern Italy.
    b. Prussia.
    c. Hungary.
    d. Poland.

13. The result of the Hungarian nobility's struggle against Habsburg oppression was that

a. they suffered a fate similar to the Czech nobility.
b. they gained a great deal of autonomy compared with the Austrian and Bohemian nobility.
c. they won their independence.
d. their efforts were inconclusive.

14. In 1742, as a result of the War of Austrian Succession, Maria Theresa
    a. was forced to abdicate.
    b. was forced to give up the province of Silesia to Prussia.
    c. gained Prussian possessions.
    d. was unable to keep Hungary in the Austrian Empire.

15. The Viking invaders in early Russian history were principally interested in
    a. controlling vast new lands politically.
    b. spreading their religion.
    c. establishing and controlling commercial interests.
    d. none of the above

16. The Muscovite princes gained their initial power through
    a. services rendered to the Vikings.
    b. strategic marriages.
    c. services rendered to the Mongols.
    d. none of the above

17. The rise of the Russian monarchy was largely a response to the external threat of the
    a. French monarchy.
    b. Asiatic Mongols.
    c. Prussian monarchy.
    d. English monarchy.

18. The Time of Troubles was caused by
    a. a dispute in the line of succession.
    b. Turkish invasions.
    c. Mongol invasions.
    d. severe crop failures resulting in starvation and disease.

19. In order to strengthen the Russian military, Peter the Great
    a. made the nobility serve in the civil administration or army for life.
    b. established schools and universities to train Russian youth.
    c. searched out and brought talented foreigners into his service.
    d. all of the above

20. The real losers in the growth of eastern Europe absolutism were the
    a. peasants.
    b. peasants and middle classes.
    c. nobility.
    d. nobility and the clergy.

GEOGRAPHY

1. Show on the outline map the area covered by the principality of Moscow in 1300. Was the principality of Moscow an important state at that time?

2. Shade in with different colors the territories acquired by the principality of Moscow from 1300 to 1689. How successful was Moscow in expanding before 1689?

3. Shade in the acquisitions of Peter the Great. How do these acquisitions suggest that Russia was becoming more western and European and less eastern and Asiatic during Peter the Great's reign?

4. Using your knowledge of Russian geography and the information in the textbook, explain how Russia's history has been influenced by its geography. For example, does Russia's geographic setting contribute to its absolutism?

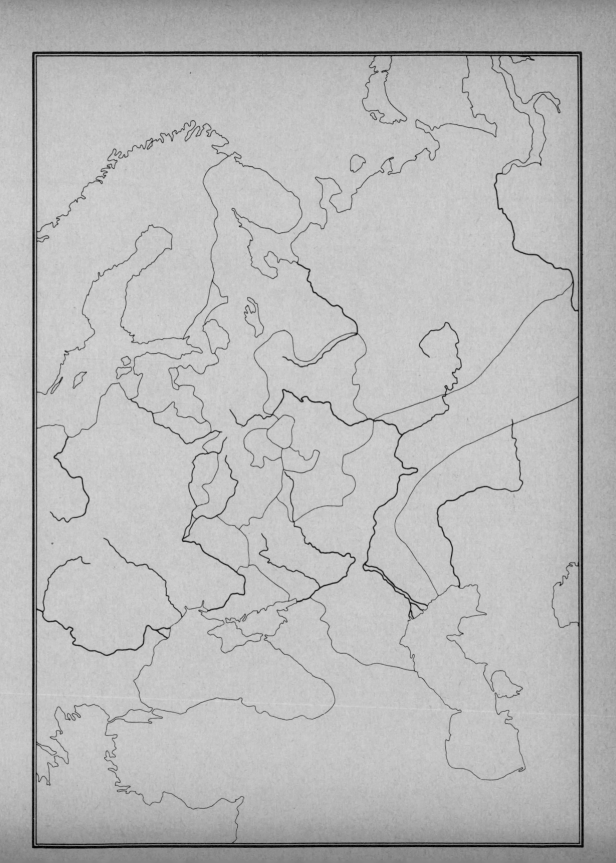

5. Looking at Map 17.1 in the text, identify the three territorial parts of the Habsburg (Austrian) state and explain how they came to be united. Do these geographic facts help explain the development of absolutism and militarism in Austria?

UNDERSTANDING HISTORY THROUGH READING AND THE ARTS

For centuries the Moscow Kremlin was the axis of Russian culture—that is, it was the place where works of great historical and artistic significance were amassed. Many examples of painting and applied art of the Kremlin are discussed and illustrated in *Treasures of the Kremlin** published by the Metropolitan Museum of Art, New York (1979). See also, T. Froncek, ed., *The Horizon Book of the Arts of Russia* (1970), and G. Hamilton, *The Art and Architecture of Russia* (1975). For the greatest architectural symbol of absolutism in France the student should turn to G. Walton, *Louis XIV's Versailles** (1986).

Baroque music, the dominant musical style in the age of absolutism, was often written for a particular monarch or princely court. The mathematical and harmonic emphasis of baroque music and its aristocratic patronage are illustrated in the six Brandenburg Concertos by Johann Sebastian Bach, written for the margrave of Brandenburg in the early eighteenth century, and in George F. Handel's *Water Music*, written for George I of England at about the same time. Both of these are available on numerous recordings. For the history of baroque music see M. F. Bukofzer, *Music in the Baroque Era* (1947).

PROBLEMS FOR FURTHER INVESTIGATION

The personality and reign of Tsar Peter the Great have generated considerable controversy for many years. Many ideas for further research can be found in M. Raeff, *Peter the Great* (rev. ed., 1972), and in L. J. Oliva, ed., *Russia and the West from Peter to Khrushev* (1965).

*Available in paperback.

CHAPTER 18

TOWARD A NEW WORLD-VIEW

CHAPTER OBJECTIVES

After reading and studying this chapter you should be able to answer the following questions:

Q-1. Why did the world-view of the educated classes change from a primarily religious one to one that was primarily secular and scientific?
Q-2. How did this new outlook on life affect society and politics?

CHAPTER SYNOPSIS

This chapter shows how the educated classes moved from a world-view that was basically religious to a world-view that was primarily secular in the course of the seventeenth and eighteenth centuries. The development of scientific knowledge was the key cause of this intellectual change. This change was momentous because it laid the groundwork for both enlightened absolutism and the spirit of revolution.

Until about 1500, scientific thought reflected the Aristotelian-medieval world-view, which taught that a motionless earth was at the center of a universe made up of planets and stars in ten crystal spheres. These and many other beliefs showed that science was primarily a branch of religion. Beginning with Copernicus, who taught that the earth revolved around the sun, Europeans slowly began to reject Aristotelian-medieval scientific thought. They developed a new conception of a universe based on natural laws, not on a personal God. Isaac Newton, standing on the shoulders of earlier mathematicians, physicists, and astronomers, formulated the great scientific synthesis: the law of universal gravitation. Newton's work was the culminating point of the scientific revolution.

The chapter examines the causes of the scientific revolution, its relationship to religion, and its impact on nonscientific thought. The new science was more important for intellectual development than for economic activity or everyday life, for above all it promoted critical thinking. Nothing was to be accepted on faith; everything was to be submitted to the rational, scientific way of thinking. This critical examination of everything, from religion and education to war and politics, was the program of the Enlightenment and the accomplishment of the philosophes, a group of thinkers who propagandized the new world-view across Europe and the North American colonies.

The philosophes were reformers, not revolutionaries. Yet reform of society from the top down—that is, by the absolute monarchs through what is called "enlightened absolutism"—proved to be impossible because the enlightened monarchs could not ignore the demands of their conservative nobilities. In the end, it was revolution, not enlightened absolutism, that changed and reformed society.

STUDY OUTLINE

I.   The scientific revolution: the origin of the modern world
   A.   Historians now recognize that the history of science and the history of society must be brought together
   B.   Scientific thought in 1500
      1.   Until the early 1500s, European ideas about the universe were based on Aristotelian-medieval ideas
         a.   Central to this view was the belief in a motionless earth fixed at the center of the universe
         b.   Around the earth moved ten crystal spheres
         c.   Beyond the spheres was heaven
      2.   Aristotle's scheme fit into Christianity because it made human beings the center of the universe and established a home for God
   C.   The Copernican hypothesis
      1.   Copernicus, a Polish astronomer, claimed that the earth revolved around the sun—that the sun was the center of the universe
      2.   This heliocentric theory was a great departure from the medieval system
      3.   Copernicus's theory created doubts about traditional religion
   D.   From Tycho Brahe to Galileo
      1.   Brahe set the stage for the modern study of astronomy by building an observatory and collecting data
      2.   His assistant, Kepler, formulated three laws of planetary motion that proved the precise relationships among planets in a sun-centered universe
      3.   Galileo discovered the laws of motion using the experimental method— the cornerstone of modern science

      4. Galileo was tried by the Inquisition for heresy and forced to recant his views

  E. Newton's synthesis

      1. Newton integrated the astronomy of Copernicus and Kepler with the physics of Galileo

         a. He formulated a set of mathematical laws to explain motion and mechanics

         b. The key feature in his synthesis was the law of universal gravitation

      2. Henceforth, the universe could be explained through mathematics

  F. Causes of the scientific revolution

      1. Medieval universities provided the framework for the new science

      2. The Renaissance stimulated science by rediscovering ancient mathematics

      3. The navigational problems of sea voyages generated scientific research

      4. New ways of obtaining knowledge improved scientific methods

         a. Bacon advocated empirical, experimental research

         b. Descartes stressed mathematics and deductive reasoning

      5. After the Reformation the Catholic church discouraged science while Protestantism tended to favor it

  G. Some consequences of the scientific revolution

      1. There arose a scientific community whose primary goal was the expansion of knowledge

      2. A modern scientific method arose that rejected traditional knowledge and logic

      3. Because the link between pure science and applied technology was weak, the scientific revolution was more an intellectual than material revolution

II. The Enlightenment

  A. Enlightenment ideas

      1. Natural science and reason can explain all aspects of life

      2. The scientific method can explain the laws of human society

      3. It is possible to create better societies and better people

  B. The emergence and results of the Enlightenment

      1. The French philosophes popularized Enlightenment ideas

      2. The Enlightenment and the scientific revolution were directly connected— the former popularized the latter

      3. The Enlightenment encouraged the growth of uncertainty about religious truth, cultural superiority, and the role of experience in learning

  C. The philosophes and their ideas

      1. The philosophes acquainted the elite of western Europe with the ideas of the new world-view

      2. They were committed to the reformation of society and humanity, although they often had to cloak attacks on church and state in satire

      a. Montesquieu used social satire to criticize existing practices

      b. He proposed that power be divided and shared by all classes by adopting the principle that "power checks power"

      c. Voltaire challenged traditional Catholic theology and exhibited a characteristic philosophe belief in a distant God who let human affairs take their own course

      d. Diderot and d'Alembert edited a great encyclopedia that examined all of human knowledge and attempted to teach people how to think critically and rationally

         (1) The *Encyclopedia* exalted science and knowledge over religion

         (2) As a summary of the Enlightenment world-view it was extremely influential

D. The later Enlightenment built rigid and dogmatic systems

    1. D'Holbach argued that humans were completely controlled by outside forces

    2. Hume's skepticism argued that the mind can produce only empirical knowledge

    3. Rousseau attacked rationalism and civilization and claimed that children needed to be protected from society

    4. His *Social Contract* centered on the idea of the general will of the people

E. The social setting of the Enlightenment

    1. Enlightenment ideas were spread by salons of the upper classes

    2. The salons were often presided over by women like the brilliant Geoffrin and Deffand

III. The evolution of the "Greats": absolutism

A. Many believed that "enlightened" reform would come by way of "enlightened" monarchs

B. Frederick II and Catherine II of Russia

    1. Frederick II used the War of the Austrian Succession to expand Prussia into a Great Power

    2. Renewed conflict in 1756 (the Seven Years' War, 1756-1763) saw Prussia aligned against Austria and Russia

    3. Frederick allowed religious freedom and promoted education

    4. He reformed the legal system and bureaucracy and encouraged agriculture and industry to improve the life of his subjects

    5. Catherine imported Western culture to Russia and corresponded with the philosophes

      a. Her ideas about reforming serfdom changed after Pugachev's uprising in 1773, however, and she restricted the serfs even more

      b. Catherine also succeeded in annexing Poland

C. Absolutism in France and Austria

1. With the duke of Orleans and the Parliament of Paris the French nobility enjoyed a revival of power following the death of Louis XIV, and the monarchy lost the power of taxation
2. The French minister began the restoration of royal absolutism under Louis XV
3. With the reign of Louis XVI royal absolutism once again declined and noble power revived
4. The Austrian emperor Joseph II was a dedicated reformer who abolished serfdom, taxed all his subjects equally, and granted religious freedom
5. Joseph failed, however, because of aristocratic opposition; his reforms were short-lived

D. An overall evaluation
1. In France, the rise of judicial and aristocratic opposition combined with a public educated in liberalism put absolutism on the defensive
2. In eastern Europe, however, the results of "enlightened absolutism" were modest and therefore absolutism remained entrenched
3. By combining state-building with the Enlightenment these absolutists underscored the long tradition of the role of the state in society

REVIEW QUESTIONS

Q-1. Contrast the old Aristotelian-medieval world-view with that of the new science of the sixteenth and seventeenth centuries. What were the contributions of Copernicus, Brahe, Kepler, Galileo, and Newton? What is meant by Newton's "synthesis"?

Q-2. How did the new scientific theory and discoveries alter the concept of God and religion? Did science, in fact, come to dictate humanity's concept of God?

Q-3. The author tells us that Copernicus hit upon "an old Greek idea being discussed in Renaissance Italy." How does this help explain the origins of the new science?

Q-4. Discuss the origins and the momentum of the scientific revolution in terms of (a) its own "internal logic" and (b) external and nonscientific causes.

Q-5. How did Bacon and Descartes contribute to the development of the modern scientific method?

Q-6. Did the Catholic and Protestant churches retard or foster scientific investigation? Explain.

Q-7. What are the consequences of the rise of modern science?

Q-8. Were the philosophes interested in popular rule by or the political education of the people? Were their dreams of reform from above utopian?

Q-9. What was the effect of Catherine's reign on (a) the Russian nobility, (b) the Russian serfs, and (c) the position of Russia in the European balance of power?

Q-10. Describe the nature of the power struggle in France following the death of Louis XIV in 1715.

Q-11. Discuss: "Joseph II [of Austria] was a heroic but colossal failure."

Q-12. Since the enlightened absolutists tried but failed to make life better for commen men and women, who were the real enemies of the people? Why was the system of absolutism resistant to change?

STUDY-REVIEW EXERCISES

Define the following key concepts and terms.

deductive reasoning

rationalism

the idea of progress

skepticism

Parlement of Paris

Enlightenment

enlightened absolutism

Aristotelian world-view

empirical method

Identify each of the following and give its significance.

Gresham College

Diderot

Bayle

Kepler

Galileo

Newton

Montesquieu

Voltaire

Copernicus

Brahe

Catherine the Great

Frederick the Great

Louis XV

Joseph II

philosophes

Bacon

Descartes

D'Holbach

<u>Explain</u> the general significance of the following books and indicate how these works and their authors influenced one another.

On the Revolutions of the Heavenly Spheres, Copernicus

New Astronomy or Celestial Physics, Kepler

Two New Sciences, Galileo

Principia, Newton

<u>Explain</u> the new ideas of the following books introduced into Englightenment society and some of the consequences of these ideas.

Conversations on the Plurality of Worlds of 1686, Fontenelle

Historical and Critical Dictionary, Bayle

The Spirit of the Laws, Montesquieu

Essay Concerning Human Understanding, Locke

Philosophical Dictionary, Voltaire

Encyclopedia: The Rational Dictionary of the Sciences, the Arts, and the Crafts, D'Alembert, Diderot

Social Contract, Rousseau

Test your understanding of the chapter by answering the following questions.

1. According to Aristotle, the sublunar world was made up of four elements: air,

   fire, _____, and _____ .
2. Copernicus *did/did not* attempt to disprove the existence of God.
3. Galileo claimed that *motion/rest* is the natural state of all objects.

4. The key feature in Newton's synthesis was the law of _____ .
5. In the medieval universities, science emerged as a branch of

   _____ .
6. The method of finding latitude came out of study and experimentation in the

   country of _____ .
7. The idea of "progress" *was/was not* widespread in the Middle Ages.
8. In the seventeenth and eighteenth centuries a close link between pure (theoretical) science and applied technology *did/did not* exist.

9. A _____ is one who believes that nothing can ever be known beyond all doubt.

10. Voltaire believed that _____ was history's greatest man because he gave humanity truth.
11. Overall, Joseph II of Austria *succeeded/failed* as an enlightened monarch.

MULTIPLE-CHOICE QUESTIONS

1. Catherine the Great did all but which one of the following?
   a. Annexed part of Poland
   b. Freed the Russian serfs
   c. Allowed limited religious tolerations
   d. Supported the philosophes of France

2. "Enlightened" monarchs believed in
   a. reform.
   b. democracy.
   c. urbanization.
   d. all of the above

3. Geoffrin and Deffand were
   a. scientific writers.
   b. religious leaders.
   c. "enlightened" women.
   d. leaders of the serf uprising.

4. The philosophes were
   a. mainly university professors.
   b. generally hostile to monarchial government.
   c. enthusiastic supporters of the Catholic church.
   d. satirist writers who wished to reform society and humanity.

5. The social setting of the Enlightenment
   a. excluded women.
   b. was characterized by poverty and boredom.
   c. was dominated by government officials.
   d. was characterized by witty and intelligent conversation.

6. Catherine the Great
   a. believed the philosophes were dangerous revolutionaries.
   b. freed the serfs to satisfy Diderot.
   c. increased the size of the Russian Empire.
   d. established a strong constitutional monarchy.

7. According to medieval thought, the center of the universe was the
   a. sun.
   b. earth.
   c. moon.
   d. heaven.

8. The Aristotelian world-view lasted two thousand years because
   a. it provided understandable answers for what people could see happening around them.
   b. its ideas were workable within the realm of Christian theology.
   c. its ideas placed human beings at the center of the universe.
   d. all of the above

9. Copernicus' theory of a sun-centered universe
   a. suggested the universe was small and closed.
   b. challenged the idea that crystal spheres moved the stars around the earth.
   c. ruled out the belief that the worlds of heaven and earth were different.
   d. suggested an enormous and possibly infinite universe.

10. The first astronomer to prove his theories through the use of mathematical equations was
   a. Galileo.
   b. Johannes Kepler.
   c. Tycho Brahe.
   d. Isaac Newton.

11. D'Holbach, Hume, and Rousseau are examples of the later Enlightenment trend toward
   a. rigid systems.
   b. social satire.
   c. religion.
   d. the idea of absolutism.

12. The French philosopher who rejected his contemporaries and whose writings influenced the romantic period was
   a. Rousseau.
   b. Voltaire.
   c. Diderot.
   d. Condorcet.

13. The gathering ground for many who wished to discuss the ideas of the French Enlightenment was the
   a. salon.
   b. lecture hall.
   c. palace at Versailles.
   d. the University of Paris.

14. Frederick II was considered an enlightened despot because he
    a. freed the serfs.
    b. wrote poetry, allowed religious freedom, and improved the legal and bureaucratic systems.
    c. kept the Junkers in a dominant position socially and politically.
    d. avoided war.

15. Catherine the Great of Russia hardened her position on serfdom after the _____ rebellion.
    a. Pugachev
    b. Moscow
    b. Polish
    c. "Five Year"

16. After Louis XIV's death,
    a. the nobility made a drastic comeback in power.
    b. the nobility secured judicial positions in the Parlements.
    c. the French government struggled with severe economic difficulties.
    d. all of the above

17. He used the War of the Austrian Succession to expand Prussia into a great power.
    a. Joseph II
    b. Frederick II
    c. William I
    d. None of the above

18. The imperialist aggressiveness of Prussia, Austria, and Russia led to the disappearance of this eastern European kingdom from the map after 1795.
    a. Hungary
    b. Sweden
    c. Brandenburg
    d. Poland

19. Francis Bacon's great contribution to scientific methodology was
    a. the geocentric theory.
    b. the notion of logical speculation.
    c. the philosophy of empiricism.
    d. analytic geometry.

20. This man set the stage for the modern study of astronomy by building an observatory and collecting data.
   a. Darwin
   b. Hume
   c. Newton
   d. Brahe

UNDERSTANDING HISTORY THROUGH READING AND THE ARTS

The upsurge of creativity in the arts in the seventeenth and eighteenth centuries, which was greatly influenced by the Enlightenment, is known as the age of the baroque. The meaning of this highly creative and dynamic style and the achievements of its great artists are discussed in M. Kitson, *The Age of the Baroque* (1966). See also Chapter 6 in N. Pevsner, *An Outline of European Architecture* (7th ed., 1963). Few artists captured English life as well as did the painter Hogarth, whose *Rake's Progress* and *Harlot's Progress* point to the consequences of moral decay. Hogarth's paintings can be seen and studied in W. Gaunt, *The World of William Hogarth* (1978), and D. Bindman, *Hogarth** (1981).

The two greatest philosophes of the age of Enlightenment were Rousseau and Voltaire. Rousseau's ideas on education and natural law are interestingly set forth in his *Emile*, and Voltaire's most-praised work is *Candide*, a funny and sometimes bawdy parody on eighteenth-century life and thought. Much of the new fiction writing of the eighteenth century reflects, often in satire, the spirit of the new world-view—Jonathan Swift, *Gulliver's Travels*; Daniel Defoe, *Moll Flanders*; and Henry Fielding, *Tom Jones*, are just a few. In Germany, the *Sturm und Drang* (storm and stress) movement, which produced works such as Lessing's *Nathan the Wise* which stressed a universal religion, was devoted to the ideas of the Enlightenment and romanticism.

PROBLEMS FOR FURTHER INVESTIGATION

Those interested in pursuing the topic of the Enlightenment will want to begin with two books that set forth some of the major issues and schools of interpretation on the subject: B. Tierney, et al., eds., *Enlightenment—The Age of Reason** (1967), and R. Wines, ed., *Enlightened Despotism** (1967).

Why was it not until the seventeenth century that rational science emerged? What has been the relationship between science and religion in Western society? What ideas did Darwin and modern biology draw from the Scientific Revolution of 1500-1800? These are just a few of the questions asked by scholars of the subject. Begin your

*Available in paperback.

investigation with a general reference and bibliography such as G. Sarton, *Introduction to the History of Science* (1927-1948, 5 vols.), and L. Thorndike, *History of Magic and Experimental Science* (1923-1958). On particular figures in science see F. S. Taylor, *Galileo and the Freedom of Thought* (1938), A. Armitage, *Copernicus, the Founder of Modern Astronomy* (1938), M. Casoar, *Johannes Kepler* (1959, trans. C. Hellman), L. T. More, *Isaac Newton* (1934), and I. Cohen, *Franklin and Newton* (1956).

READING WITH UNDERSTANDING
EXERCISE 4

LEARNING TO CLASSIFY INFORMATION ACCORDING TO SEQUENCE

As you know, a great deal of historical information is classified by sequence, in which things follow each other in time. This kind of *sequential order* is also known as *time order* or *chronological order*.

Attention to time sequence is important in the study of history for at least two reasons.

1. It helps us organize historical information effectively.

2. It promotes historical understanding. If the student knows the order in which events happened, he or she can think intelligently about questions of cause and effect. The student can begin to evaluate conflicting interpretations.

Since time sequences are essential in historical study, the authors have placed a number of timelines in the text to help you organize the historical information.

Two Fallacies Regarding Time Sequences

One common fallacy is often known by the famous Latin phrase *post hoc, ergo propter hoc:* "after this, therefore because of this." This fallacy assumes that one happening that follows another *must* be caused by the first happening. Obviously, some great development (such as the Protestant Reformation) could come after another (the Italian Renaissance) without being caused by it. *Causal relationships must be demonstrated, not simply assumed on the basis of the "after this, therefore because of this" fallacy.*

A second common, if old-fashioned, fallacy assumes that time sequences are composed only of political facts with precise data. But in considering social, intellectual, and economic developments, historians must often speak with less chronological exactitude—in terms of decades or even centuries, for example. Yet they still use time sequences, and students of history must recognize them. For example, did you realize that the sections on "The Scientific Revolution" and "The Enlightenment" in Chapter 18 are very conscientious about time sequence, even though they do not deal with political facts?

Exercise

Reread the large section in Chapter 18 on "The Scientific Revolution" with an eye for dates and sequential order. Then take a sheet of notebook paper and with the book open make a "Timeline for the Scientific Revolution." Pick out at least a dozen important events and put them in the time sequence, with a word or two to explain the significance when possible.

Suggestion: Do not confine yourself solely to specific events with specific dates. Also, integrate some items from the subsection on the causes of the Scientific Revolution into the sequence. You may find that constructing timelines helps you organize your study.

After you have completed your timeline, compare it with the one on the following page, which shows how one of the authors of the text did this assignment.

Timeline on the Scientific Revolution

(1300-1500)	Renaissance stimulates development of mathematics
early 1500s	Aristotle's ideas on movement and universe still dominant
1543	Copernicus publishes *On the Revolution of the Heavenly Spheres*
1572, 1577	New star and comet create more doubts about traditional astronomy
1546-1601	Tycho Brache—famous astronomer, creates mass of observations
1571-1630	Johannes Kepler—his three laws prove Copernican theory and demolish Aristotle's beliefs
1589	Galileo Galilei (1564-1642) named professor of mathematics
1610	Galileo Galilei studies moon with telescope and writes of experience
1561-1626	Francis Bacon—English scientific enthusiast, advocates experimental (inductive) method
1596-1650	Rene Descartes—French philosopher, discovers analytical geometry in 1619 and advocates theoretical (deductive) method
to about 1630	All religious authorities oppose Copernican theory
about 1632	Galileo tried by papal inquisition
1622	Royal Society of London founded—brings scientists and practical men together
1687	Isaac Newton publishes his *Principia*, synthesizing existing knowledge around idea of universal gravitation
to late 1700s	Consequences of Scientific Revolution primarily intellectual, not economic

CHAPTER 19

THE EXPANSION OF EUROPE IN THE
EIGHTEENTH CENTURY

CHAPTER OBJECTIVES

After reading and studying this chapter you should be able to answer the following questions:

Q-1. How did the European economy expand and change in the eighteenth century?
Q-2. What were the causes of this expansion?
Q-3. How did these changes affect people and their work?

CHAPTER SYNOPSIS

How did our "modern" world begin? This chapter discusses the important economic and demographic changes of the eighteenth century, which led up to the Industrial Revolution. It also prepares us for understanding the life of ordinary people in the eighteenth century, which is the subject of the following chapter.

The chapter covers four important and interrelated subjects. First, the centuries-old open-field system of agricultural production, a system that was both inefficient and unjust, is described. This system was gradually transformed into a more productive system of capitalistic farming, first in the Low Countries and then in England. Some English peasants suffered in the process, but on the whole the changes added up to a highly beneficial agricultural revolution. The second topic is the explosive growth of European population in the eighteenth century. This growth, still imperfectly understood, was probably due largely to the disappearance of the plague and to new and better foods, such as the potato. Doctors and organized medicine played a very minor role in the improvements in health. Third, the chapter discusses the movement of manufacturing from urban shops to cottages in the countryside. Rural families worked there as units in the new domestic system, which provided employment for many in the growing population. The domestic system was particularly effective in the textile industry, which this chapter examines in detail.

Finally, the chapter shows how the mercantilist economic philosophy of the time resulted in world wars for trade and colonies. Mercantilism also led to the acquisition of huge markets for British manufactured goods, especially cloth. The demand from these new markets fostered the continued growth of the domestic system and put pressure on it. This eventually led to important inventions and the development of the more efficient factory system. Thus the modern world was born. It is important to look for the interrelatedness of these changes and to keep in mind that it was in only one country, Great Britain, that all of these forces were fully at work.

STUDY OUTLINE

I. Agriculture and the land
    A. The hazards of an agrarian economy
        1. The agricultural yields in seventeenth-century Europe were not much higher than in ancient Greece
        2. Frequent poor harvests and bad weather led to famine and disease
    B. The open-field system
        1. The open-field system divided the land into a few large fields, which were then cut up into long, narrow strips
        2. The fields were farmed jointly by the community, but a large portion of the arable land was always left fallow
        3. Common lands were set aside for community use
        4. The labor and tax system throughout Europe was unjust, but eastern European peasants suffered the most
        5. By the eighteenth century most peasants in western Europe were free from serfdom and many owned some land
    C. The agricultural revolution of the late seventeenth and eighteenth centuries
        1. Crop rotation eliminated the need for fallowing and broke the old cycle of scarcity; more fodder meant more animals, which meant more food
        2. Enclosure of the open fields to permit crop rotation also meant the disappearance of common land
    D. The leadership of the Low Countries and England
        1. By the middle of the seventeenth century, the Low Countries led in intensive farming
        2. Dutch engineers such as Vermuyden helped England drain its marshes to create more arable land
        3. Population pressure, the growth of towns, and economic freedom in the Low Countries led to agricultural expansion

4. Tull and Townsend in England advocated new crops and new methods

E. The debate over enclosure

1. The fencing of open fields probably did not harm the poor people who lived off the land, as some historians have claimed

2. Enclosure resulted in more, not less, agricultural employment for wage workers

II. The beginning of the population explosion

A. The limitations on population growth up to 1700

1. The traditional checks on growth were famine, disease, and war

2. Quarantine of ports and the victory of the brown rat helped reduce the plague

3. These checks kept Europe's population growth rate fairly low

B. The new pattern of population growth in the eighteenth century

1. The basic cause of population growth was fewer deaths, partly owing to the disappearance of the plague

2. Advances in medicine, such as inoculation against smallpox, did little to reduce the death rate

3. An increase in the food supply meant fewer famines and epidemics

4. The growing population often led to overpopulation and increased rural poverty

III. The growth of cottage industry

A. Rural industry

1. The rural poor took in manufacturing work to supplement their income

2. This cottage industry challenged the monopoly of the urban craft guilds

B. The putting-out system

1. It was based on rural workers producing cloth in their homes for merchant-capitalists, who supplied the raw materials and paid for the finished goods

2. This system reduced the problem of rural unemployment and provided cheap goods

3. England led the way in the conversion from urban to rural textile production

C. The textile industry in England as an example of the putting-out system

1. The English textile industry was a family industry: the women would spin and the men would weave

2. A major problem was that there were not enough spinners to make yarn for the weaver

3. Strained relations often existed between workers and capitalist employers

4. The capitalist found it difficult to control the worker and the quality of the product

IV. Building the Atlantic economy in the eighteenth century

A. Mercantilism and colonial wars

1. Mercantilism is an economic system whereby the state uses a variety of means to regulate the economy
2. The mercantilists claimed that a favorable balance of trade was necessary for the nation's survival
3. The Navigation Acts were a form of economic warfare
   a. They required that goods exported to England be carried mostly on British ships
   b. These acts gave Britain a virtual trade monopoly with its colonies
4. The French quest for power in Europe and North America led to international wars
   a. The loss of the War of the Spanish Succession forced France to cede parts of Canada to Britain
   b. The Seven Years' War was the decisive struggle in the French-British competition for colonial empire, and France ended by losing all its North American possessions; Spain's empire expanded
B. Land and wealth in North America
   1. Colonies helped relieve European poverty and surplus population as settlers eagerly took up farming on the virtually free land
   2. The English mercantilist system benefited American colonists
   3. The population of the North American colonies grew very quickly during the eighteenth century
C. The growth of foreign trade
   1. The English colonists made up for a decline in English trade on the Continent
   2. These colonies also encouraged industrial growth in England
D. Revival in colonial Latin America
   1. Spain's political success was matched by economic involvement in its colonies
   2. In much of Latin America Creole landowners dominated the economy and the Indian population
   3. Compared to North America, racial mixing was more frequent in Spanish America

REVIEW QUESTIONS

Q-1. How did the open-field system work? Why was much of the land left uncultivated while the people sometimes starved?

Q-2. What changes brought the open-field system to an end?

Q-3. Where did the modern agricultural revolution originate? Why?

Q-4. What is meant by "enclosure"? Was this movement a great swindle of the poor by the rich, as some have claimed?

Q-5. Was the dramatic growth of population in the eighteenth century due to a decreasing death rate or an increasing birthrate? Explain.

Q-6. How did the "revolution in the animal kingdom" break the force of the deadly bubonic plague?

Q-7. What improvements in the eighteenth century contributed to the decline of disease and famine?

Q-8. The movement of production from town to country is commonly known as the growth of the domestic or putting-out system. Using textile production as an example, explain how the system worked and why it grew.

Q-9. What were the advantages and disadvantages of the putting-out system for the merchant-capitalist? For the worker?

Q-10. What was mercantilism? How could it have been a cause of war? Of economic growth?

Q-11. How do the careers of English businessmen like Mun and Child illustrate the theory of mercantilism?

Q-12. The eighteenth century witnessed a large number of expensive and drawn-out wars. Who was attempting to alter the balance of power? Were the causes of these wars economic or political?

Q-13. Did the American colonists and the American colonial economy benefit or suffer from the British mercantilistic colonial system?

Q-14. "The Spanish settlers strove to become a genuine European aristocracy, and they largely succeeded." Explain.

Q-15. What was the cause of the Spanish War of Succession and who won?

STUDY-REVEW EXERCISES

Define the following key concepts and terms.

famine foods

common land

open-field system

enclosure

mercantilism

cottage industry

putting-out system

fallow fields

asiento

crop rotation

mestizos

primogeniture

Creole elite

Identify each of the following and give its significance.

the Asiatic brown rat

Jethro Tull

Charles Townsend

Cornelius Vermuyden

Navigation Acts

Treaty of Paris

Peace of Utrecht

spinning jenny

turnips

Explain the following wars in the age of mercantilism by providing the appropriate information.

Name of War	Dates	Participants	Causes	Outcome
Anglo-Dutch wars				

War of the Spanish Succession

War of the Austrian Succession

Seven Years' War

Fill in the blank with the letter of the correct answer.

_____ 1. Disappearance of this encouraged population growth

_____ 2. Agricultural land set aside for general village use

_____ 3. The area with highest average standard of living in the world

_____ 4. After 1763 the major power in India

_____ 5. West African slave trade

_____ 6. Led Europe in agricultural improvement

_____ 7. Products of racial miscegenation

_____ 8. The most important new eighteenth-century food

a. Low Countries
b. mestizos
c. commons
d. Thirty Years' War
e. American colonies
f. potato
g. *asiento*
h. France
i. bubonic plague
j. Britain

MULTIPLE-CHOICE QUESTIONS

1. All but which one of the following is a reason for Dutch agricultural success in the eighteenth century?
   a. The nature of the people themselves
   b. Their excellent teachers, the British
   c. The extensive urbanization of the lowlands
   d. The dense population of the lowlands

2. Which of the following was *not* a shortcoming of the cottage textile industry?
   a. An imbalance between spinning and weaving
   b. Strained labor relations
   c. Difficulty in controlling the quality of the product
   d. Not enough demand for the product

3. All but which one of the following is a characteristic of eighteenth-century economic change?
   a. Increased world trade
   b. The switch from the cottage system of production to the factory system
   c. The creation of more common lands and open fields for production
   d. The increase in both population and food supply

4. The battle in England against the enclosure movement has often been exaggerated. Proof of this is the fact that
   a. no English land at all had been enclosed by 1750.
   b. parliamentary actions after 1760 initiated the enclosure movement.
   c. the proportion of landless laborers was very large after 1830.
   d. enclosure actually created jobs.

5. The agricultural improvements of the mid-eighteenth century were based on the elimination of
   a. livestock farming.
   b. the open-field system.
   c. rotation of fields.
   d. nitrogen-producing plants, such as peas and beans.

6. Which of the following prevented eighteenth-century peasants from gaining a profit on their land?
   a. The combination of oppressive landlords and poor harvests
   b. The plague
   c. The relatively light taxes imposed on them by landlords
   d. Their reliance on crop rotation

7. The mercantilist attitude toward the state was that
   a. the government should regulate the economy.
   b. governmental power should be increased at the expense of private profit.
   c. using governmental economic power to help private interests is unethical.
   d. the economy should be left to operate according to its natural laws.

8. The new farming system consisting of crop rotation and the use of nitrogen-sorting crops caught on quickly in
   a. the Low Countries and England.
   b. Russia.
   c. eastern Europe as a whole.
   d. Scandinavia.

9. The rapid development of Dutch farming was the result of
    a. a dense population.
    b. the increasing number of cities and towns.
    c. an unencumbered political and economic system.
    d. all of the above

10. A fair description of population fluctuation figures before 1700 in Europe would be that the
    a. population was remarkably uniform in its growth.
    b. population increased steadily on account of very young marriages and large families.
    c. population decreased slightly on account of war, famine, and disease.
    d. population grew slowly and erratically.

11. After 1720, the plague did not reappear because of
    a. quarantining in Mediterranean ports.
    b. the practice of isolating carriers of the dread disease.
    c. the invasion of the Asiatic brown rat.
    d. all of the above

12. In the mid-seventeenth century, England's major maritime competitor was
    a. France.
    b. the Netherlands.
    c. Spain.
    d. Denmark.

13. The Seven Years' War (1756-1763) between France and Britain resulted in
    a. British dominance in North America and India.
    b. French dominance in North America and India.
    c. a stalemate.
    d. British dominance only in North America.

14. The slow growth of industry in America during the colonial period was caused by
    a. excessive availability of land and the high cost of labor.
    b. a lack of capital for investment.
    c. a scorn for industry.
    d. none of the above

15. The black-to-white ratio in America by 1774 was
    a. one to four.
    b. one to eight.
    c. one to ten.
    d. one to two.

16. The abundance of land in the American colonies encouraged
    a. increased population through natural increase and immigration.
    b. a higher standard of living.
    c. economic equality.
    d. all of the above

17. Which of the following did not result from the British mercantile system?
    a. It reduced sales on the continent caused by the closing of French markets.
    b. It further exploited British colonial markets.
    c. It balanced and diversified English exports.
    d. It stagnated the British foreign trade economy.

18. The group that used the new farming methods to the fullest in England was
    a. independent farmers.
    b. well-financed, profit-minded tenant farmers.
    c. large landowners.
    d. small landowning wage laborers.

19. The dominant political and economic group in Spanish America was the
    a. Creoles.
    b. Indians.
    c. mestizos.
    d. none of the above

20. The landowners who dominated the economy and the Indian population of Spain's Latin American empire are known as
    a. mestizos.
    b. Creoles.
    c. mercantilists.
    d. warlords.

GEOGRAPHY

1. Locate on the outline map and shade in with different colors the four main European countries that had large holdings in the New World in 1701.

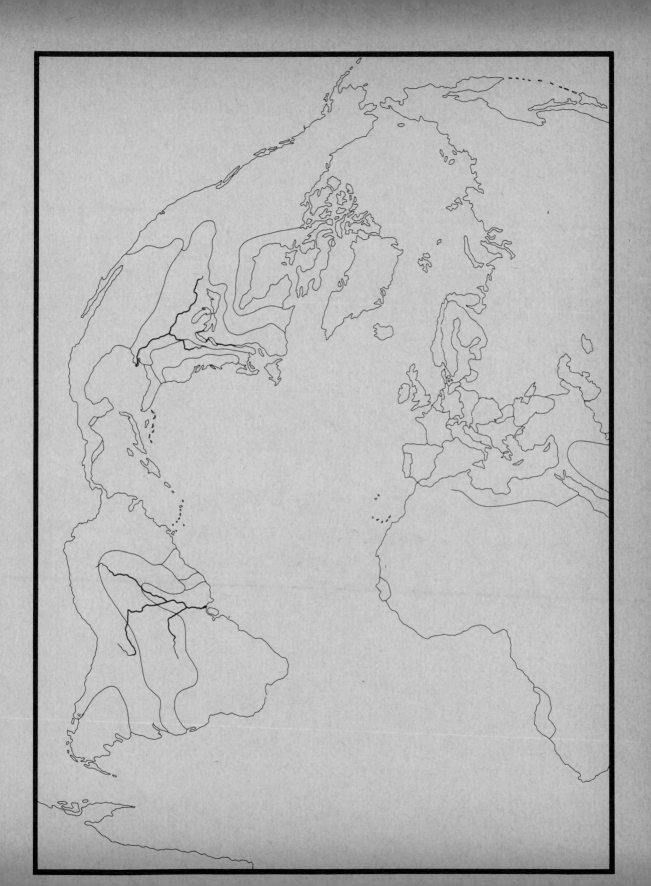

2. Using the same shading scheme, shade in the respective colonial holdings in North and South America, referring to Map 19.1 if necessary. Did the largest colonial holdings go to the largest European countries? Or was a position on the Atlantic the key factor?

3. Redraw the outline map to show territorial changes in the Americas after 1763. Which European country was the big winner? The big loser?

4. Draw in and label arrows that show the main paths of trade in the Atlantic Basin in the eighteenth century. In what ways do these trade routes illustrate the doctrines of mercantilism at work?

UNDERSTANDING HISTORY THROUGH READING AND THE ARTS

The relationship between people and agriculture makes for interesting reading. For more on the agricultural life in Britain the reader should start with J. D. Chambers and G. E. Mingay, *The Agricultural Revolution (1750-1880)* (1966), and on the subject of soil, climate, land tenure, and the routine of peasant life in Russia before 1917 turn to R. Pipes, *Russia Under the Old Regime** (1974, 1982). For Europe in general, F. Huggett, *The Land Question and European Society Since 1650** (1975), presents a picture of how agricultural changes have affected the development of European society.

PROBLEMS FOR FURTHER INVESTIGATION

Was the enclosure a blessing or a great swindle for the British farmer? This question has been debated by historians and social commentators since the movement toward

*Available in paperback.

business agriculture began in sixteenth-century England. The general argument against enclosure was first set out in the sixteenth century by Sir Thomas More, who claimed (in his book *Utopia*) that it resulted in rural unemployment and rural crime. It is the enclosures between 1750 and 1850, however, that are the most controversial. The best contemporary coverage of the debate is G. E. Mingay, *Enclosure and the Small Farmer in the Age of the Industrial Revolution** (1968), which also contains a useful bibliography.

*Available in paperback.

CHAPTER 20

THE LIFE OF THE PEOPLE

CHAPTER OBJECTIVES

After reading and studying this chapter you should be able to answer the following questions:

Q-1. Why did traditional marriage and sex practices begin to change in the late eighteenth century?
Q-2. What was it like to be a child in preindustrial society?
Q-3. How adequate was the diet and health care of the people of the eighteenth century? Were there any signs of improvement?
Q-4. What influence did religion hold in everyday life and what was *pietism*?

CHAPTER SYNOPSIS

Until recently scholars have not been very interested in how men and women lived in preindustrial society. The aspects of everyday life, such as family relations, sex, marriage, health, and religion, took a secondary place in history. As a result, much of our understanding of these subjects is often based on myth rather than on solid historical research and interpretations. This chapter corrects some of the long-standing myths and provides a close look at the life of the people.

Contrary to early belief, for example, it appears that in western Europe the nuclear family was very common among preindustrial people. Furthermore, preindustrial people did not marry in their early teens, and illegitimacy was not as common as usually thought, and certainly less so than today. The concept of childhood as we know it hardly existed. The author also shows that the diet of poor people was probably almost as nutritionally sound as that of rich people—when the poor got enough to eat. As for medical science, it probably did more harm than good in the eighteenth century. Also explained in this chapter are the reasons for a kind of "sexual revolution" beginning in the mid-eighteenth century—with young people engaging in sex at an earlier age and with illegitimacy on the rise.

In the area of religion the eighteenth century witnessed a tug of war between the Enlightenment's attempt to demystify Christianity and place it on a more rational basis and a popular movement to retain traditional ritual, superstition, and religious mysteries. In Protestant and Catholic countries alike, rulers and religious leaders sought to purify religion by eliminating many ritualistic practices. The response to this "reform" by the common people in Catholic countries was a resurgence of religious ritual and mysticism, while in Protestant Germany and England there occurred a popular religious revival based on piety and emotional "conversion." Meanwhile, most of Europe—Catholic and Protestant—saw the state increase its control over the church.

STUDY OUTLINE

I.   Marriage and the family in preindustrial society
    A.   Extended and nuclear families
        1.   Contrary to popular belief, the extended family was not common in western Europe
        2.   Also, early marriage was not common prior to 1750, and many people never married at all
        3.   Marriage was commonly delayed because of poverty and/or local law and tradition
    B.   Work away from home
        1.   Many boys left home to work as craftsmen or laborers
        2.   Girls left to work as servants
    C.   Premarital sex and birth-control practices
        1.   Illegitimate children were not common in preindustrial society
        2.   Premarital sex was common, but marriage usually followed
        3.   Coitus interruptus was the most common form of birth control
    D.   New patterns of marriage and illegitimacy after about 1750
        1.   The growth of cottage industry resulted in people marrying earlier—and for love
        2.   The explosion of births and the growth of prostitution from about 1750 to 1850 had several causes
            a.   Increasing illegitimacy signified rebellion against laws that limited the right of the poor to marry
            b.   Pregnant servant girls often turned to prostitution, which also increased illegitimacy

E. The question of sexual emancipation for women
   1. Women in cities and factories had limited economic independence
   2. Poverty kept many people single—leading to premarital sex and illegitimate births

II. Women and children in preindustrial society
  A. Child care and nursing
    1. Infant mortality was very high
    2. Breast-feeding of children was common among poor women
    3. Middle- and upper-class women hired wet nurses
    4. The occupation of wet-nursing was often exploitative of lower-class women
  B. Foundlings and infanticide
    1. "Killing nurses" and infanticide were forms of population control
    2. Foundling hospitals were established but could not care for all the abandoned babies
  C. Attitudes toward children
    1. Attitudes toward children in preindustrial society were different from those of today
     a. Parents and doctors were generally indifferent to children
     b. Children were often neglected or treated brutally
    2. The Enlightenment brought about more humane treatment of children
  D. Schools and education
    1. The beginnings of education for common people lie in the seventeenth and eighteenth centuries
    2. Protestantism encouraged popular education
    3. Literacy increased, especially in France and Scotland, between 1700 and 1800

III. The Europeans' food
  A. Life expectancy
    1. The life span of Europeans increased from twenty-five years to thirty-five years between 1700 and 1800
    2. Life expectancy increased because diet improved and plagues and economic crises decreased
  B. Diet and nutrition
    1. The diet of ordinary people improved
     a. Poor people ate mainly grains and vegetables
     b. Milk and meat were rarely eaten
    2. Rich people ate quite differently from the poor
     a. Their diet was rich in meat and wine
     b. They spurned fruits and vegetables
  C. The impact of diet on health

       1. There were nutritional advantages and disadvantages to the diet of the poor
         a. Their breads were very nutritious
         b. Their main problem was getting enough green vegetables and milk
       2. The rich often ate too much rich food
   D. New foods and new knowledge about diet
       1. The potato substantially improved the diet of the poor
       2. There was a growth in market gardening and an improvement in food variety in the eighteenth century
       3. There was some improvement in knowledge about diet, although Europeans did not entirely cast off their myths
       4. Greater affluence caused many to turn to less nutritious food such as white bread and sugar
IV. Medical science and the sick
   A. The medical professionals
       1. The demonic view of disease was common, and faith healers were used to exorcise the demons
       2. Pharmacists sold drugs that were often harmful to their patients
       3. Surgeons often operated without anesthetics and in the midst of dirt
       4. Physicians frequently bled or purged people to death
   B. The terrible conditions at hospitals
       1. Patients were crowded together, often several to a bed
       2. There was no fresh air or hygiene
   C. Mental illness
       1. Mental illness was misunderstood and treated inhumanely
       2. Some attempts at reform occurred in the late eighteenth century
   D. Medical experiments and research
       1. Much medical experimentation was creative quackery
       2. The conquest of smallpox was the greatest medical triumph of the eighteenth century
         a. Jenner's vaccination treatment, begun in 1796, was a great medical advance
         b. Smallpox soon declined drastically in Europe
V. Religion and Christian churches
   A. The institutional church
       1. Despite the critical spirit of the Enlightenment, the local parish church remained important in daily life
       2. The Protestant belief in individualism in religion was tempered by increased state control over the church and religion
   B. Catholic piety
       1. In Catholic countries the old religious culture of ritual and superstition remained popular

2. Catholic clergy reluctantly allowed traditional religion to survive
C. Protestant revival
    1. Pietism stressed religious enthusiasm and individualism
    2. In England, Wesley was troubled by religious corruption, decline, and uncertainty
    3. His "Methodist" movement rejected Calvinism and stressed salvation through faith
    4. Wesley's ministry brought on a religious awakening, particularly among the lower classes

REVIEW QUESTIONS

Q-1. It is often believed that the typical preindustrial family consisted of an extended family. Do you agree? Define "extended" and "nuclear" family.

Q-2. In *Romeo and Juliet*, Juliet was just fourteen and Romeo was not too many years older. Is this early marriage typical of preindustrial society? Why did so many people not marry at all?

Q-3. When did the custom of late marriage begin to change? Why?

Q-4. Did preindustrial men and women practice birth control? What methods existed?

Q-5. How do you explain that prior to 1750 there were few illegitimate children but that there was a growth of illegitimacy thereafter?

Q-6. It is often claimed that factory women, as opposed to their rural counterparts, were sexually liberated. Is this claim correct? Explain.

Q-7. How and why did life expectancy improve in the eighteenth century?

Q-8. What were the differences in the diets of the rich and the poor in the eighteenth century? What nutritional deficiencies existed?

Q-9. How important was the potato in the eighteenth century? Is it important enough to merit more attention from historians?

Q-10. How important were the eighteenth-century advances in medical science in extending the life span?

Q-11. What was the demonic view of disease?

Q-12. It is said that when it came to medical care, the poor were better off than the rich because they could not afford doctors or hospitals. Why might this have been true?

Q-13. Why was there so much controversy over the smallpox inoculation? Was it safe? What contribution did Edward Jenner make to the elimination of this disease?

Q-14. How was mental illness regarded and treated in the eighteenth century?

Q-15. What effect did changes in church-state relations have on the institutions of the Church?

Q-16. Describe the forms in which popular religious culture remained in Catholic Europe.

Q-17. Define *pietism* and describe how it is reflected in the work and life of John Wesley.

STUDY-REVIEW EXERCISES

Define the following key concepts and terms.

extended family

demonic view of disease

nuclear family

preindustrial childhood

illegitimacy explosion

Methodists

coitus interruptus

purging

"killing nurses"

Jesuits

Identify each of the following and give his or her significance.

Saint Vincent de Paul

Lady Mary Montague

Edward Jenner

James Graham

Joseph II

John Wesley

Test your understanding of the chapter by answering the following questions.

1. It is apparent that the practice of breast-feeding *increased/limited* the fertility of lower-class women.
2. The teenage bride *was/was not* the general rule in preindustrial Europe.
3. Prior to about 1750, premarital sex usually *did/did not* lead to marriage.

4. In the eighteenth century, the _____ was the primary new food in Europe.
5. People lived *longer/shorter* lives as the eighteenth century progressed.
6. The key to Jenner's inoculation discovery was the connection between immun-

    ity from smallpox and _____ , a mild and not contagious disease.
7. In Catholic countries it was largely *the clergy/the common people* who wished to hold on to traditional religious ritual and superstition.
8. The Englishman who brought religious "enthusiasm" to the common folk of

    England was _____ .

MULTIPLE-CHOICE QUESTIONS

1. One of the chief deficiencies of the diet of both rich and poor Europeans was the absence of sufficient
    a. meat.
    b. fruit and vegetables.
    c. white bread.
    d. wine.

2. A family in which three or four generations live under the same roof under the direction of a patriarch is known as a(n)
    a. nuclear family.
    b. conjugal family.
    c. industrial household.
    d. extended family.

3. Prior to about 1750, marriage between two persons was more often than
   not
   a. undertaken freely by the couple.
   b. controlled by law and parents.
   c. based on romantic love.
   d. undertaken without economic considerations.

4. The establishment of foundling hospitals in the eighteenth century was an
   attempt to
   a. prevent the spread of the bubonic plague.
   b. isolate children from smallpox.
   c. prevent willful destruction and abandonment of newborn children.
   d. provide adequate childbirth facilities for rich women.

5. All but which one of the following is true about preindustrial society's attitudes
   toward children?
   a. Parents often treated their children with indifference and
       brutality.
   b. Poor children were often forced to work in the early factories.
   c. Doctors were the only people interested in the child's welfare.
   d. Killing of children by parents or nurses was common.

6. It appears that the role of doctors and hospital care in bringing about improvement in health in the eighteenth century was
   a. very significant.
   b. minor.
   c. helpful only in the area of surgery.

7. In the seventeenth and early eighteenth centuries people usually
   married
   a. surprisingly late.
   b. surprisingly early.
   c. almost never.
   d. with enormous frequency.

8. Which of the following was *not* a general characteristic of the European family
   of the eighteenth century?
   a. The nuclear family
   b. Late marriages
   c. Many unmarried relatives
   d. The extended family

9. The overwhelming reason for postponement of marriage was
   a. that people didn't like the institution of marriage.
   b. lack of economic independence.
   c. the stipulation of a legal age.
   d. that young men and women valued the independence of a working life.

10. In the second half of the eighteenth century, the earlier patterns of marriage and family life began to break down. Which of the following was *not* a result of this change?
    a. A greater number of illegitimate births
    b. Earlier marriages
    c. Marriages *exclusively* for economic reasons
    d. Marriages for love

11. The "illegitimacy explosion" of the late eighteenth century was encouraged by all but which one of the following?
    a. The laws, especially in Germany, concerning the poor's right to marry
    b. The mobility of young people needing to work off the farm
    c. The influence of the French Revolution, which repressed freedom in sexual and marital behavior
    d. The exploitation of girls in the servant class

12. Which of the following statements best describes the attitude toward children in the first part of the eighteenth century?
    a. They were protected and cherished.
    b. They were never disciplined.
    c. They were treated as they were—children living in a child's world.
    d. They were ignored, often brutalized, and often unloved.

13. Most of the popular education in Europe of the eighteenth century was sponsored by
    a. the church.
    b. the state.
    c. private individuals.
    d. parents, in the home.

14. Which of the following would most likely be found in an eighteenth-century hospital?
    a. Isolation of patients
    b. Sanitary conditions
    c. Uncrowded conditions
    d. Uneducated nurses and poor nursing practices

15. The greatest medical triumph of the eighteenth century was the conquest
    of
    a. starvation.
    b. smallpox.
    c. scurvy.
    d. cholera.

16. The practice of sending one's newborn baby to be cared for by a poor woman
    in the countryside was known as
    a. the cottage system.
    b. infanticide.
    c. wet-nursing.
    d. all of the above

17. Which of the following was not a common food for the European
    poor?
    a. Vegetables
    b. Beer
    c. Dark bread
    d. Milk

18. It appears that the chief dietary problem of European society was the lack of
    an adequate supply of
    a. vitamins A and C.
    b. vitamin B complex.
    c. meat.
    d. sugar.

19. Most probably the best thing an eighteenth-century sick person could do with
    regard to hospitals would be to
    a. enter only if an operation was suggested by a doctor.
    b. enter only if in need of drugs.
    c. enter only a hospital operating under Galenic theory.
    d. stay away.

20. The country that led the way in the development of universal education
    was
    a. Britain.
    b. Prussia.
    c. France.
    d. none of the above

UNDERSTANDING HISTORY THROUGH READING AND THE ARTS

Painting is one of the major sources of information for the history of childhood. Preindustrial childhood is the subject of *Children's Games*, by Pieter Brueghel the Elder. It is a lively and action-packed painting of over two hundred children engaged in more than seventy different games, and it is the subject of an interesting article by A. Eliot, "Games Children Play," *Sports Illustrated* (January 11, 1971): 48-56.

Tom Jones, eighteenth-century England's most famous foundling, was the fictional hero of Henry Fielding's *Tom Jones* and the subject and title of director Tony Richardson's highly acclaimed, award-winning film version of Fielding's novel. Starring Albert Finney, Susannah York, and Dame Edith Evans, the film re-creates, in amusing and satirical fashion, eighteenth-century English life. A more recent film adaptation is Richardson's *Joseph Andrews*, based on another Fielding novel.

London was the fastest-growing city in the eighteenth century. How people lived in London is the subject of two highly readable and interesting books: M. D. George, *London Life in the Eighteenth Century** (3rd ed., 1951), and R. J. Mitchell and M. D. R. Leys, *A History of London Life** (1963).

Few men in preindustrial society earned enough to support a family. This, in part, explains why and when women married, and why most women worked. The preindustrial woman, therefore, was not in any modern sense a homemaker. The subject of women and the family economy in eighteenth-century France is discussed by O. Hufton in *The Poor of Eighteenth-Century France* (1974).

PROBLEMS FOR FURTHER INVESTIGATION

Did medical science contribute to an improvement in eighteenth-century life? Until about twenty years ago, it was fashionable to believe that the population explosion was due to improvements made by medical science. Although this theory is generally disclaimed today, it appears to be enjoying a slight revival. For both sides, read the following journal articles (which also have bibliographies): T. McKeown and R. G. Brown, "Medical Evidence Related to English Population Change," *Population Studies* 9 (1955); T. McKeown and R. G. Record, "Reasons for the Decline in Mortality in England and Wales During the Nineteenth Century," *Population Studies* 16 (1962); and P. Razzell, "Population Change in Eighteenth-Century England: A Reinterpretation," *Economic History Review*, 2nd series, 18-2 (1965); and on the history of disease see D. Hopkins, *Princes and Peasants: Smallpox in History* (1977).

*Available in paperback.

CHAPTER 21

THE REVOLUTION IN POLITICS,
1775-1815

CHAPTER OBJECTIVES

After reading and studying this chapter you should be able to answer the following questions:

Q-1. What were the causes of the political revolutions between 1775 and 1815 in America and France?
Q-2. What were the ideas and objectives of the revolutionaries in America and France?
Q-3. Who won and who lost in these revolutions?

CHAPTER SYNOPSIS

The French and American revolutions were the most important political events of the eighteenth century. They were also a dramatic conclusion to the Enlightenment, and both revolutions, taken together, formed a major turning point in human history. This chapter explains what these great revolutions were all about.

The chapter begins with liberalism, the fundamental ideology of the revolution in politics. Liberalism had deep roots and called for freedom and equality at a time when monarchs and aristocrats took their great privileges for granted. The author sees the immediate origins of the American Revolution in the British effort to solve the problem of war debts, which was turned into a political struggle by the American colonists, who already had achieved considerable economic and personal freedom. The American Revolution stimulated reform efforts throughout Europe.

It was in France that the ideas of the Enlightenment and liberalism were put to their fullest test. The bankruptcy of the state gave the French aristocracy the chance to grab power from a weak king. This move backfired, however, because the middle class grabbed even harder. It is significant that the revolutionary desires of the middle class depended on the firm support and violent action of aroused peasants and poor urban workers. It was this action of the common people that gave the revolution its driving force.

In the first two years of the French Revolution, the middle class, with its allies from the peasantry and urban poor, achieved unprecedented reforms. The outbreak of an all-European war against France in 1792 then resulted in a reign of terror and a dictatorship by radical moralists, of whom Robespierre was the greatest. By 1795, this radical patriotism wore itself out. The revolutionary momentum slowed and the Revolution deteriorated into a military dictatorship under the opportunist Napoleon. Yet until 1815 the history of France was that of war, and that war spread liberalism to the rest of Europe. French conquests also stimulated nationalism. The world of politics was turned upside down.

STUDY OUTLINE

I. The new ideas of liberty and equality
   A. Liberty
      1. In the eighteenth century, liberty meant human rights and freedoms and the sovereignty of the people
   B. Equality
      1. This meant equal rights and equality of opportunity
   C. The roots of liberalism
      1. The Judeo-Christian tradition of individualism, reinforced by the Reformation, supported liberalism
      2. Liberalism's modern roots are found in the Enlightenment's concern for freedom and legal equality
      3. Liberalism was attractive to both the aristocracy and the middle class, but it lacked the support of the masses
II. The American Revolution (1775-1789)
   A. Some argue that the American Revolution was not a revolution at all but merely a war for independence
   B. The origins of the Revolution are difficult to ascertain
      1. The British wanted the Americans to pay their share of imperial expenses
         a. Parliament passed the Stamp Act (1765) to raise revenue
         b. Vigorous protest from the colonies forced the act's repeal (1766)
      2. Many Americans believed they had the right to make their own laws
      3. The issue of taxation and representation ultimately led to the outbreak of fighting
   C. The independence movement was encouraged by several factors

1. The British refused to compromise, thus losing the support of many colonists
2. The radical ideas of Thomas Paine, expressed in the best-selling *Common Sense*, greatly influenced public opinion in favor of independence
3. The Declaration of Independence, written by Thomas Jefferson and passed by the Second Continental Congress (1776), further increased the desire of the colonists for independence
4. Although many Americans remained loyal to Britain, the independence movement had wide-based support from all sections of society
5. European aid, especially from the French government and from French volunteers, contributed greatly to the American victory in 1783

D. The Constitution and Bill of Rights consolidated the revolutionary program of liberty and equality
1. The federal, or central, government was given important powers, the right to tax, the means to enforce its laws, the regulation of trade—but the states had important powers too
2. The executive, legislative, and judicial branches of the government were designed to balance one another
3. Some people (the Anti-Federalists) feared that the central government had too much power; to placate them, the Federalists wrote the Bill of Rights, which spells out the rights of the individual

E. The American Revolution encouraged European revolution

III. The French Revolution: the revolution that began the modern era in politics
A. The influence of the American Revolution
1. Many French soldiers, such as Lafayette, served in America and were impressed by the ideals of the Revolution
2. The American Revolution influenced the French Revolution, but the latter was more violent and more influential

B. The breakdown of the old order
1. By the 1780s, the government was nearly bankrupt
2. The French banking system could not cope with the fiscal problems, leaving the monarchy with no choice but to increase taxes

C. Legal orders and social realities: the three estates
1. The first estate, the clergy, had many privileges and much wealth, and it levied an oppressive tax on the peasantry
2. The second estate, the nobility, also had great privileges, wealth, and power, and it too taxed the peasantry
3. The third estate, the commoners, was a mixture of a few rich members of the middle class, urban workers, and the mass of peasants

D. The formation of the National Assembly of 1789
1. Louis XVI's economic reform plan to tax landed property was opposed by the notables

    2. Louis called for a meeting of the Estates General, the representative body of the three estates

        a. Traditionally, historians have viewed the bourgeoisie's class and economic interests as pushing it into a revolutionary role

        b. Revisionist historians, however, claim that the bourgeoisie's interests did not differ from the interests of the upper class

        a. The nobility represented both conservative and liberal viewpoints

        b. The third estate representatives were largely lawyers and government officials

        c. The third estate wanted the three estates to meet together so the third estate would have the most power

    3. The dispute over voting in the Estates General led the third estate to break away and form the National Assembly

    4. Louis tried to reassert his monarchial authority and assembled an army

  E. The revolt of the poor and the oppressed

    1. Rising bread prices in 1788-89 stirred the people to action

    2. Fearing attack by the king's army, angry Parisians stormed the Bastille (July 14, 1789)

        a. The people took the Bastille, and the king was forced to recall his troops

        b. The uprising of the masses saved the National Assembly

    3. The peasants revolted, forcing the National Assembly to abolish feudal dues, and won a great victory

  F. A limited monarchy established by the bourgeoisie

    1. The National Assembly's Declaration of the Rights of Man (1789) proclaimed the rights of all citizens and guaranteed equality before the law and a representative government

    2. Meanwhile, the poor women of Paris forced the king and government to move to Paris

    3. The National Assembly established a constitutional monarchy and passed major reforms of France's laws and institutions

    4. The National Assembly attacked the power of the church by seizing its land and subjugating the church to the state

    5. This attack on the church turned many people against the Revolution

IV. World war and republican France (1791-1799)

  A. War began in April 1792

    1. The European attitude toward the French Revolution was mixed

        a. Liberals and radicals such as Priestly and Paine praised it as the triumph of liberty

        b. Others such as Burke and Gentz predicted it would lead to tyranny

2. Fear among European kings and nobility that the revolution would spread resulted in the Declaration of Pillnitz (1791), which threatened the invasion of France by Austria and Prussia

3. In retaliation, the patriotic French deputies declared war on Austria in 1792, but France was soon retreating before the armies of the First Coalition

4. In 1792 a new assembly (the National Convention) proclaimed France a republic

B. The "second revolution" and rapid radicalization in France
   1. Louis XVI was tried and convicted of treason by the National Convention and guillotined in early 1793
   2. French armies continued the "war against tyranny" by declaring war on nearly all of Europe
   3. In Paris, the republicans—divided between the Girondists and the Mountain—struggled for political power
   4. The sans-culottes—the laboring poor—allied with the Mountain and helped Robespierre and the Committee of Public Safety gain power

C. Total war and the Reign of Terror (1793-94)
   1. Robespierre established a planned economy to wage total war and aid the poor
   2. The Reign of Terror was instituted to eliminate opposition to the revolution, and many people were jailed or executed
   3. The war became a national mission against evil within and outside of France

D. The "Thermidorian reaction" and the Directory (1795-1799)
   1. Fear of the Reign of Terror led to the execution of its leader, Robespierre
   2. The period of the "Thermidorian reaction" following Robespierre's death was marked by a return to bourgeois liberalism
      a. Economic controls were abolished
      b. The Directory, a five-man executive body, was established
      c. Riots by the poor were put down
   3. The poor lost their fervor for revolution
   4. A military dictatorship was established in order to prevent a return to peace and monarchy

V. The Napoleonic era (1799-1815)
   A. Napoleon's rule
      1. Napoleon appealed to many, like abbé Sieyés who looked for authority from above
      2. Napoleon became the center of a plot to overturn the weak Directory and was named first consul of the republic in 1799
      3. He maintained order and worked out important compromises

        a. His civil code of 1804 granted the middle-class equality under the law and safeguarded their right to own property

        b. He confirmed the gains of the peasants

        c. He centralized the government, strengthened the bureaucracy, and granted amnesty to nobles

        d. He signed the Concordat of 1801, which guaranteed freedom of worship for Catholics

    4. He betrayed the ideals of the Revolution by violating the rights of free speech and press, and free elections

  B. Napoleon's wars and foreign policy

    1. He defeated Austria (1801) and made peace with Britain (1802)

    2. Another war (against the Third Coalition—Austria, Russia, Sweden, and Britain) resulted in British naval dominance at the battle of Trafalgar (1805)

    3. Napoleon used the fear of a conspiracy to return the Bourbons to power to get himself elected emperor

    4. The Third Coalition collapsed at Austerlitz (1805), and Napoleon gained much German territory

    5. In 1806, Napoleon defeated Prussia and gained even more territory

    6. Napoleon's Grand Empire meant French control of continental Europe

    7. The beginning of the end for Napoleon came with the Spanish revolt and the British blockade

    8. The French invasion of Russia in 1812 was a disaster for Napoleon

    9. He was defeated by the Fourth Coalition and abdicated his throne in 1814—only to be defeated again at Waterloo in 1815

VI. Was the French Revolution a success?

  A. Yes, the liberal revolution in France succeeded in giving great benefits to the people

  B. Although the Revolution brought the Reign of Terror and a dictatorship, the old order was never re-established, and thus a substantial part of the liberal philosophy survived

REVIEW QUESTIONS

Q-1. Define liberalism. What did it mean to be a "liberal" in the eighteenth and nineteenth centuries? How does this compare to twentieth-century liberalism?

Q-2. Were great differences in wealth contradictory to the revolutionaries' idea of equality? Explain.

Q-3. How did the writers of the Enlightenment differ on the method of establishing liberty?

Q-4. According to Locke, what is the function of government?

Q-5. Think back to the English Revolution of 1688 (Chapter 16). How does Locke's theory justify the English action of getting rid of their king and contracting for a new one?

Q-6. Which side, American or British, had the better argument with regard to the taxation problem? How do the Seven Years' War, the Stamp Act, and the Boston Tea Party fit into your explanation?

Q-7. Why is the Declaration of Independence sometimes called the world's greatest political editorial?

Q-8. What role did the European powers play in the American victory? Did they gain anything?

Q-9. What was the major issue in the debate between the centralists and the Anti-Federalists?

Q-10. How did Americans interpret "equality" in 1789? Has it changed since then? Are the definitions of liberalism and equality unchangeable, or do they undergo periodic redefinition?

Q-11. Did the American Revolution have any effect on France?

Q-12. Why was there fear in France that the tax-reform issue would have "opened a Pandora's box of social and political demands"?

Q-13. Describe the three estates of France. Who paid the taxes? Who held the wealth and power in France?

Q-14. With the calling of the Estates General, "the nobility of France expected that history would repeat itself." Did it? What actually did happen?

Q-15. Discuss the reforms of the National Assembly. Do they display the application of liberalism to society?

Q-16. What were the cause and the outcome of the peasants' uprising of 1789?

Q-17. What role did the poor women of Paris play in the Revolution?

Q-18. Why were France and Europe overcome with feelings of fear and mistrust?

Q-19. Why did the Revolution turn into war in 1792?

Q-20. What effect did the war have on the position of the French king and aristocracy?

Q-21. Were the French armies conquerors or liberators?

Q-22. Who were the sans-culottes? Why were they important to radical leaders such as Robespierre? What role did the common people play in the Revolution?

Q-23. Why did the Committee of Public Safety need to institute a Reign of Terror?

Q-24. What event led to the takeover by Napoleon?

Q-25. Was Napoleon a son of the Revolution or just another tyrant? Explain.

Q-26. Describe the Grand Empire of Napoleon. Was he a liberator or a tyrant?

Q-27. What caused Napoleon's downfall?

STUDY-REVIEW EXERCISES

Define the following key concepts and terms.

liberalism

Montesquieu's "checks and balances"

natural or universal rights

republican

popular sovereignty

tithe

Identify each of the following and give its significance.

Stamp Act

battle of Trafalgar

American Bill of Rights

American Loyalists

American Constitutional Convention of 1787

Jacobins

Reign of Terror

National Assembly

Declaration of the Rights of Man

Bastille

sans-culottes

Girondists

the Mountain

Explain who the following people were and give their significance.

"the baker, the baker's wife, and the baker's boy"

Lord Nelson

Thomas Paine

Edmund Burke

Marie Antoinette

Marquis de Lafayette

Thomas Jefferson

Robespierre

John Locke

abbé Sieyés

Test your understanding of the chapter by answering the following questions.

1. Napoleon's plan to invade England was made impossible by the defeat of the French and Spanish navies in the battle of

    _____ in 1805.

2. Overall, the common people of Paris played *a minor/an important* role in the French Revolution.

3. The author of the best-selling radical book *Common Sense* was

    _____ .

4. Prior to the crisis of the 1760s, American colonists had exercised *little/a great deal of* political and economic independence from Britain.

5. The peasant uprising of 1789 in France ended in *victory/defeat* for the peasant class.

6. By the mid 1790s, people like Sieyés were increasingly looking to *the people/ a military ruler* to bring order to France.

MULTIPLE-CHOICE QUESTIONS

1. Eighteenth-century liberals laid major stress on
   a. economic equality.
   b. equality in property holding.
   c. equality of opportunity.
   d. racial and sexual equality.

2. Which came first?
   a. Formation of the French National Assembly
   b. Execution of King Louis XVI
   c. American Bill of Rights
   d. Seven Years' War

3. The French Jacobins were
   a. aristocrats who fled France.
   b. monarchists.
   c. priests who supported the Revolution.
   d. revolutionary radicals.

4. The French National Assembly was established by
   a. the middle class of the Third Estate.
   b. King Louis XVI.
   c. the aristocracy.
   d. the sans-culottes.

5. The National Assembly did all but which one of the following?
   a. Nationalized church land
   b. Issued the Declaration of the Rights of Man
   c. Established the metric system of weights and measures
   d. Brought about the Reign of Terror

6. In 1789 the influential abbé Sieyés wrote a pamphlet in which he argued that France should be rule by the

a. nobility.
b. clergy.
c. people.

7. In the first stage of the Revolution the French established
   a. a constitutional monarchy.
   b. an absolutist monarchy.
   c. a republic.
   d. a military dictatorship.

8. Edmund Burke's *Reflections on the Revolution in France* is a defense of
   a. the Catholic church.
   b. Robespierre and the Terror.
   c. the working classes of France.
   d. the English monarchy and aristocracy.

9. Generally, the people who did *not* support eighteenth-century liberalism were the
   a. elite.
   b. members of the middle class.
   c. masses.
   d. intellectuals.

10. Most eighteenth-century demands for liberty centered on
    a. the equalization of wealth.
    b. a classless society.
    c. better welfare systems.
    d. equality of opportunity.

11. Americans objected to the Stamp Act because the tax it proposed
    a. was exorbitant.
    b. was required of people in Britain.
    c. would have required great expense to collect.
    d. was imposed without their consent.

12. The American Revolution
    a. had very little impact on Europe.
    b. was supported by the French monarchy.
    c. was not influenced by Locke or Montesquieu.
    d. was supported by almost everyone living in the United States.

13. Which of the following was *not* a cause of the outbreak of revolution in France in 1789?
    a. An enormous national debt
    b. An economic crisis and a bad harvest
    c. The demand of the nobility for greater power and influence
    d. The invasion of France by foreign armies

14. The first successful revolt against Napoleon began in 1808 in
    a. Spain.
    b. Russia.
    c. Germany.
    d. Italy.

15. Napoleon appealed to
    a. French peasants.
    b. French businessmen.
    c. French soldiers.
    d. all of the above

16. Prior to about 1765, the American people were
    a. fairly independent of the British government.
    b. subject to heavy and punitive British controls.
    c. paying a majority share of British military costs.
    d. under the direct control of the East India Company.

17. The major share of the tax burden in France was carried by the
    a. peasants.
    b. bourgeoisie.
    c. clergy.
    d. nobility.

18. The participation of the common people of Paris in the revolution was initially attributable to
    a. their desire to be represented in the Estates General.
    b. the soaring price of food.
    c. the murder of Marat.
    d. the large number of people imprisoned by the king.

19. For the French peasants, the Revolution of 1789 meant
    a. a general movement from the countryside to urban areas.
    b. greater land ownership.
    c. significant political power.
    d. few, if any, gains.

20. The group that announced that it was going to cut off Marie Antoinette's head, "tear out her heart, [and] fry her liver" was the
    a. National Guard.
    b. Robespierre radicals.
    c. revolutionary committee.
    d. women of Paris.

21. The group that had the task of ridding France of any internal opposition to the revolutionary cause was the
    a. Revolutionary Army.
    b. secret police.
    c. republican mob of Paris.
    d. Committee of Public Safety.

GEOGRAPHY

1. Show on the outline map the boundaries of France before the outbreak of war in 1792. Now shade in the areas acquired by France by 1810. Was Napoleon successful in 1810 in expanding the boundaries of France? Who inhabited the territories newly acquired by France?

2. Shade in the dependent states in 1810. What nationalities inhabited these states? Were these large, powerful states?

3. Look closely at Map 21.1. Can you find the four small British fortified outposts scattered throughout Europe? How were these outposts necessary to and a reflection of Britain's military power? What did these outposts mean for smugglers and Napoleon's efforts to stop British trade with continental countries?

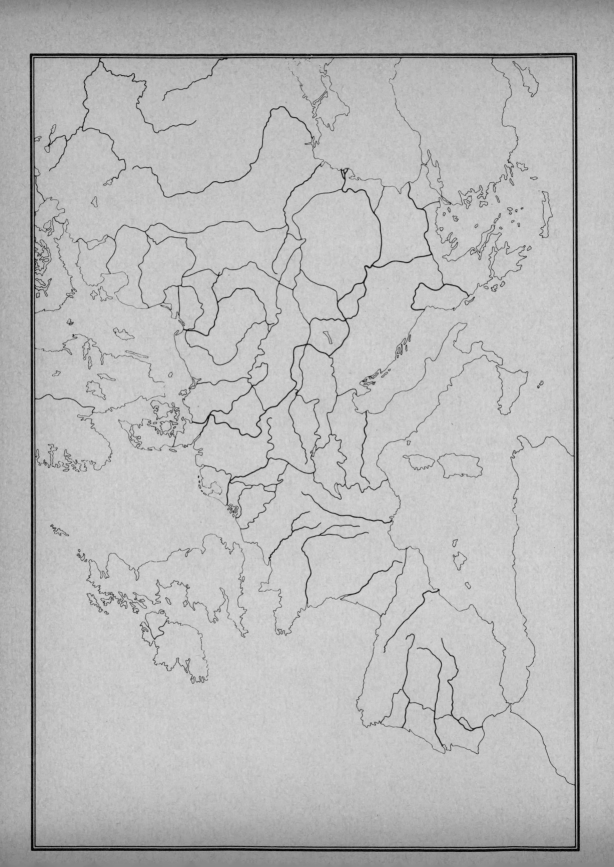

PROBLEMS FOR FURTHER INVESTIGATION

This era of revolution is ideal for the study of both individual and group actions. The various arguments of scholars over the motives and contributions of Napoleon are brought together in D. H. Pinkney, ed., *Napoleon: Historical Enigma** (1969), and the story of Admiral Lord Nelson, Britain's hero and victor of great sea battles, is interestingly told in R. Hough, *Nelson, A Biography* (1980). King George III of England has often been viewed, in American history, as the arch-enemy of liberty and constitutionalism. Is this a fair assessment? The debate over his role has gone on for a number of years and is the subject of a book of collected opinions, *George III: Tyrant or Constitutional Monarch?** (1964), edited by E. A. Reitan.

Group action in a revolution makes for an equally interesting study. The role of women in the revolution in France (and in other times) is well handled in Elise Boulding, *The Underside of History: A View of Women Through Time* (1976). The "people" (which includes the Paris mob) who participated in the revolution in France are the subject of the interesting study by George Rude, *The Crowd in the French Revolution** (1959).

Students interested in the origins of the French revolution will want to check R. W. Greenlaw, ed., *The Economic Origins of the French Revolution** (1958), and those interested in political theory may want to consider a study of liberalism beginning with H. Schultz, ed., *English Liberalism and the State—Individualism or Collectivism?** (1972).

*Available in paperback.

READING WITH UNDERSTANDING
EXERCISE 5

LEARNING HOW TO IDENTIFY MAIN POINTS
THAT ARE CAUSES OR REASONS

In Exercise 3 we considered cause and effect and underlined a passage dealing with effects or results. This exercise continues in this direction by focusing on causes or reasons.

Exercise

Read the following passage as a whole. Reread it and underline or highlight each cause (or factor) contributing to the Industrial Revolution in England.

Note that there are several causes and that they are rather compressed. (This is because the author is summarizing material presented in previous chapters before going on to discuss other causes or factors—notably technology and the energy problem—in greater detail.) Since several causal points are presented in a short space, this is a very good place to number the points (and key subpoints) in the margin. After you have finished, compare your underlining or highlighting with that in the suggested model on pages E-4 to E-5.

Eighteenth-Century Origins

The Industrial Revolution grew out of the expanding Atlantic economy of the eighteenth century, which served mercantilist England remarkably well. England's colonial empire, augmented by a strong position in Latin America and in the African slave trade, provided a growing market for English manufactured goods. So did England itself. In an age when it was much cheaper to ship goods by water than by land, no part of England was more than twenty miles from navigable water. Beginning in the 1770s, a canal building boom greatly enhanced this natural advantage (see Map 22.1). Nor were there any tariffs within the country to hinder trade, as there were in France before 1789 and in politically fragmented Germany.

Agriculture played a central role in bringing about the Industrial Revolution in England. English farmers were second only to the Dutch in productivity in 1700, and they were continuously adopting new methods of farming as the century went on. The result, especially before 1760, was a period of bountiful crops and low food prices. The ordinary English family did not have to spend almost everything it earned just to buy bread. It could spend more on other items, on manufactured goods—leather shoes or a razor for the man, a bonnet or a shawl for the woman, toy soldiers for the son, and a doll for the daughter. Thus, demand for goods within the country complemented the demand from the colonies.

England had other assets that helped give rise to the Industrial Revolution. Unlike eighteenth-century France, England had an effective central bank and well-developed credit markets. The monarchy and the aristocratic oligarchy, which had jointly ruled the country since 1688, provided stable and predictable government. At the same time the government let the domestic economy operate fairly freely and with few controls, encouraging personal initiative, technical change, and a free market. Finally, England had long had a large class of hired agricultural laborers, whose numbers were further increased by the enclosure movement of the late eighteenth century. These rural wage earners were relatively mobile—compared to village-bound peasants in France and western Germany, for example—and along with cottage workers they formed a potential industrial labor force for capitalist entrepreneurs.

All these factors combined to initiate the Industrial Revolution, which began in the 1780s—after the American war for independence and just before the French Revolution. Thus the great economic and political revolutions that have shaped the modern world occurred almost simultaneously, though they began in different countries. The Industrial Revolution was, however, a longer process. It was not complete in England until 1830 at the earliest, and it had no real impact on continental countries until after the Congress of Vienna ended the era of revolutionary wars in 1815.

Eighteenth-Century Origins

causes

1

a

b

c

2

a

b

c

3

4

5

6

The Industrial Revolution grew out of the expanding Atlantic economy of the eighteenth century, which served mercantilist England remarkably well. England's colonial empire, augmented by a strong position in Latin America and in the African slave trade, provided a growing market for English manufactured goods. So did England itself. In an age when it was much cheaper to ship goods by water than by land, no part of England was more than twenty miles from navigable water. Beginning in the 1770s, a canal building boom greatly enhanced this natural advantage (see Map 22.1). Nor were there any tariffs within the country to hinder trade, as there were in France before 1789 and in politically fragmented Germany.

Agriculture played a central role in bringing about the Industrial Revolution in England. English farmers were second only to the Dutch in productivity in 1700, and they were continuously adopting new methods of farming as the century went on. The result, especially before 1760, was a period of bountiful crops and low food prices. The ordinary English family did not have to spend almost everything it earned just to buy bread. It could spend more on other items, on manufactured goods—leather shoes or a razor for the man, a bonnet or a shawl for the woman, toy soldiers for the son, and a doll for the daughter. Thus, demand for goods within the country complemented the demand from the colonies.

England had other assets that helped give rise to the Industrial Revolution. Unlike eighteenth-century France, England had an effective central bank and well-developed credit markets. The monarchy and the aristocratic oligarchy, which had jointly ruled the country since 1688, provided stable and predictable government. At the same time the government let the domestic economy operate fairly freely and with few controls, encouraging personal initiative, technical change, and a free market. Finally, England had long had a large class of hired agricultural laborers, whose numbers were further increased by the enclosure movement of the late eighteenth century. These rural wage earners were relatively mobile—compared to village-bound peasants in France and western Germany, for example—and

a

along with cottage workers they formed a potential industrial labor force for capitalist entrepreneurs.

All these factors combined to initiate the Industrial Revolution, which began in the 1780s—after the American war for independence and just before the French Revolution. Thus the great economic and political revolutions that have shaped the modern world occurred almost simultaneously, though they began in different countries. The Industrial Revolution was, however, a longer process. It was not complete in England until 1830 at the earliest, and it had no real impact on continental countries until after the Congress of Vienna ended the era of revolutionary wars in 1815.

READING WITH UNDERSTANDING
EXERCISE 6

LEARNING HOW TO MAKE HISTORICAL COMPARISONS

An important part of studying history is learning how to *compare* two (or more) related historical developments. Such comparisons not only demonstrate a basic understanding of the two objects being compared, but also permit the student-historian to draw distinctions that indicate real insight.

For these reasons, "compare-and-contrast" questions have long been favorites of history professors, and they often appear on essay exams. Even when they do not, they are an excellent study device for synthesizing historical information and testing your understanding. Therefore, as the introductory essay suggests, *try to anticipate* what compare-and-contrast questions your instructor might ask. Then work up your own study outlines that summarize the points your essay answer would discuss and develop. The preparation of study outlines of course is also a useful preparation for essay questions that do not require you to compare and contrast.

Exercise

Read the brief passage below. Reread it and underline or highlight it for main points. Now study the passage in terms of "compare and contrast." Prepare a brief outline (solely on the basis of this material) that will allow you to compare and contrast the Russian and German revolutions (of 1917-1919). After you have finished, compare your outline with the model on page F-3. Remember: the model provides a *good* answer, not the *only* answer.

The German Revolution of November 1918 resembled the Russian Revolution of March 1917. In both cases a genuine popular uprising toppled an authoritarian monarchy and established a liberal provisional republic. In both countries liberals and moderate socialists took control of the central government, while workers' and soldiers' councils formed a "countergovernment." In Germany, however, the moderate socialists won and the Lenin-like radical revolutionaries in the councils lost. In communist terms, the liberal, republican revolution in Germany in 1918 was only "half" a revolution: a "bourgeois" political revolution without a communist second installment. It was Russia without Lenin's Bolshevik triumph.

There were several reasons for the German outcome. The great majority of Marxian socialist leaders in the Social Democratic party were, as before the war, really pink and not red. They wanted to establish real political democracy and civil liberties, and they favored the gradual elimination of capitalism. They were also German nationalists, appalled by the prospect of civil war and revolutionary terror. Moreover, there was much less popular support among workers and soldiers for the extreme radicals than in Russia. Nor did the German peasantry, which already had most of the land, at least in western Germany, provide the elemental force that has driven all great modern revolutions, from the French to the Chinese.

Of crucial importance also was the fact that the moderate German Social Democrats, unlike Kerensky and company, accepted defeat and ended the war the day they took power. This act ended the decline in morale among soldiers and prevented the regular army with its conservative officer corps from disintegrating. When radicals headed by Karl Liebknecht and Rosa Luxemburg and their supporters in the councils tried to seize control of the government in Berlin in January, the moderate socialists called on the army to crush the uprising. Liebknecht and Luxemburg were arrested and then brutally murdered by army leaders. Finally, even if the moderate socialists had taken the Leninist path, it is very unlikely they would have succeeded. Civil war in Germany would certainly have followed, and the Allies, who were already occupying western Germany according to the terms of the armistice, would have marched on to Berlin and ruled Germany directly. Historians have often been unduly hard on Germany's moderate socialists.

Comparison of Russian and German Revolutions (1917-1918)

Similarities

1. Both countries had genuine liberal revolutions.
   a. Russia—March 1917
   b. Germany—November 1918

2. In both countries moderate socialists took control.

Differences

1. Russia had a second, radical (Bolshevik) revolution; Germany did not.

2. In Germany workers and peasants gave radicals less support than in Russia.

3. In Germany the moderate Socialists stopped the war immediately and therefore the German army, unlike the Russian army, remained intact to put down radical uprisings.

ANSWERS TO OBJECTIVE QUESTIONS

CHAPTER 1

Test your understanding.

1. Charles Darwin
2. Hammurabi
3. pharaoh
4. Hyksos
5. Akhenaten
6. Egyptian and Hittite
7. Babylon
8. were
9. could
10. Neolithic
11. Tigris, Euphrates
12. was
13. c

Number the following events.

1. 6
2. 3
3. 5
4. 2
5. 4
6. 1

Multiple-choice questions.

1. c
2. b
3. d
4. b
5. c
6. a
7. d
8. a
9. a
10. a
11. b
12. d
13. b
14. b
15. a
16. c
17. b
18. b
19. d
20. a
21. b

CHAPTER 2

Test your understanding.

1. a
2. more
3. Yahweh

4. did
5. Medes, Persians

6. east
7. satrapies

Multiple-choice questions.

1. c
2. b
3. b
4. b
5. b

6. c
7. c
8. a
9. d
10. d

11. b
12. c
13. d
14. a
15. d

16. c
17. d
18. b
19. d

CHAPTER 3

Fill in the blank lines.

1. f
2. d

3. b
4. a

5. c
6. e

7. h

Test your understanding.

1. Athens, Sparta, Thebes
2. were
3. did

4. Philip of Macedonia
5. divine law

6. were
7. supported

Multiple-choice questions.

1. b
2. c
3. c
4. b
5. d

6. d
7. a
8. a
9. d
10. d

11. b
12. a
13. d
14. b
15. a

16. d
17. d
18. d
19. c
20. d

CHAPTER 4

Test your understanding.

1. no
2. Stoicism
3. discard
4. Diogenes
5. did not

6. 330 B.C.
7. did not
8. Antigonid, Ptolemaic, Seleucid, Pergamene

9. increase
10. fate or chance
11. tolerant
12. Isis

Multiple-choice questions.

1. c	6. c	11. d	16. c
2. d	7. c	12. d	17. c
3. b	8. a	13. b	18. a
4. b	9. d	14. d	19. d
5. b	10. a	15. c	20. d

CHAPTER 5

Test your understanding.

1. Carthage
2. did
3. Sicily, North Africa
4. did not
5. more
6. Jupiter
7. realistic
8. did not
9. patrician

Number the following events.

1. 3
2. 6
3. 1
4. 4
5. 5
6. 2

Multiple-choice questions.

1. d	6. d	11. a	16. c
2. b	7. c	12. b	17. b
3. a	8. b	13. c	18. b
4. d	9. d	14. d	19. d
5. a	10. b	15. b	20. b

CHAPTER 6

Test your understanding.

1. did
2. Byzantium (Constantinople)
3. Livy
4. increase
5. A.D. 380
6. did
7. increase
8. minor
9. expansion

Number the following events.

1. 5
2. 3
3. 2
4. 1
5. 4
6. 6

Multiple-choice questions.

1. b	7. d	12. b	17. d
2. d	8. a	13. c	18. d
3. b	9. c	14. b	19. c
4. d	10. d	15. c	20. a
5. c	11. b	16. a	21. a
6. b			

CHAPTER 7

Test your understanding.

1. did	5. was	9. Hegira
2. Constantine	6. Augustine of Hippo	10. *City of God*
3. wergeld	7. German chieftains	11. emperor
4. east	8. retarded	

Multiple-choice questions.

1. c	7. b	13. d	19. c
2. d	8. c	14. a	20. a
3. c	9. b	15. b	21. b
4. b	10. a	16. d	22. d
5. a	11. d	17. c	23. b
6. d	12. b	18. b	24. b

CHAPTER 8

Test your understanding.

1. Saint Augustine	4. less	6. Alciun
2. Bede	5. good	7. Salerno
3. increase		

Multiple-choice questions.

1. c	6. d	11. c	15. d
2. c	7. b	12. d	16. d
3. c	8. a	13. a	17. b
4. c	9. c	14. c	18. d
5. c	10. b		

CHAPTER 9

Test your understanding.

1. increase/deteriorated
2. warmer
3. Peace of God
4. decrease, increase
5. Cluny
6. clergy, emperor
7. Gorze

Multiple-choice questions.

1. d	6. a	11. d	16. c
2. c	7. d	12. d	17. d
3. a	8. b	13. c	18. c
4. a	9. a	14. b	19. d
5. a	10. b	15. a	20. a

CHAPTER 10

Test your understanding.

1. swaddling
2. uncertain
3. greater
4. did
5. "manor"
6. never
7. bride
8. late
9. knighthood
10. was not
11. horse

Multiple-choice questions.

1. d	7. a	12. a	17. c
2. c	8. b	13. d	18. d
3. c	9. b	14. c	19. d
4. b	10. d	15. c	20. d
5. c	11. c	16. c	21. c
6. d			

CHAPTER 11

Test your understanding.

1. *Unam Sanctam*
2. Exchequer
3. Frederick Barbarossa
4. *Domesday Book*
5. England
6. Sicily
7. Magna Carta
8. Chartres
9. Romanesque
10. *summa*
11. Hanseatic League
12. Peter Abelard
13. Thomas Becket
14. Parlement of Paris

Multiple-choice questions.

1. d	6. b	11. b	16. c
2. b	7. d	12. d	17. a
3. c	8. b	13. a	18. b
4. d	9. c	14. a	19. a
5. b	10. d	15. d	20. c

CHAPTER 12

Provide approximate dates.

1. 1348	4. 1414-1418	6. 1358
2. 1309-1372	5. 1346	7. 1321
3. 1337-1453		

Test your understanding.

1. did not	3. England, France	5. economic
2. bad	4. Lollards	6. decrease

Multiple-choice questions.

1. d	6. a	11. c	16. b
2. d	7. c	12. c	17. d
3. a	8. d	13. a	18. c
4. c	9. b	14. c	19. b
5. b	10. d	15. b	20. c

CHAPTER 13

Test your understanding.

1. Niccolo Machiavelli	3. increased	5. declined
2. less	4. Thomas More	6. is not

Multiple-choice questions.

1. a	7. c	13. c	18. b
2. d	8. d	14. b	19. a
3. d	9. a	15. b	20. d
4. b	10. d	16. d	21. a
5. b	11. d	17. b	22. b
6. b	12. a		

CHAPTER 14

Test your understanding.

1. did
2. king
3. political
4. Martin Luther
5. Alexander VI
6. was
7. weaken
8. Protestant

Multiple-choice questions.

1. c
2. d
3. b
4. a
5. b
6. b
7. c
8. c
9. a
10. b
11. a
12. d
13. d
14. d
15. c
16. c
17. b
18. c
19. a
20. c

CHAPTER 15

Test your understanding.

1. Thirty Years' War
2. Cortez
3. Las Casas
4. Edict of Nantes
5. sixteenth
6. Gustavus Adolphus
7. the United Provinces of the Netherlands
8. Amsterdam
9. Elizabeth I
10. skepticism
11. Charles V
12. Concordat of Bologna
13. Portugal

Multiple-choice questions.

1. d
2. b
3. d
4. d
5. d
6. b
7. a
8. b
9. d
10. c
11. a
12. d
13. a
14. c
15. b
16. b
17. b
18. d
19. d
20. c
21. a
22. d

CHAPTER 16

Test your understanding.

1. stadholder
2. Colbert
3. entered
4. disaster
5. John Churchill
6. Laud

Multiple-choice questions.

1. b	7. c	12. d	17. d
2. d	8. b	13. d	18. a
3. a	9. a	14. b	19. c
4. d	10. d	15. b	20. c
5. d	11. c	16. d	21. a
6. a			

CHAPTER 17

Test your understanding.

1. Peter the Great
2. Johann Sebastian Bach
3. increased
4. Suleiman the Magnificent
5. maintained
6. Frederick II (the Great)
7. (1) 4   (2) 1   (3) 3   (4) 2   (5) 5   (6) 6
8. weaker

Multiple-choice questions.

1. d	6. b	11. b	16. c
2. c	7. d	12. c	17. b
3. c	8. b	13. b	18. a
4. a	9. a	14. b	19. d
5. c	10. d	15. c	20. b

CHAPTER 18

Test your understanding.

1. water, earth
2. did not
3. motion
4. universal gravitation
5. philosophy
6. Portugal
7. was not
8. did not
9. skeptic
10. Newton
11. failed

Multiple-choice questions.

1. b	6. c	11. a	16. d
2. a	7. b	12. a	17. b
3. c	8. d	13. a	18. c
4. d	9. a	14. b	19. c
5. d	10. b	15. a	20. d

CHAPTER 19

Fill in the blank line.

1.	i	3.	e	5.	g	7.	b
2.	c	4.	j	6.	a	8.	f

Multiple-choice questions.

1.	b	6.	a	11.	d	16.	d
2.	d	7.	a	12.	b	17.	d
3.	c	8.	a	13.	a	18.	b
4.	d	9.	d	14.	a	19.	a
5.	b	10.	d	15.	a	20.	b

CHAPTER 20

Test your understanding.

1.	limited	4.	potato	7.	the common people
2.	was not	5.	longer	8.	Wesley
3.	did	6.	cowpox		

Multiple-choice questions.

1.	b	6.	b	11.	c	16.	c
2.	d	7.	a	12.	d	17.	d
3.	b	8.	d	13.	a	18.	a
4.	c	9.	b	14.	d	19.	d
5.	c	10.	c	15.	b	20.	b

CHAPTER 21

Test your understanding.

1.	Trafalgar	3.	Thomas Paine	5.	victory
2.	an important	4.	a great deal of	6.	military ruler

Multiple-choice questions.

1.	c	7.	a	12.	b	17.	a
2.	d	8.	d	13.	d	18.	b
3.	d	9.	c	14.	a	19.	b
4.	a	10.	d	15.	d	20.	d
5.	d	11.	d	16.	a	21.	d
6.	c